POSITIVE PEDAGOGY FOR SPORT COACHING

The concept of positive pedagogy has transformed the way we understand learning and coaching in sport. Presenting examples of positive pedagogy in action, this book is the first to apply its basic principles to individual sports such as swimming, athletics, gymnastics and karate.

Using the game based approach (GBA) (an athlete-centred, inquiry-based method that involves game-like activities), this book demonstrates how positive pedagogy can be successfully employed across a range of sports and levels of performance, while also providing insight into coaches' experiences of this approach. Divided into three sections that focus on the development, characteristics and applications of positive pedagogy, it fills a gap in coaching literature by extending the latest developments of GBA to activities beyond team sports. It pioneers a way of coaching that is both efficient in improving performance and effective in promoting positive experiences of learning across all ages and abilities.

Positive Pedagogy for Sport Coaching: Athlete-centred coaching for individual sports is invaluable reading for all sports coaching students as well as any practising coach or physical education teacher looking for inspiration.

Richard Light is Professor of Sport Pedagogy in the College of Education, Health and Human Development at the University of Canterbury, Christchurch, New Zealand. A prominent figure in research on, and the development of, athlete-centred coaching, his work situates learning and coaching within social and cultural contexts to emphasize the subjective, affective and whole-person nature of experience and learning in sport. His work, which draws on contemporary learning theory, social theory and his experiences of coaching and teaching across a range of cultural settings, has developed into a distinctive approach to sport coaching pedagogy.

POSITIVE PEDAGOGY FOR SPORT COACHING

Athlete-centred coaching for individual sports

Richard Light

Routledge
Taylor & Francis Group

LONDON AND NEW YORK

First published 2017
by Routledge
2 Park Square, Milton Park, Abingdon, Oxon OX14 4RN

and by Routledge
711 Third Avenue, New York, NY 10017

Routledge is an imprint of the Taylor & Francis Group, an informa business

British Library Cataloguing in Publication Data
A catalogue record for this book is available from the British Library

Library of Congress Cataloging in Publication Data
Names: Light, Richard, 1951- author.
Title: Positive pedagogy for sport coaching : athlete-centred coaching for individual sports / Richard Light.
Description: Abingdon, Oxon ; New York, NY : Routledge is an imprint of the Taylor & Francis Group, an Informa Business, [2017] | Includes bibliographical references and index.
Identifiers: LCCN 2016020414 | ISBN 9781138215580 (hardback) | ISBN 9781138215597 (pbk.) | ISBN 9781315443720 (ebk)
Subjects: LCSH: Coaching (Athletics) | Coaching (Athletics)--Psychological aspects. | Athletes--Psychology.
Classification: LCC GV711 .L54 2017 | DDC 796.07/7--dc23
LC record available at https://lccn.loc.gov/2016020414

ISBN: 978-1-138-21558-0 (hbk)
ISBN: 978-1-138-21559-7 (pbk)
ISBN: 978-1-315-44372-0 (ebk)

Typeset in Bembo
by Taylor & Francis Books

CONTENTS

ACKNOWLEDGEMENTS

I would like to thank my wife, Chiho, and daughter, Amy, for their support and tolerance of what, at times, must have seemed like my 'absent presence' in the home due to the time and effort I devoted to writing this book. Beginning in October last year it took me six months to write it with barely a day passing without me committing significant time to working on it – even on the family holiday in Hawaii. At home in Christchurch I was often up at 4.30am writing before I drove to the office and often up late at night when 'on a roll' and not wanting to lose momentum. I made similar comments about my *Game Sense* book, published in 2013, and suggested it had, at best, only fleeting relevance for them. This one is a little different because both of them were interested in the ideas underpinning it and happy to occasionally engage in discussion about ideas and issues that I was thinking about. In particular, Amy's decision to change to a major in philosophy at university and her work as a swimming coach has enhanced our recent conversations about Positive Pedagogy in coaching. While dialogue with colleagues helps develop ideas and knowledge at one level, conversations with my family and with non-academics (including my students) helped keep me grounded while writing.

I would also like to thank Dr Jenny Clarke, who coordinates the Bachelor of Sport Coaching at the University of Canterbury (UC), for her curiosity at both an intellectual and practical level and the many conversations we had about this book and my ideas on coaching. For someone who earned a doctorate at Oxford University in theoretical physics her knowledge of, and interest in, Positive Pedagogy for coaching and the ideas that inform it were initially surprising but always stimulating. Interaction with Jenny and other colleagues, my family and students that I have taught and worked with around the world was pivotal to building and refining the conceptual understanding needed to write this book. I am also grateful for all the opportunities I have had to develop my ideas on coaching and teaching across a range of cultures and sports since becoming an academic. These range from coaching a primary school 4×100 metre track relay team in Sydney to running workshops on touch rugby in Taiwan and Japan, some of which I have drawn on in Part III.

Although this is a sole-authored book, I asked two colleagues and two of my Ph.D. students to draw on their experiences of coaching to co-write a chapter each with me. With each of them we talked about their experiences and I set them a type of template for them to write a draft chapter. When this was done we collaborated in writing a chapter that provides insight into their experiences and which is linked to Positive Pedagogy. Dr Jenny Clarke worked with me to write chapter 9 on croquet and Dr Chris North (University of Canterbury) co-authored chapter 12 on coaching the roll in kayaking. Ph.D. student Mohammad Shah Razak, who is a former head of a secondary school physical education department in Singapore and teaches in athlete-centred coaching at the University of Canterbury, co-authored chapter 13 on rock climbing with me. Bianca Couto de Aguiar, who is also a Ph.D. student of mine, co-authored chapter 14 on gymnastics.

I would also like to acknowledge the contribution of Associate Professor Stephen Harvey towards writing chapter 1 (An outline of Positive Pedagogy for sport coaching) and chapter 5 (Questioning for learning). Chapter 1 draws on a previous publication that we co-authored in *Sport, Education and Society* (Harvey and Light, 2015) with chapter 5 drawing on an article published in *Asia-Pacific Journal of Health, Sport and Physical Education* (Harvey and Light, 2015).

CONTRIBUTORS

Dr Jenny Clarke (chapter 9) completed a DPhil in Theoretical Elementary Particle Physics at the University of Oxford, UK in 2000. While studying in the UK, Jenny played women's county cricket and was introduced to the sport of croquet. She has competed internationally since 2003, winning the 2010 Australian Open title and the 2012 Women's World Championships and was a member of the New Zealand team, which won the 2014 World Team Championships, among many team and individual titles. In 2008, Jenny combined her love of sport with her training in physics to become a lecturer in Sport Science at the University of Canterbury. Her research interests have grown to include teaching and coaching pedagogy, with a particular emphasis on experiential learning and athlete empowerment. Jenny has coached croquet from beginner to elite levels, and in recent years has developed a coaching programme based around Game Sense and Positive Pedagogy.

Dr Stephen Harvey (chapter 1 and chapter 5) is an Associate Professor in Instructional Methods at West Virginia University, USA. Stephen's research is focused on teacher/coach pedagogy and practice and its influence on student/player learning, and he has been invited to deliver presentations and workshops on these topics at international, national and regional conferences. Stephen is co-author of *Advances in Rugby Coaching: An Holistic Approach* and co-editor of two additional books, *Ethics in Youth Sport* and *Contemporary Developments in Games Teaching*, all published by Routledge (London & New York). Additionally, Stephen is co-developer of the Coach Analysis Intervention System (CAIS) iPad application by Axis Coaching Technology. Stephen is Secretary for the International Association for Physical Education in Higher Education Teaching Games for Understanding Special Interest Group, a role he has held since January 2009.

Dr Chris North (chapter 12) lectures in outdoor and environmental education at the University of Canterbury, New Zealand. His teaching background includes secondary and tertiary institutions in New Zealand and North America. He has worked as a teacher, tourist guide and outdoor instructor and holds a number of instructor qualifications including rock climbing, white water kayaking, backpacking and alpine climbing. Chris' research focus is in the areas of outdoor education practices, adventure education, environmental education and initial teacher education.

Mohammad Shah Razak (chapter 13) is completing a Ph.D. at the University of Canterbury, New Zealand on 'Moral and ethical learning in sports in secondary schools' under the supervision of Professor Richard Light. He has an extensive background in teaching physical education and coaching sport, both at the recreational and competitive levels in Singapore over an 18-year period that includes coaching rock climbing, football and outdoor education in both primary and secondary schools. As a previous head of a physical education department he is currently a tutor teaching on athlete-centred coaching at the University of Canterbury.

Bianca Couto de Aguiar (chapter 14) is completing a Ph.D. at the University of Canterbury, New Zealand on games teaching in secondary schools under the supervision of Professor Richard Light. She has an extensive background in gymnastics in Portugal where she competed in artistic gymnastics for eight years and won several national titles. She has also coached acrobatic gymnastics in Coimbra at recreation, development and competition levels and taught physical education, including gymnastics, at the primary and intermediate years of schooling. She is currently coaching gymnastics at Christchurch School of Gymnastics in Christchurch, New Zealand where she coaches pre-school, recreational and competitive classes.

INTRODUCTION

While teaching pre-service physical education teachers about Game Sense at the University of Sydney in 2006 a student asked me, 'Richard, we are convinced about how good Game Sense is for teaching games and team sports and I will definitely be using it when I start teaching but what about other sports like swimming and athletics that are not team sports? How can Game Sense help teach them?' I replied by saying that, as they were not games you couldn't use Game Sense, per se, but that you could apply its principles to any sport. This question started me thinking about what the principles of Game Sense actually were with a suggestion for four pedagogical features set out in my book, *Game Sense: Pedagogy for Performance, Participation and Enjoyment* (Light, 2013a). Writing this book encouraged me to think about how these principles could be modified to help teach individual sports like swimming in which technique is so important. While there are tactical aspects of swimming in the longer events there can be no doubt about the central importance of technique (see Light and Wallian, 2008; Lang and Light, 2010). By individual, sports I mean sports in which participants most commonly compete as an individual, such as swimming, archery, croquet, golf, martial arts such as judo and karate, canoeing, diving and surfing. In all these sports, and many other individual sports, there are team events, which could be seen as not being individual competition but the dominant form of competition is on an individual basis. Individual sports are also distinct from team sports due to the comparative lack of interaction between teammates and because they have less tactical complexity.

At the time of being asked how Game Sense can inform coaching and teaching individual sports at the University of Sydney, my daughter was a successful age-group swimmer who won several events at the NSW state championships the following year. As a parent of a committed swimmer I lived in the world of age-group swimming, which provided me with some useful insights into young people's experiences of competitive swimming (see Light, 2016), the culture of the sport and its coaching. I had come to know her coach, Dene Roulstene, well and respected him as a thinking coach who developed excellent relationships with his swimmers and was very good at helping young swimmers realize their talent. I talked with him about applying the features of Game Sense pedagogy to swimming with a focus on reflection, dialogue and inquiry and invited him to come to the university to work with my students in a unit in which I wanted to begin to answer my student's question about using Game Sense when teaching or coaching individual sports. He was open to my ideas and happy to design and coach a session on reducing resistance in dives and pushing off the wall that emphasized reflection upon experience, dialogue and collaborative problem solving, which helped me develop my ideas on how athlete-centred coaching could be employed in swim coaching. Like most good collaborations we both learned something from the experience, as I suspect the students did.

In 2007, I spent four months as Invited Professor at the Université de Franche-Comté (France) where I engaged in many conversations with Dr Nathalie Wallian (she was an associate professor at the time) on using constructivist perspectives to inform pedagogy for teaching and coaching individual sports. Our discussions led to the publication of what I think is a significant article on informing the teaching of swimming with constructivism, which I believe was the first such study (Light and Wallian, 2008). I have since written a number of articles on learner-centred, inquiry-based approaches to coaching swimming in French and English (see Light and Lémonie, 2012; Light, 2014a) and have had a number of discussions with some excellent swimming coaches such as Australian Olympic coach Rohan Taylor.

Establishing a dialectic between theory and practice is central to my development of, and research on, coaching pedagogy and is something that Nathalie Wallian emphasized in our conversations in Franche-Comté and in our article on a constructivist-informed approach to teaching swimming (Light and Wallian, 2008). This encouraged me to put theory into action by offering to coach my daughter's primary school 4 x 100 metre track relay team to work through some ideas I had on coaching individual sports while helping out the school. As a busy academic I no longer have the time or opportunity to coach and to develop and test pedagogical ideas in practice. Running workshops with teachers, coaches and academics provides the opportunity to reflect in and on practice, but opportunities to coach in real-life settings and introduce innovation do not often arise. This experience of coaching is reported on in more detail in chapter 10 but, briefly, I was interested in taking on the challenge of employing a learner-centred, inquiry-based approach in a very technique-intensive aspect of the track relay. From being a parent coach for the beach sprint in the nippers (junior lifesaving), I knew that the quickest way to get improvement was by focusing on starts and baton changes and so chose to focus on changing the baton.

I began with a direct instruction approach where I showed them the precise technique I wanted them to use, but used an athlete-centred approach to help them learn how to do efficient changes as a shared task involving two young athletes in practice through reflection and discussion between pairs and between all four girls.

We experienced great success in terms of results, enjoyment, learning how to learn and developing a better understanding of each other. This experience made a significant contribution to the development of my ideas on applying Game Sense pedagogy to individual sports and suggested to me that this approach can work in practice.

I continued to develop my ideas and to think about the importance of understanding the core ideas or concepts of Game Sense and other GBAs and how humans learn for pre-service teachers who could go out and make a difference. This led me to think about what the core features of Game Sense pedagogy were to offer a framework within which teachers and coaches could develop their own approaches to it. As I am very clear about in my book on Game Sense (Light, 2013a), I did not want to be prescriptive and set out 'non-negotiables'. Instead, I wanted to frame what a Game Sense approach looked like and what its features were to offer coaches and physical education teachers some room to interpret and develop their coaching and teaching along these lines.

I have since strengthened my ideas on this to avoid talking or writing about what is or isn't an authentic version of a GBA or referring to models that teachers or coaches should follow. Once I had identified the four core features of Game Sense it was quite a simple task to modify them so that they could be applied to coaching individual sports and other activities with me reducing them to three features. The emphasis of my research and teaching is on helping coaches and/or physical education teachers develop a sound understanding of theories of human learning and the philosophy underpinning GBA and Positive Pedagogy to enable them to interpret them and adapt them to their existing knowledge and dispositions. A very similar argument for helping teachers and coaches learn to employ a Teaching Games for Understanding (TGfU) and Game Sense approach to games teaching has recently been proposed by Stolz and Pill (2015).

While in Melbourne from 2011 to 2014, I read an article on Positive Psychology that was having a significant influence on teaching in many Melbourne schools, with the Dean of the Melbourne Graduate School of Education at The University of Melbourne, Professor Field Rickards, planning to set up a Positive Psychology centre. As I read further on Positive Psychology I was encouraged to think about my experiences of teaching practical classes in Game Sense and how this seemed to facilitate the positive wellbeing that Positive Psychology works at promoting. Indeed, my experiences of teaching and coaching using TGfU and Game Sense since 2000 have always been satisfying, not only due to the learning I see but also the happiness and joy that seems to accompany discovery, learning and the positive social interaction that is present in a good Game Sense class or session (see Light, 2002).

I felt Positive Psychology had something to offer in the development of pedagogy for coaching and teaching that was not limited to team sports and by enhancing the positive experiences of learning that GBA promote. By this time I felt I had progressed well with modifying and adapting Game Sense pedagogy so that it could be applied to individual sports and other activities that were not team sports but could not think of a suitable name for it, so I decided to call it Positive Pedagogy. A subsequent search for others' use of the term suggested to me that, although there were some differences between them and what I was doing, there were also basic similarities. In particular, George's (2006) ideas on Positive Pedagogy for teaching music resonated with my ideas and feelings.

My reading of, and thinking about, Positive Psychology and how I could use it to inform and support Positive Pedagogy brought to mind some work I had read by medical sociologist Anton Antonovsky that was informing the development of the new Australian national physical education curriculum through the concept of a strengths-based approach to teaching (see McCuaig et al., 2013). This work draws on the strengths-based approach used in social work that takes a positive approach to help clients deal with adversity by being 'future focused' and drawing on the strengths they bring with them to solve or deal with the problem(s) they face. Antonovsky's concern with the affective and social dimensions of life and his focus on experience fits in well with the same focus in my work on teaching and coaching. By aligning with what GBA pedagogy can develop in learners, the three elements of his Sense of Coherence (SoC) model that most contribute towards wellbeing offer a means of enhancing the positive learning experiences that Positive Pedagogy can offer.

In this book there are frequent references made to 'traditional' ways of coaching that are contrasted with GBA and Positive Pedagogy and which I feel oblige me to outline what I mean by 'traditional' coaching. I use the term 'traditional' in reference to long-established practice that favours direct instruction and the reduction of complex movement to distinct components, that (in reference to teaching) Davis and Sumara (1997, 2003) call a 'complicated' (mechanistic) approach they compare with complex approaches. This is similar to Dewey's 'progressive' ideas on teaching that he compares to traditional teaching to suggest that 'the history of educational theory is marked by opposition between the idea that education is development from within and that it is formed from without' (Dewey, 1938a, p. 1). The traditional approach to teaching is guided by the principles of behaviourism, a mechanism that involves the 'manipulation of students toward predetermined ends and ignores the experience of the students themselves, viewing it as a contamination of the process' (Hopkins, 1994, p. 12).

Writing on, and thinking about, educational theory and approaches to sport coaching tends to exaggerate differences and split different approaches into exclusive opposites such as instruction versus facilitation, passive versus active learning and traditional versus progressive approaches which is something I try to avoid, as best I can, in this book. As Light, Evans, Harvey and Hassanin (2015) suggest, there is not one 'traditional' approach in coaching but, instead, a spectrum of coaching approaches ranging from coaches who rely exclusively on direct instruction, skill-drill, monologue and the reduction of the sport or activity to discrete components to coaches who almost exclusively use an athlete-centred, inquiry-based approach.

The book

This book comprises fifteen chapters preceded by the introduction and followed by reflections in 'Concluding thoughts'. The core of the book is divided into three parts which are: (I) The development of Positive Pedagogy, (II) Pedagogical features of Positive Pedagogy and (III) Applications.

Part I: The development of Positive Pedagogy

Chapter 1 provides an overview of Positive Pedagogy that explains its development from game based approaches (GBAs) to coaching team sport. It draws on an article I published with Associate Professor Stephen Harvey (Light and Harvey, 2015) to suggest how the learner-centred pedagogy of GBA inherently encourages positive personal and social development whether or not this is its aim. It then outlines and explains how the four pedagogical features of Game Sense (Light, 2013a) have been modified and reduced to three features to guide Positive Pedagogy coaching and how drawing on Positive Psychology and Antonovsky's concept of salutogenesis can enhance positive learning experiences.

Chapter 2 examines the range of theories that I have used to explain and enhance learning in Positive Pedagogy with a focus on constructivist learning theory that includes CLT and the complementary theories of enactivism and situated learning theory while also discussing the notion of embodied cognition. Chapter 3 examines Positive Psychology and Antonovsky's salutogenesis (origins of health) through which he asked what creates health and what the origins of health are instead of looking for the causes of disease. It then outlines how both these positive approaches have been appropriated to enhance positive learner/ athlete experiences and to foster positive personal and social development in athletes.

Part II: Pedagogical features of Positive Pedagogy

Chapter 4 focuses on the design and management of learning activities as the first step in the Positive Pedagogy approach, and probably the most important. Drawing on Dewey (1916/1997) it explains how, in Positive Pedagogy for coaching, learning occurs through experience in two ways: (1) engagement with the physical learning activity, and (2) reflection upon this experience through social interaction. It deals with issues that are central to coaching using Positive Pedagogy for individual sports such as the use of constraints with different aims and the interaction between articulated knowledge and knowledge-in-action for athlete learning. Chapter 5 begins with a discussion of why coaches need to ask questions and what the aim of questioning is in Positive Pedagogy. Just as athletes need to know *why* and *when* they should take particular action or perform a skill and not just *how*, it is imperative that coaches know why they are asking questions. After suggesting why coaches need to ask questions this chapter discusses what questions to ask and when to ask them.

The emphasis of Positive Pedagogy on inquiry requires reflection in and on action, dialogue and the collaborative formulation of ideas or suggestions to be tested. It is very different to traditional coaching that emphasizes the coach-to-athlete monologue of direct instruction and feedback, and the pursuit of correct technical execution. Its inquiry-based approach differentiates it from a coach-centred, instructional coaching approach and requires a very different set of relationships between coach and athletes and between athletes and traditional approaches. It requires and develops better understanding and trust between coach and athlete that can be uncomfortable for athletes who are unused to this approach and not ready to open up and to trust their peers and coach. Chapter 6 discusses the inquiry-based nature of Positive Pedagogy and the need to establish and nurture a culture, or socio-moral environment, that encourages athletes to open up, take risks, discover and engage in inquiry.

Part III: Applications

Chapter 7 draws on a keynote presentation I delivered at the 2015 ACHPER (Australian Council for Health, Physical Education and Recreation) International Conference convened in Adelaide. It suggests how to use Positive Pedagogy to focus on skill development when using a Game Sense approach by narrowing the focus and intended outcomes through the use of 'game-like activities'. This approach focuses on a particular skill while still providing some of the complexity needed for the transfer of skill practice to the full game by ensuring that each activity requires and develops awareness and decision-making. It maintains the flow and enjoyment of learning provided by achieving the appropriate level of challenge needed to generate the positive experiences of learning that are so important for youth sport and physical education in particular.

Chapter 8 provides two examples of how Positive Pedagogy can be applied to coaching swimming technique by drawing on learning activities that I developed from watching and talking to experienced swim coaches. Both examples aim to develop an understanding of the two fundamental concepts of swimming, which are: (a) maximizing thrust/propulsion and (b) reducing resistance, from which the swimmer can interpret instruction on technique and adapt it to his/her way of swimming. It aims to enhance embodied and reflective understanding of how performance of the technique influences propulsion and/or resistance as part of the complex act of swimming.

Chapter 9 is co-authored with Dr Jenny Clarke from the University of Canterbury, New Zealand. In it she reflects on using Positive Pedagogy to coach older athletes in a croquet workshop. As a multiple world champion in croquet and coordinator of the Sport Coaching program at the University of Canterbury, Jenny has recently applied Positive Pedagogy to coaching croquet with this being the focus of this chapter. In it she reflects upon her use of Positive Pedagogy with a focus on feel to improve the performance of older athletes in striking the ball.

Although there is a tactical dimension to running that is particularly important over longer distances there is a clear need for athletes to develop technical proficiency that chapter 10 deals with. This may require some direct instruction but, even with a strong focus on learning technique, coaches can take a Positive

Pedagogy approach to helping athletes learn technique. This chapter draws on my experiences of coaching children's running that sees learning as an ongoing 'conversation' between pre-reflective and reflective learning aimed at developing knowledge-in-action (Schön, 1983).

Chapter 11 provides an example of an inquiry-based approach to coaching children and young adolescents in the javelin throw, but in a way that has relevance for other throwing events and throwing in general such as in team games like softball or handball. Although it draws on my experience of teaching pre-service teachers, it is relevant for coaching outside schools. It first sets out some group activities through which the young athletes learn the 'root movements' of throwing through solving the problems posed by throwing a range of objects not normally thrown in a guided discovery approach. These are then adapted and applied to throwing the javelin. The next chapter (chapter 12) is co-authored with Dr Chris North from the University of Canterbury. In it he provides suggestions for drawing on Positive Pedagogy to help students learn how to roll a kayak. In this chapter he recognizes the significance of the fluid environment in which the kayaker learns and uses a focus on feel and sensations to help his students perform a roll that is a single smooth, graceful and powerful movement.

In the application of Positive Pedagogy here, the teacher or leader does not design a learning environment but learning is grounded in experience and facilitated with questioning to promote interaction and thinking within an inquiry-based approach. The session outlined for helping students learn to roll a kayak recognizes and accounts for the fluid environment in which the skill is executed with a focus on feel and flow and the fact that learning cannot be separated from the physical context.

In chapter 13, Mohammad Shah Razak reflects upon his experiences of teaching primary school–aged children rock climbing in Singapore to identify the similarity between the pedagogy he used and Positive Pedagogy. He recounts his experience while offering suggestions for improving it by drawing on Positive Pedagogy. In the session that he recounts, he focuses on developing awareness of the body's centre of gravity and shifting it to make climbing more efficient. This is followed by a chapter on coaching gymnastics by Bianca Couto de Aguiar. Bianca is a Ph.D. student of mine at the University of Canterbury and has extensive experience competing in gymnastics and coaching in Portugal and, more recently, coaching in Christchurch, New Zealand. She draws on her experiences of taking a more athlete-centred and inquiry-based approach to coaching aspects of gymnastics while making suggestions for improving it by drawing more on Positive Pedagogy. Chris, Jenny, Shah and Bianca's using athlete-centred and inquiry-based approaches, and their suggestions for taking this approach, provide useful insights for readers into practitioners' experiences of using Positive Pedagogy and the learning emerging from it that is enhanced by adopting a reflective disposition.

In the final practical example (chapter 15) I draw on my background in Japanese martial arts to recount my experience teaching karate, in which I experimented with athlete-centred teaching. In karate there are three main aspects of training, which are (1) basic technique (*kihon waza*) (2) predetermined forms (*kata*) and (3) sparring (*kumite*). In this chapter I recount and discuss teaching *waza* for *kumite*. In the first activity I teach the skill of delivering a powerful *gyakuzuki* (reverse punch) with a focus on generating power and speed and adjusting to varying distance to a moving target. I do this by using hit pads with an emphasis on feel and kinaesthetic feedback. In the second activity I recount working with a karate practitioner (*karateka*) to develop tactical understanding of footwork and positioning by allowing each *karateka* to use only one technique.

Concluding thoughts

The book closes with some reflections that identify three core themes and factors that shape and influence the use of Positive Pedagogy. First it discusses the importance of socio-cultural context when taking up a Positive Pedagogy approach, which is also important for any approach to coaching. Context or environment is not restricted to the context of the specific learning activity or natural settings, as in chapter 13, and the socio-cultural environment that the coach establishes and maintains to support inquiry-based learning. It also considers how larger cultural, social and institutional contexts influence learning and coaching and how they need to be accounted for. I then discuss two distinguishing features of Positive Pedagogy for sport coaching that form strong themes through the book. They are the humanistic and holistic nature of Positive Pedagogy for sport coaching.

PART I

The development of Positive Pedagogy

1

AN OUTLINE OF POSITIVE PEDAGOGY FOR SPORT COACHING

With Stephen Harvey

GBAs such as Game Sense offer excellent opportunities for delivering high-quality coaching in team sports due to the nature of their athlete-centred, inquiry-based approach. However, with a few exceptions there has been little interest shown in adapting GBA pedagogy to individual sports and other physical activity (see Light, 2014a). This chapter provides an overview of Positive Pedagogy that begins with its development from Game Sense pedagogy (Light, 2013a) through the adaptation of the core pedagogical features of Game Sense to coaching individual sports and other physical activity.

Game Sense and other GBA

Game-based coaching and teaching can improve team performance by developing tactical knowledge, informed decision-making, awareness and the ability to adapt at non-conscious and conscious levels of cognition in match conditions across a range of team sports (see Light, Harvey et al., 2014; Chappell and Light, 2015; Jones, 2015). They generate positive experiences of practice sessions for athletes and foster the transfer of learning from practice to competition games (Jones, 2015). This occurs across a range of cultural and institutional settings from primary school physical education in Australia (Chen and Light, 2006) and secondary school physical education in Hong Kong (Wang and Ha, 2009) to university sport in the USA (Harvey, 2009) and professional sport played at the most elite levels in New Zealand and Japan (Evans, 2012; Jones, 2015). They can also foster positive personal, social and moral development as an important outcome of participation in any sport and of particular importance in youth sport. The potential for GBA to improve performance, make practice enjoyable, foster the ability and inclination to learn, and the 'value added' personal, social and moral learning it can encourage arises from their learner/athlete-centred, inquiry-based pedagogy that emphasizes reflection, collaboration, dialogue and collective inquiry.

Although its roots can be traced back several decades before Bunker and Thorpe's publication in 1982, TGfU can be seen as the father of an increasing range of variations that have been influenced by their different foci and the cultural contexts from which they have emerged. They do however share a reasonably common focus on the game, locating learning in modified games and emphasizing questioning over instruction (Light, 2013a; Stolz and Pill, 2015). In my book, *Game Sense: Pedagogy for Performance, Participation and Enjoyment* (Light, 2013a) I identify what the fundamental pedagogical features of Game Sense coaching and teaching are to suggest a framework for coaching and teaching that this book draws on to set out a framework for coaching beyond team sports. *Positive Pedagogy in Sports Coaching: An athlete-centered approach to coaching individual sports* reduces the four pedagogical features of Game Sense to three by combining features 3 and 4 to emphasize the importance of the inquiry-based approach to learning in individual sports.

Within the range of GBAs typically referred to in the literature, Game Sense (den Duyn, 1997; Light, 2013a) and Play Practice (Launder and Piltz, 2013) were developed for coaching but have been applied to physical education teaching as well. Rod Thorpe worked with the Australian Sports Commission and local coaches to develop Game Sense as a variation of TGfU for sport coaching. Launder's (see Launder 2001; Launder and Piltz, 2013) Play Practice was developed from his wide experience as a coach with a broader coaching focus but was not developed from TGfU, as he emphasized at the 2003 International TGfU conference held in Melbourne, Australia. The influence of the broader concept of athlete-centred coaching (see Kidman, 2005) is evident across a range of coaching in New Zealand from the development of youth sport programmes to the coaching of the All Blacks as one of the most successful sports teams of all time (see Smith, 2005; Cassidy and Kidman, 2010; Evans, 2012, 2014).

While these approaches focus on developing better performance, the process of learning involved can generate positive experiences that are enjoyable and satisfying, and which facilitate learning how to learn (see Light, 2003). The learning experiences provided by this pedagogy can also contribute towards positive social, moral and personal development (see Dyson, 2005; Sheppard and Mandigo, 2009; Light, 2013b) but should not be seen as an automatic outcome of adopting GBA. The same applies to coaching individual sports using Positive Pedagogy.

The literature suggests a range of positive outcomes that arise from athlete-centred coaching, a growing influence on coaching, and increasing research interest in it. However, with a few exceptions in sport coaching (see Light 2014a) and physical education (see Chen and Rovegno, 2000; Chen, 2001), this has not extended far beyond team sports with little thought given to applying the principles and ideas underpinning GBA to individual sports. Team sports (and invasion games in particular) provide ideal contexts for the application of GBAs. However, the undeniable importance of technique and skill in many individual sports, and the hegemony of the technical approach, leave little space for consideration of athlete-centred approaches to coaching and seem to have discouraged any significant consideration of its possible application to individual sports (Light and Wallian, 2008).

Play Practice (Launder, 2001; Launder and Piltz, 2013) applies to sport other than team sport and there have been some suggestions made for applying the principles of GBA to coaching individual sports (see Light and Wallian, 2008; Light and Kentel, 2015) but this is an area that is desperately underdone and in need of research attention. The notion of Positive Pedagogy presented in this book draws on the Game Sense framework (Light, 2013a), the positive approach to wellbeing proposed by Antonovsky (1987) and work in Positive Psychology to outline what a positive approach to coaching has to offer.

Coaching beyond team sports

There are a number of teaching/coaching approaches specifically focused on pro-moting positive development for young people through sport and other physical activity. These include Positive Youth Development (see Holt et al., 2012), Sport Education (Siedentop, 1994) and Teaching Personal and Social Responsibility (Hellison, 2003). Although not specifically aimed at promoting personal develop-ment, GBA can foster its development with the learner-centred, inquiry-based coaching used in these approaches prompting a critical examination of traditional 'folk pedagogies' (Bruner, 1999) that have long influenced sport coaching (Nelson et al., 2014).

These holistic and humanistic approaches challenge traditional approaches that are informed by behaviourist perspectives on learning that objectify athletes and reduce performance in sport to a number of discrete components. Typically, they are characterized by the dominance of direct instruction, feedback, and demon-strations based upon the assumption that the more the coach intervenes the more the athletes will improve (Williams and Hodges, 2005). Even for confident and experienced athletes who have the necessary skills to meet expectations of perfor-mance in this approach, the learning involved is not necessarily positive because it can promote a fear of failure that limits their capacity to learn from mistakes (Partington et al., 2014). While it may allow the more skilled athletes to demon-strate competency it does not help them learn to learn or foster the development of positive personal or psychological attributes that a Positive Pedagogy approach can. Indeed, it can promote selfishness, egotism and a lack of empathy or compassion for others, which is counterproductive in building a team, squad or club identity, cohesion and sense of common purpose. In coaching individual sports as well as team sports, it fails to teach real teamwork.

In regard to team sport, technical approaches to coaching assume that learning to play team games requires a level of technical competence *before* playing them. Assuming that there is one ideal form of technical execution that learners must strive to master, this approach focuses upon reducing errors and moving the athlete closer to the 'correct' performance of the technique. This view of learning as a process of correcting mistakes highlights what athletes *cannot* do and is exacerbated when less confident young athletes attempt to perform these skills under the gaze of their peers and their coach. Conversely, in GBAs such as Game Sense, mistakes actually provide opportunities for learning rather than being something used to control and pressure athletes (Renshaw et al., 2012) and should be seen as constructive errors that play an important role in learning (Light, 2013a; Light et al., 2015).

Making learning positive

The pedagogical features of Game Sense (Light, 2013a) inherently encourage positive learning experiences, but Positive Pedagogy for coaching draws on Antonovsky's salutogenic theory and SoC model (1979, 1987) and Positive Psychology (Seligman and Csikszentmihalyi, 2000) to foster positive experiences of learning by athletes of any age.

Antonovsky's salutogenic theory and SoC model

Antonovsky's (1979, 1987) salutogenic theory and SoC model focuses on the socially constructed resources that allow people to achieve and maintain good health. To facilitate positive experiences of learning in sport I have appropriated Antonvsky's SoC as a framework for considering what is needed to make learning positive.

Antonovsky (1979) developed the concept of 'salutogenesis' in reference to the origins of health to take a positive, holistic approach that emphasizes what supports health and wellbeing, rather than what causes disease or the 'lifestyle' approach that focuses on identifying risk factors (Antonovsky, 1996). His holistic approach is concerned more with the affective and social dimensions of life and a focus on experience than with its cognitive aspects. His SoC model comprises three elements that most encourage good health, which are: (a) comprehensibility, (b) manageability and (c) meaningfulness. Here I briefly explain these elements and suggest how they can be used as elements of coaching that contribute towards positive learning experiences.

Comprehensibility. Developed through experience, comprehensibility refers to the extent to which things make sense for the individual and the extent to which they see events and situations being ordered and consistent. For learning to be comprehensible in sport it should help athletes know not only how to do something, but also when, where and why to do it. It should also foster deep learning that involves understanding the concepts or 'big ideas' (Fosnot, 1996) that constructivist perspectives on learning suggest underpin it. It should also involve understanding by doing and the embodied learning this involves. This is because comprehensive understanding involves not only rational, conscious and articulated knowing, but also a practical understanding, or a practical sense of things (Bourdieu, 1986). This is developed through experience and engagement in a process of learning as the unfolding of knowledge that includes learning how to learn. It is evident in the emphasis placed on athletes understanding the fundamental concepts of manipulating space and time in team sports when using GBAs such as Game Sense. It is emphasized in Positive Pedagogy for individual and more skill-intensive sports such as swimming or throwing events in athletics (see Light, 2014a; Light and Kentel, 2015) as is evident in all of the practical examples presented in Part III of this book. For example, the core concepts underpinning swimming can be seen to be the maximization of propulsion (or thrust) and the minimization of resistance, whether swimming, diving or turning and streamlining off the wall (see chapter 8).

Manageability. Manageability is the extent to which an individual feels s/he has the resources at hand to manage stress and challenge. Resources can be objects such as tools and equipment, skills, intellectual ability, social and cultural capital and so on. In Positive Pedagogy this includes the resources available from interaction within groups and teams and/or the whole team in dialogue and the debate of ideas (Gréhaigne et al., 2005). In Positive Pedagogy learning is seen to be manageable when the challenges set extend the athlete but with him/her feeling that s/he can manage the task. The concept of *manageability* aligns with the aim of the coach in managing learning activities to provide an optimal level of challenge and learning as a pedagogical feature of Positive Pedagogy.

Challenges are manageable when they can be met by drawing on individual resources such as skill, physical capacity and/or the social resources available from social interaction with peers and the teacher/coach. The provision of a supportive socio-moral environment assists in making challenges manageable and rewarding. For a task to seem manageable the athlete should feel that s/he has the skill and understanding and can draw on the resources of teammates and the coach to meet them. The collective, social element is of prime importance here.

Meaningfulness. Meaningfulness refers to how much the individual feels that life makes sense and that its challenges are worthy of commitment. According to Antonovsky, meaningfulness promotes a positive expectation of life and the future and encourages people to see challenges as being interesting, relevant and worthy of their emotional commitment. When activities engage learners affectively and socially as well as physically and intellectually they are likely to be meaningful. The Game Sense approach in team sport makes learning/practice meaningful because it is situated within the game or game conditions to make practice and what the athletes feel they have learned relevant.

Engagement gives meaning to tasks and experiences because the athletes understand what they are trying to achieve and why. Learning is meaningful in team and other sports when its comprehensibility gives meaning to the tasks and activities because they make sense within the 'big picture'. Positive Pedagogy coaching should make learning meaningful by making the links clear between detailed foci on particular aspects of the sport, its most fundamental concepts and the end aims of the activity. Having the coach explain what each session involves and why would add to making it engaging and meaningful, as would players knowing the strategy and plans for the season. This should not just involve cognitive processes but also the affective, emotional and corporeal learning that encourages long-term engagement with the activity (Renshaw et al., 2012).

Positive Psychology

Positive Psychology sets out to redress a preoccupation of psychology with pathologies and repairing the 'worst aspects' of life by promoting its positive qualities (Seligman and Csikszentmihalyi, 2000). It focuses on wellbeing and satisfaction in the past, on happiness and the experience of 'flow' in the present and on hope and optimism in the future (Jackson and Csikszentmihalyi, 1999). It aims to build 'thriving individuals, finding and nurturing talent and making normal life more fulfilling', drawing on the concepts of *flow* and *mindfulness* as positive states that generate learning (Seligman and Csikszentmihalyi, 2000, p. 5). Flow has also been proposed as a way of explaining the experiences possible when learning through sport and practice/modified games that provide appropriate levels of challenge (Jackson and Csikszentmihalyi, 1999; Kretchmar, 2005; Harvey et al., 2014) and which can be experienced when using GBAs such as TGfU (Lloyd and Smith, 2010). It refers to a state of being absorbed in the experience of action through intense concentration, as the athlete is 'lost' in the flow of experience to provide optimal (non-conscious) learning.

Although Positive Pedagogy does not specifically focus on developing wellbeing or happiness, all five elements of Seligman's (2012) PERMA (positive emotions, engagement, relations, meaning and achievement) model are evident in it, which suggests the positive experiences of learning it can provide. The Positive Pedagogy of GBA can generate positive emotions such as enjoyment or delight (Kretchmar, 2005), engagement in learning, the building of relationships and a sense of belonging (Light, 2008a), meaning, and opportunities for achievement, both individually and collectively. Positive Pedagogy emphasizes what the learner *can* do and how s/he can draw on existing individual and social resources to meet learning challenges through reflection and dialogue. It is forward focused.

Pedagogical features of Positive Pedagogy

This section examines the ways in which the core pedagogical features of Positive Pedagogy foster positive learning experiences for athletes in individual sports. It also notes some of the significant challenges facing coaches taking up Positive Pedagogy that are discussed more fully in Part II. The pedagogical features of Positive Pedagogy are that: (1) it emphasizes engagement with the physical learning environment or experience, (2) the coach asks questions that generate dialogue and thinking in preference to telling players/athletes what to do, and (3) it adopts an inquiry-based approach to provide opportunities for athletes to collectively formulate, test and evaluate solutions to problems supported by a socio-moral environment in which making mistakes is accepted as an essential part of learning.

Designing and managing the learning environment/experience

When coaching team sports using Positive Pedagogy the game is seen as a complex phenomenon within which learning to play well involves adapting to its dynamics with tactical knowledge, skill execution and decision-making all interconnected as knowledge-in-action (Light 2013a). Learning is located within modified games or game-like activities based on the assumption that it occurs through engagement with the learning environment and not through direct instruction (Dewey 1916/1997). This is also initially learning that largely takes place as a process of adaptation at a non-conscious level and forms the basis of ensuing learning experiences as attempts are made to bring it to consciousness through language. This means that the ability of the coach to manage the activities or a game to establish and sustain the appropriate level of challenge is of pivotal importance. Indeed, designing practice activities and managing them through the analysis of performance is probably the biggest challenge facing coaches in implementing a Positive Pedagogy approach. Some recent attention has been paid to this (see Turner, 2014; Light, 2015) and it forms the focus of chapter 4.

Adopting a Positive Pedagogy approach for individual sports such as running and swimming adopts a similar approach but typically involves providing learning experiences that place constraints on the athlete. These are usually used to create problems to be solved and processes of non-conscious thinking and conscious thinking but can also be used just to develop awareness of a technique, such as discussed in chapter 10 on using the arms in sprinting. They typically involve structuring learning in a way that restricts possible solutions compared with coaching in team sports and which could be seen as being a guided discovery teaching style (Mosston and Ashworth, 1986).

When a coach introduces a new group or individual athlete to a Positive Pedagogy approach, s/he should begin with a more structured approach that the athletes are used to and move gradually towards empowering them. As athletes adapt to the approach and embrace it they can take on more autonomy, ownership and responsibility to participate in the design, modification and evaluation of learning games or activities (Almond, 1983) as well as the formulation, testing and evaluation of tactical solutions. This leads to increasing empowerment achieved through a growing understanding of games and of how to learn. As players/athletes adapt and become more prepared to engage in purposeful social interaction they rely less upon the coach and begin to take more responsibility for their own learning, which is an important and positive learning experience. This typically involves a coach–athlete relationship that is more equitable in the repositioning of the coach and the empowerment of the athlete.

Learning by doing occurs at a non-conscious level as a process of adaptation that is emphasized by psychological constructivism (Piaget, 1950), enactivism (Varela et al., 1991) and CLT (Davis and Sumara, 2003). The use of practice games designed to achieve particular outcomes suggests that they improve player motivation in a range of team sports (see, for example, Light, 2004; Evans and Light, 2008; Harvey, 2009). While some practice games can be designed to focus on particular skills they should still include developing awareness and some decision-making and can be social in nature, even when there is no verbal interaction (see Tan et al., 2011 and Turner, 2014 for an overview of learning game design using GBAs).

Ask questions to generate dialogue and thinking

Questioning is one of the central mechanisms employed for promoting player/athlete-centred learning in Game Sense and one that typically presents challenges for coaches (Wright and Forrest, 2007; Roberts, 2011; Forrest, 2014). In Positive Pedagogy questions are employed to promote thinking and dialogue but it takes time for coaches to become skilful enough with questioning to achieve these aims. Questions should create a range of possible answers or solutions rather than lead to predetermined answers that are deemed to be either correct or incorrect, but this can vary when coaching a skill or skill-intensive sport. Wright and Forrest (2007) identify the problems involved with questioning in GBA through their criticism of the sequencing of questions suggested in some TGfU texts and the ways in which it limits the possible responses instead of expanding them. The commonly used Initiation, Response, Evaluation (IRE) questioning shuts down interaction between the coach and the athletes and between the athletes, with Forrest (2014) suggesting use of the reflective toss (van Zee and Minstrell, 1997) in which the coach prompts and probes different learners' perspectives of game play.

Positive Pedagogy also requires the coach avoiding or at least minimizing being critical or telling learners they are wrong as part of a coach disposition towards promoting divergent thinking and creativity. When a solution developed by an athlete (or group) does not work the coach should asked them to reflect upon why it did not work and to consider how it could be modified to work or decide it cannot work and seek a different solution. This is a 'solution-focused' approach that focuses the athlete's attention on the goals of the activity and what they can do to achieve these goals (Clarke and Dembowski, 2006; Grant, 2011). Here the athletes solve problems by drawing on the resources they have available and within the constraints of the rules or limits of the task that shape the solution and the learning taking place. This approach ensures that discussions are future-paced and focused directly on solutions to help prevent the athletes disengaging from the task (Grant, 2011) while aligning with Antonovsky's notion of *manageability*.

Whether it is a discussion between two swimmers about how to compensate for the reduction in thrust when doing one-arm butterfly or between members of a team playing small-sided games, there will be some disagreement because this is the nature of debate, but as the athletes develop their ability to debate and interact to achieve a common purpose this interaction will be more effective (Gréhaigne et al., 2005; Harvey and Light, 2015; Light, 2014b). Athletes unused to this empowerment and taking responsibility for actions and learning may also take some time to realize the opportunities on offer (see Roberts, 2011). This can also be demanding for the coach because it requires skill in shaping and facilitating productive interaction that can foster players'/athletes' abilities to negotiate, compromise and arrive at outcomes without making any participants feel 'wrong' or excluded and disengaged.

Developing effective questioning is not an easy task for coaches used to telling athletes what to do. The coach's contribution here is to promote a positive experience of inquiry and ask questions about what options or strategies might be appropriate to guide inquiry or to guide discovery when working on skills. This approach should help athletes learn to learn independently of the coach and that making mistakes is an essential part of learning when approached in this positive way. Such learning experiences can also promote resiliency, creativity, social learning, collective effort and an enjoyment of inquiry and discovery (Forrest, 2014).

Adopt an inquiry-based approach to athlete learning

Positive Pedagogy adopts an inquiry-based approach to learning. In the practice games used in Game Sense the teams are given opportunities to have 'team talks' at appropriate times (Light, 2013a) to collectively formulate strategies that they test and evaluate. The same approach is adopted in Positive Pedagogy whether it is two relay runners testing ideas for improving their baton changeover in a relay or groups of young people testing ideas for finding the best way to throw an object. After this they gather again to critically reflect upon how the strategy worked. If it didn't work they are asked to identify why it didn't work and formulate a new strategy or plan and test it.

While more confident and experienced players/athletes may initially dominate discussion the less experienced can make valuable contributions when encouraged by the coach. This way, athletes improve while developing confidence in their ability to become independent learners and problem solvers and so remain motivated to participate in the activity for the longer term (Renshaw et al., 2012). The productive social interaction involved in this process can also lead to athletes understanding each other as more than objects on the field or court. It encourages empathy, compassion, meaningful relationships, a sense of connection and care for each other as well, both on and off the field.

Regardless of age, to get athletes to speak up, take risks and be creative, coaches have to build an environment in which they feel secure enough to do so. This must involve coaches making it clear that mistakes are essential for learning and that they provide opportunities for learning (Renshaw et al., 2012). From a Positive Pedagogy perspective, mistakes are seen as constructive errors that are made into positive learning experiences with the provision of opportunities for adequate reflection and analysis. This can be facilitated though a focus on the longer term of the season or the development trajectories of teams or athletes so that they do not feel immediate pressure to succeed (Renshaw et al., 2010). The idea that 'mistakes are often the best teachers' (Rach et al., 2013, p. 22) helps develop an awareness of the process of learning and can make it meaningful enough to make it worthy of emotional commitment (Antonovsky, 1979).

Discussion

The challenges

This chapter outlines the Positive Pedagogy framework for coaching to encourage positive and effective learning in and through sport and other activities but there is no suggestion that this would be a smooth and unproblematic process. It offers ideas for Positive Pedagogy as a loose framework for coaches and others in teaching roles to think about, and draw on, to shape athlete learning but with no intention of being prescriptive. It also recognizes the challenges involved in undertaking such significant change in practice. There is no proposition here for a model with 'non-negotiable' components but, instead, broader suggestions about a pedagogical approach that coaches could draw on to make their coaching more positive and effective.

As is the case with GBAs such as Game Sense, the challenges involved in taking up a Positive Pedagogy approach can be confronting for many coaches. Designing and managing learning experiences and managing the constraints placed on the athletes requires the ability of a coach to analyze performance in practice and adjust the activity to get the best results. The effective use of questioning to stimulate thinking and interaction as part of its inquiry-based approach is also a substantial challenge, particularly for coaches who have previously relied upon direct instruction (see Roberts, 2011).

Research on Game Sense identifies how coaches can struggle with the different relationships required between coach and players and the perceptions of others (Evans, 2014). Others' perceptions of a good coach being explicitly in charge, transmitting knowledge, and of his/her practice session looking ordered and running smoothly typically contrast with the sometimes chaotic appearance of a Game Sense session (Light, 2004). The problems that this presents for coaches taking up GBA or Positive Pedagogy are tied into issues of power in coaching that have received some recent attention (see Taylor and Garrett, 2010). Some of the discomfort caused by shifting from being 'in command' to adopting a more equal relationship with athletes is largely due to the ways in which it challenges accepted power relationships in sport between athletes and the coach.

Taking up Positive Pedagogy can also be hindered by inadequate or partial understanding as is evident in Light and Evans' (2010) study on rugby coaches' interpretations of Game Sense. The same problem with shallow or limited understandings of the approach can occur on a larger scale. For example, the RFU (Rugby Football Union, England) chose to use Game Sense to guide the ongoing development of its coaching programmes but a recent study suggests that the lack of deep knowledge of Game Sense from the top down to coach educators and practising coaches is limiting its potential to make a significant contribution to improving coaching at a national level (Light et al., 2015).

Despite the challenges involved in taking up Positive Pedagogy and the need to account for them, the Positive Pedagogy framework can provide a means of making learning more positive across a wide range of sports settings. This approach emphasizes learning through the social interaction that has been strongly linked to joyful experiences (see for example Kretchmar, 2005; Harvey, 2009; Renshaw et al., 2012) with large-scale research in psychology also suggesting strong links between happiness, social interaction and social networks within which people respect others and are respected by them (see Fowler and Christakis, 2008). The social nature of learning emphasized in Positive Pedagogy and its inclusive nature can also facilitate a sense of belonging and self-esteem (see for example Light, 2002) with Deci and Ryan (2000) arguing that *relatedness* is a psychological requirement for human growth and the promotion of wellbeing. This is further emphasized in Seligman's PERMA model that Positive Pedagogy draws upon to make practice positive. The 'relationships' element of the PERMA model emphasizes the importance of supportive personal connections and the need to respect other people and feel respected to promote wellbeing.

The possibilities

In her Positive Pedagogy approach to teaching music, George (2006) argues that taking an approach to teaching that focuses on 'fixing' mistakes prevents learners experiencing the joy of self-discovery that can build self-confidence and autonomy. She contends that basing learning on the teacher correcting mistakes leads to a lack of learner focus, engagement and motivation, which are significant problems associated with directive, coach-centred approaches that focus on technical mastery of the sport skills approach (see Kirk 2005b, 2010). These attributes of Positive Pedagogy for learning music are surely as important for sport coaching and particularly when coaching children and young people.

Positive Pedagogy for coaching maintains a focus on the core aim of most coaching, which is the improvement of performance, but also helps athletes learn how to learn and develop both the motivation and confidence to learn. It also encourages the secondary learning of many of the same positive personal traits that Positive Psychology aims to develop such as compassion, resilience, self-confidence and creativity, or the competence, coping ability, health, resilience, and the wellbeing that Positive Youth Development through Sport aims at promoting (Holt et al., 2012). It can also facilitate positive social learning and social skills that participation in sport and physical activity are commonly assumed to deliver but which merely playing games will not necessarily teach (see De Martelaer et al., 2012; Light, 2013b). Although not specifically aimed at developing positive personal and social learning and social skills, the nature of Positive Pedagogy can encourage this development. For children's and youth sport coaches who value this secondary learning it can be enhanced by an explicit focus on it (Harvey et al., 2014).

Positive Pedagogy emphasizes the holistic, social nature of learning, and the role of experience, the body and its senses in it. It encourages the development of the social skills involved in engaging in purposeful dialogue, a willingness and ability to negotiate and compromise and the understanding of democratic processes involved in making and enacting collective decision-making while making learning enjoyable. Learning to learn and the positive inclinations towards learning it can generate, and some of the social learning that can accompany it, are more likely to transfer into life off the court, pool, track or field than improved sport technique and fitness are.

The way in which it can develop a positive inclination towards learning, and the contribution it can make towards wellbeing, would clearly be beneficial for children and young people participating in sport. It would also be of benefit for improving performance at any level and could make a contribution towards helping elite-level, professional athletes meet the challenges of developing post-playing careers while enhancing their wellbeing during this often difficult transition.

2

MAKING SENSE OF LEARNING

An holistic approach

This book follows on from *Advances in rugby coaching: An holistic approach*, which I wrote with John Evans, Stephen Harvey and Rémy Hassanin (2015), to further develop an holistic approach to coaching but with a focus on individual sports. Holism is a philosophical concept that sees parts of a whole as being intimately interconnected to the point that they cannot exist independently of the whole and cannot be understood without reference to the whole. As Aristotle claimed, 'The whole is greater than the sum of its parts'. Holism is opposed to epistemological reductionism, which claims that a complex system can be explained and understood by reducing it to its fundamental parts. From an ontological perspective, holism is opposed to atomism, which sees the world as being composed of an indefinite number of things exclusively characterized by intrinsic properties. However, this does not mean that taking an holistic position necessarily denies access to the tools of analytic analysis and particularly in regard to intentional phenomena (Esfeld, 1998).

The Game Sense approach to coaching team sports provides an example of a coaching approach that sits upon holistic philosophy. It focuses on the game as a whole and considers all aspects of play such as tactical knowledge, skill execution, awareness and decision-making as being inseparably interconnected. Conversely, coaching that divides the game into fundamental techniques that are drilled and refined out of the context of the game is underpinned by epistemological reductionism and atomistic ontology. It reduces the game to discrete components. My reference to an holistic coaching approach in this book includes views of a skill such as throwing or running as complex phenomena in which the various techniques involved are interrelated and, although they can be focused on in coaching, must be developed in relation to the whole skill. It also refers to an holistic view of humans as complex beings that cannot be reduced to component parts such as the mind, body, emotions and spirit. Drawing on Davis, Sumara and Luce-Kapler (2000), it could be described as being a complex approach rather than a complicated (mechanistic) one.

Theories of learning

The approach to coaching I present in this book finds its origins in Bunker and Thorpe's (1982) original ideas on TGfU that were first published over thirty years ago and which were influenced by earlier developments in teaching and coaching team sports such as the work of Mahlo (1974) and Wade (1967). Bunker and Thorpe's ideas for TGfU were a practical response to a practical problem with little effort devoted to theorizing how learning occurred (Light, 2013a). They identified how students who had been taught to play games with a focus on technique became technically sound but did not become good games players. They dealt with this by locating learning in modified games and emphasizing asking questions over telling students what to do. They did not suggest the use of any particular theory of learning that underpinned their work but, as it drew more interest from researchers in physical education and coaching from the 1990s, suggestions were made for theorizing the learning that TGfU generated.

Since then many suggestions have been made for theorizing learning in and through GBA which include constraints-led theory (see Renshaw et al., 2010), self-determination theory (see Mandigo et al., 2008), constructivism (see Richard and Wallian, 2005), CLT (see Light, 2014a) and situated learning theory (see Kirk and MacPhail, 2002). In this chapter I draw primarily on social constructivism but also on some of Piaget's individual constructivism, and particularly through CLT, complementary work in enactivism, and the notion of embodied cognition, to explain how Positive Pedagogy enhances learning in and through sport. All these approaches are based upon constructivist epistemology that sees knowledge as being constructed and contingent upon convention, human perception and social experience. Epistemology is a branch of philosophy concerned with answering the questions, what is knowledge and how do we acquire it?

Constructivism

There are various forms of constructivism that draw on different streams of thought with tensions and contradiction between them but, at a very basic level, constructivism contends that learning occurs by doing rather than observing and is a process of knowledge construction shaped by previous experience and knowledge. The different, and often competing, forms of constructivism are generally considered to fall into the two main camps of (1) psychological (also referred to as individual, personal or cognitive) constructivism that arises from the work of Jean Piaget, and social (or socio-cultural) constructivism originating in the work of Lev Vygotsky.

Many others have contributed to the ongoing development of constructivism for over half a century and the work of Dewey and Bruner has made a major contribution. Bruner originally followed and developed the work of Piaget but from the 1960s picked up on Vygotsky's work after its publication in English. Dewey is widely considered to be the most influential thinker in education over the twentieth century and has had a strong influence on my views on coaching and teaching. Recently his work has been effectively applied to understanding learning in and through GBA and the influence of context by Quay and Stolz (2014).

Psychological constructivism

Psychological constructivism originates in the work of Jean Piaget. A Swiss biologist, Piaget rejected the traditional idea that learning involved the passive assimilation of objective knowledge to propose that it is a dynamic process of cognitive adaptation. For Piaget, learning involves processes of cognitive adaptation to a 'perturbation' that disturbs cognitive equilibrium in response to which the learner draws on existing knowledge and experience to maintain or re-establish cognitive equilibrium (Piaget, 1975/1985). This is not a process of merely adding on new knowledge but instead one through which the learner interprets and constructs unique personal knowledge through the interaction of his or her previous experience and knowledge, and new experiences. This involves the learner both modifying the new knowledge or experience (assimilation) and changing his/her existing knowledge and cognitive structures to *accommodate* new knowledge.

Piaget's ideas on learning assume that knowledge is not merely received or taken in but, instead, that the learner actively interprets it through processes of exploration and discovery (McInerney and McInerney, 1998). Dewey's ideas on discovering knowledge encouraged the development of *discovery learning* by Bruner (1961) and guides some of the practical examples provided in Part III. Psychological constructivism emphasizes the intrapersonal dimensions of learning as a process of personal meaning-making. It sees the construction of knowledge as involving 'the activation and reorganization of existing knowledge to make a unique understanding of the world' (Chen and Rovegno, 2000, p. 357). Piaget also recognizes the importance of experience to suggest that thinking and learning are not restricted to the mind but extend to the body and its senses (Davis et al., 2000).

Social constructivism

Social constructivism is most strongly influenced by the work of Russian psychologist Lev Vygotsky, who died in 1934 but whose work did not begin to strongly influence Western thinking until its publication in English from the early 1960s (Vygotsky, 1962). Vygotsky stresses the central role of social interaction in the development of cognition (learning) as well as the importance of community for learning as a process of meaning-making and the inseparability of learning from culture (Vygotsky, 1978). His theory for the development of higher cognitive function in children proposes that reasoning emerges from practical activity within a particular social environment with an emphasis on language, and learning being contingent upon cultural practices.

The social constructivist perspective does not see cognition as being an individual process as does Piaget. Instead, it is seen as a collective process spread across the individual's world and strongly influenced by culture with understandings and capabilities that emerge from social interaction with a group seen to be greater than those that are possible at an intrapersonal level. Pedagogical approaches informed by social constructivism emphasize social interaction and dialogue, for example when children in school work in groups to share ideas and solve mathematical problems through collaboration. When coaching team sport, Game Sense provides a pedagogical approach informed by social constructivism that emphasizes collaborative problem solving between the whole team and between teams in small-sided games. In this approach the athletes are encouraged to come up with tactical solutions and develop strategies collectively that extend beyond verbal interaction to include the embodied dialogue that is possible in games as an ongoing conversation between players or students (Light and Fawns, 2001).

Positive Pedagogy is informed by social constructivism while drawing on elements of Piaget's psychological constructivism and the broader, more inclusive CLT (Davis and Sumara, 2003). However, it is worth noting the importance of not confusing a theory of human learning with pedagogy or teaching/coaching methods. Constructivism is a theory that attempts to explain how human learning occurs (Fosnot, 1996). It is not a way of teaching or coaching. Confusing learning theory with pedagogy or teaching methods leads to talk of constructivist coaching or constructivist teaching with coaches and teachers feeling obliged to *always* use questions and to *never* use direct instruction in their coaching or teaching. Such misinformed coaching is invariably stressful for the coach and fails to reach expectations of enhanced athlete learning and motivation. It can also contribute towards coaches abandoning promising practice because it doesn't work.

Piaget and Vygotsky both believed that children construct their own understanding of the world and unique knowledge but they differ significantly. Piaget's theory proposes that understanding is constructed from the learner's experiences of interactions with his/her physical world. Vygotsky believes that learning is co-constructed through interaction between the learner and other people, within which language plays a central role. He believes that children's learning and development are guided by a more knowledgeable member of their community and/or culture. This means that the knowledge constructed by the learner reflects something of the culture in which it developed but for Piaget the learner's knowledge is culture free.

The interpersonal or 'social' aspects of learning through which individuals absorb the habits and culture of their environment in a spontaneous, non-conscious and embodied way play a significant role in learning. This has implications for how we understand learning/improvement in sport and the ways in which we coach. It necessitates a repositioning of the coach and his/her role in learning so that learners are afforded the opportunity to make decisions independent of the teacher/coach. This includes being given the chance to reflect on experience, make meaning of it and reconstructing knowledge.

Complex learning theory (CLT)

Davis and Sumara (2003) proposed the concept of CLT as a means of circumnavigating some of the contradictions between different forms of constructivism. It is also influenced by their work in complexity theory that they have since further developed but is not a branch or form of it. Complexity theory is useful in describing the ways in which a range of phenomena or systems, which can range from large-scale economies to school organizations and the human brain, comprise a collective of interrelated, dynamic systems that cannot be reduced to discrete parts (Davis and Sumara 2001). Complexity theory focuses on the object of study as a complex system and, although it has been applied to education (see Davis and Sumara, 2008), and physical education (see Ovens et al., 2013), it is not a theory of learning.

Looking at improving technique in individual sports from a CLT perspective suggests that the execution of a skill is more of complex phenomena comprised of the engagement of the athlete's mind, body, sensations and emotions and the context s/he is working in. As Dewey (1934/1989, p. 246) argues, the environment (physical and socio-cultural) cannot be separated from experience and learning, because 'experience is a matter of interaction of organism with its environment' (see Quay and Stolz, 2014 for an excellent discussion of this in games teaching). Drawing on Dewey, Quay and Stolz argue that the organism does not sit inside the environment like an object in a box, but instead is part of the environment – they are inseparable. Learning in any individual sport involves more than just reproducing a predetermined, ideal technique or a collection of techniques. Even learning technique can be seen to be a process of interpretation and adaptation undertaken by the athlete with no two athletes having precisely the same technique in action (Light and Wallian, 2008).

Davis and Sumara (2003) propose three core principles that underpin CLT, which are that learning is a *social* process of *interpretation* and *adaptation*. Below I briefly outline these.

Adaptation

Reflecting the influence of Piaget, CLT sees learning as an ongoing process of adaptation and a complex, multifaceted and continuous process of change but with adaptation involving more than just a cognitive adaptation to a perturbation. It involves the whole person as a complex process with the learner inseparable from his/her environment (physical and social-cultural). This notion of adaptation draws significantly on Piaget and is influenced by complexity theory.

Social interaction

The attention paid to social interaction in CLT reflects the influence of social constructivism derived from the work of Vygotsky and others such as Dewey and Bruner. It rejects the idea of cognition as intrapersonal to see it as a process in which various thinking agents are inseparably intertwined. This means that personal knowledge and activity are enfolded in, and unfold from, social interaction, collective knowledge, knowing and activity.

Learners bring different sets of experiences, inclinations, and knowledge with them through which they interpret learning experiences that learning unfolds from. This emphasizes the notion of learning being a social process to suggest how it is deeply tied into social experience, not only at the site of the specific learning experience, but also in the individual's participation in the social and cultural practices of larger social and cultural settings. This is also emphasized in Lave and Wenger's (1991) concept of situated learning, relative to communities of practice, and legitimate, peripheral participation, which emphasizes embodied, non-conscious learning through participation in the practices of the community.

Interpretation

Common to Piaget and Vygotsky, CLT also sees learning as involving change resulting from interpretation and making sense of learning experiences. It rejects conceptions of knowledge as a representation of an external reality, learning as its internalization and the assumption of a pre-given external reality. Instead, it sees learners as constructing meaning and knowledge and interpreting learning experiences as a process that is deeply dependent upon perception.

The work of Merleau-Ponty (1962) on perception has influenced the development of contemporary learning theories such as social constructivism and enactivism (see Varela et al., 1991). Merleau-Ponty suggests that perception is a far more complex process than merely inputting information as information processing theory suggests it is. He emphasizes the connections between human biology and our *lived experiences* (see Husserl, 1962) of the world to suggest that perception is an interpretative act that involves more than just the passive reception of information fed into the brain via the body's senses. For Merleau-Ponty, perception involves the active projection of the individual's experience, which means that what we perceive varies according to our accumulated experiences. From this perspective, the world does not exist as an objective reality that is completely separate from us but, instead, as we perceive it and have experienced it, with Merleau-Ponty arguing that perception is the basis of all rationality.

Embodied learning

Recent studies on coach development highlight the powerful role that learning through experience within particular socio-cultural contexts plays in the implicit shaping of dispositions, beliefs and practice over time (see Hassanin and Light, 2014). As Bourdieu (1986, 1990) suggests, the implicit pedagogy of participation is powerful *because* it operates unnoticed at a level below the scrutiny of the conscious mind. This is illustrated in a study on the construction of coaching habitus among elite-level rugby coaches (Light and Evans, 2013). Evans' (2012, 2014) study on elite-level rugby coaches in Australia and New Zealand also illustrates how cumulative experience embodied over time operates below the level of consciousness to exert a profound influence on their beliefs about coaching and dispositions towards it and which can be seen as embodied learning. It also suggests the powerful influence of the socio-cultural contexts within which coaches learn to coach, which is the focus of Hassanin and Light's (2014) study on the development of beliefs about coaching by rugby coaches from Australia, New Zealand and South Africa.

The concept of cognition and learning underpinning this research rejects the division of the mind from the body to see the process of coach learning as being shaped by aspects of the living, experiencing body. This is also evident in Bourdieu's challenge to the cognitive bias in the social sciences (Bourdieu and Wacquant, 1992) and in the concepts of situatedness (as an agent embedded in and shaped his/her environment) and Lave and Wenger's (1991) situated learning, which highlights the implicit learning (embodiment) of culture through participation in the practices of communities of practice.

The concept of embodied learning identifies the long-term implicit learning at an embodied level that has received increasing attention in the physical education literature. It extends beyond specific learning, such as how to throw a javelin, to cultural, social and personal learning involved in cultural reproduction such as Evans, Davies and Rich's (2009) notion of embodied action. Stolz (2015) argues for the importance of embodied learning in sport and physical education by suggesting that psychological approaches to learning fail to provide an adequate explanation of how we come to understand meaningfully because they are disconnected from the role the body plays in learning and the notion of embodied learning. He argues that the notion of embodied learning offers an holistic conception of the whole person as an 'acting, feeling, thinking being-in-the-world, rather than as separate physical and mental qualities which bear no relation to each other' (Stolz, 2015, p. 474).

Embodied cognition

Attempts to account for the body and corporeal aspects of learning are also evident in the notion of embodied cognition and the embodied mind (see Maturana and Varela, 1987; Varela et al., 1991; Lakoff and Johnson, 1999; Borghi and Cimatti, 2010). These concepts largely originate from the philosophy of Kant and Merleau-Ponty, who was influenced by Husserl (1962) and his concept of phenomenological embodiment. Developed across a range of disciplines and sub-disciplines including cognitive science, social psychology, and sociology, embodied cognition recognizes the inseparability of mind and body and how the mind is not only connected to the body, but how the mind cannot function without the body. As

Stolz (2015, p. 475) suggests, 'the similarities with Merleau-Ponty's understanding of embodiment are striking'.

Embodiment

Husserl (1962) saw the body as a locus of distinctive sets of sensations that can only be experienced first-hand and as a system of movement possibilities that allow us to experience every moment of our situated, practical-perceptual life. His notion of kinaesthetic consciousness is not a consciousness *of* movement, but, instead, a subjectivity that is characterized by the ability to move freely and responsively. In Husserl's phenomenology of embodiment the body is a centre of experience that is *lived* through its ability to move and its distinctive sets of sensations, which play a central role in influencing how we encounter and relate to others as embodied agents. The body is thus not only a means of practical action but also plays a pivotal part in the deep structure of knowing and learning.

Enactive cognition

Varela et al. (1991) proposed the concept of *enaction* to emphasize how the experienced world is determined by mutual interactions between the physiology and biology of the organism, its sensorimotor circuit and the environment. Enactive cognition challenges the dualistic divisions of a pre-existing, external reality and its internal representations by arguing that it cannot account for the feedback from the actions of a situated, cognizing agent. The approach of Varela and his colleagues to embodied cognition draws on Merleau-Ponty and the phenomenological idea that cognitive agents 'bring forth' a world through the activity of their situated, lived bodies. It informs the enactivist approach discussed in the following section.

Enactivism

Enactivism proposes that cognitive processes are grounded in sensory behaviour and motor actions with Holton (2010) suggesting that it integrates the ideas of constructivism with embodied cognition, which makes it appealing as a way of understanding what learning occurs in sport and how it occurs (Lémonie et al., 2015). The notion of *agent* is central to enactivism in which learning is defined as a change in the internal structure of the agent, but it is the internal structure, or *internal dynamics*, of the agent that determines learning and not the stimulus from the environment (Proulx, 2004). Indeed, the internal dynamics of the agent shapes the environment as the agent experiences it – reflecting the influence of Merleau-Ponty. The same stimulus experienced a second time will thus not necessarily result in the same response for the same agent because the agent's system is continuously changing and so will not be the same because s/he has already learned. This is explained by the fact that experiences are understood and interpreted on the basis of the agent's existing knowledge and prior experiences, much as constructivism suggests they are.

It is the agent's internal dynamics that orient the kind of effect that an experience can have on them and what they learn from it. Indeed, the internal dynamics provide different worlds of experience for the agent because of the ways in which they shape interpretation, as explained by Varela et al. (1991, p. 9) who suggest that there are, 'many different worlds of experience – depending on the structure of the being involved and the kinds of distinctions it is able to make'. As the use of the word *being* suggests, this explanation of learning is not limited to humans, with Proulx (2004) drawing on the different ways in which animals and humans experience different worlds due to their different internal dynamics to illustrate this point. He provides an example of how different internal dynamics create different worlds of experience by comparing the different ways in which a dog and a human interpret the same seat differently. When a human sits on a seat s/he experiences it differently due to the dog's ability to pick up and interpret different smells to make sense of and give meaning to the place (its internal dynamics) that the human cannot do because of different internal dynamics.

Maturana and Varela's (1987, p. 27) suggestion that 'All doing is knowing and all knowing is doing' tells us much about enactivist perspective on learning in which knowledge is defined as *adequate/viable action in the world* (Proulx, 2004). Enactivism emphasizes the role of action and the body in learning and how cognition is not limited to the mind but is instead related to the extended body and its actions. The starting point of enactivism is the interaction between an individual and his/her environment. Here s/he is considered to be an autonomous or autopoietic (self-creating) agent (Arnoldi, 2006) who *enacts* a world of meaning through his/her actions. From an enactivist perspective, the agent initiates his/her environment through his/her internal dynamics that are, in turn, shaped by it (Varela et al., 1991). Social interactions are seen to be structured processes that emerge from the dynamics of the participants' coordination with each other and which potentially allow for building a form of intersubjectivity (Maturana and Varela, 1987). They are dialectically structuring processes in that social interactions affect the construction of meaning and the actions of individuals (De Jaegher and Di Paolo, 2007).

In enactivism *sense-making* is the capacity of an individual to *enact* a world and imbue it with significance from his/her point of view with the notion of sense-making extended to the field of social interactions through the concept of *participatory sense-making* (De Jaegher and Di Paolo, 2007). In participatory sense-making, individuals participate in and shape each other's meaning-making through social interaction as is illustrated in a recent study on teacher–student interaction in French swimming classes (Lémonie et al., 2015). From this perspective, the interaction effects can be seen as being *constructive* effects (Samurçay and Rabardel, 2004) that affect the lived experience of each individual and generate learning as a process of transformation.

Constructivism and enactivism

Constructivism has made a significant contribution towards understanding learning in and through participation in sport and physical education but there are concerns that the vocabulary used to describe learning as a process of 'construction' with references to 'knowledge' and 'mental models' does not provide an adequate account of the fluid, 'ever-changing' and elusive nature of learning (Davis and Sumara, 2003; Varvey, 2009). In social constructivism, learners are seen to interpret experience according to their existing knowledge and mental structures to construct their own understandings and new knowledge (Varvey, 2009). Enactivism sees learning in a similar way but with more attention paid to the body and action by seeing learning as being a 'stabilizing and expansionary process that sustains order and novelty within learner's [enacted] worlds' (Horn and Wilburn, 2005, p. 749). Indeed, it has been suggested that enactivism can better account for action than constructivism by suggesting that learning occurs *in* experience instead of *through* experience while emphasizing the inseparability of individual and context (Fenwick, 2001). Enactivism can also be seen to account for 'non-cognitive knowing' in the form of emotion, intuition and sensations (see Begg, 2013; Colombetti, 2014) with learning as the transformation of the world of learners enacted through interaction.

Knowledge and knowing in sport

Constructivism, CLT and enactivism reject divisions between the knower and the known and views of knowledge as an object that can be transmitted from one person to another. If we were to accept that knowledge is an object that can be passed from the coach to the athlete we might well ask whether or not the coach loses any knowledge in the process. From a constructivist perspective, the learner draws on existing knowledge, experience and dispositions to interpret learning experiences through which s/he constructs new understanding and knowledge that involves change in existing knowledge and knowing.

As I have suggested with Rod Fawns (2003), knowing something, whether it is how to throw a javelin, perform a tumble turn in swimming or strike a croquet ball accurately and with appropriate power, means being able to do it.

The body and learning

There is always some engagement of the body and its senses in cognition and learning that, at the very least, involves the act of perception (Lakoff and Johnson, 1999). The body's senses are employed in all learning, including sight, hearing, touch, motor responses, and other senses such as that of a 'sixth sense' or a practical sense of things (Bourdieu, 1986) that involves the body in more than a biological sense. There are more ways of knowing than just through rational thought and language. Perception is more than merely a biological function of the body because it involves interpretation that is shaped by experience (Merleau-Ponty, 1962; Varela et al., 1991). Infants learn through their eyes, ears, tactile sensations, combinations of senses and nonverbal social interaction well before the development of language as learning that Dewey (1916/1997, p. 142) suggests involves the use of 'organs of the process of doing something from which meaning results'.

There is no denying the central role language plays in learning but the importance placed on language in formal education can promote a view of education as a process of transmitting objective knowledge that neglects the body's role in learning. Before children enter school they have learned language through participation in 'the intercourse of life' (Dewey, 1916/1997, p. 17). By this time they are already competent in the complex tasks of language and locomotion through the interaction of their biology and their engagement in their immediate socio-cultural environment. This implicit learning is recognized in recent attempts to understand how we learn, not just in schools and universities, but also across our lives, such as in the work of Lave and Wenger (1991), Varela (see Varela et al., 1991) and others.

In sport, thinking is not restricted to a disembodied mind with recent work suggesting the inseparability of thought from action during 'at-action' decision-making in team sports (Light, Harvey et al., 2014). This work also questions simple linear explanations of the relationship between mind and body in action such as that of information processing theory. Notions of the body thinking and of embodied cognition (see Varela et al., 1991) also reflect challenges to the separation of mind from body in action.

There is some danger of taking a dualistic approach to facilitating learning when using GBA for coaching team sports by seeing the learning by doing in practice games and the learning through dialogue such as in the debate of ideas (Gréhaigne et al., 2005) as being separate. One way of avoiding this lies in conceiving of learning as an ongoing conversation between the body, expressed in action through games, and the mind, expressed in speech and in articulated reflection after action (Light and Fawns, 2003). This also requires recognition of the relationship between rational, articulated knowledge (declarative) and embodied or enacted knowledge (procedural) that is discussed in more detail in chapter 4. This is equally applicable to teaching individual sport using Positive Pedagogy.

The concept of a learning conversation between mind and body is an attempt to understand how GBA pedagogy links non-conscious, embodied learning and conscious learning as expressed through language. Such conceptions of athlete learning reflect a constructivist view of knowledge as being inseparable from the learner and of cognition as being both embodied and distributed across groups of people and not restricted to the individual mind.

Discussion

This chapter outlines the theories of learning that have shaped my thinking about coaching and athlete learning and which underpin the development of Positive Pedagogy for coaching. The approach taken to enhancing learning throughout this book sits upon holistic ontology (assumptions about the nature of being and existence) and constructivist epistemology (assumptions about what knowledge is and how we attain it). Holistic ontology can see the whole world as one holistic system or, from a more moderate perspective, to be limited to specific systems such as biological systems that are characterized by a particular principle of internal organization

(Esfeld, 1998). As one of five branches of epistemology, the constructivist epistemology Positive Pedagogy sits upon sees knowledge as being constructed and shaped by convention, human perception and social experience.

There are aspects of GBA and Positive Pedagogy that seem to lend themselves to the use of other theories proposed for understanding and improving learning in and through them but there are important differences in the epistemology that they sit upon. For example, the consideration of the interaction between individual and environment in constraints-led theory seems to fit with GBA and Positive Pedagogy. However, it sits more upon empiricist epistemology and is informed by behaviourist perspectives on learning as is evident in the idea of perception-action coupling and the notion of skill acquisition and acquiring movement patterns (see Renshaw et al., 2010). On the other hand, despite differences between various forms of constructivism, CLT and enactivism, they all sit upon the same philosophical assumptions with them also having a strong influence upon embodied cognition. This makes them reasonably complementary explanations of learning that can be drawn on in considering learning in and through Positive Pedagogy.

Clearly, social constructivism forms the most significant influence upon my development of Positive Pedagogy. This is particularly so with its emphasis on dialogue in reflection upon action and in the inquiry-based nature of this pedagogy, but aspects of Piaget's individual constructivism can also contribute towards understanding how learning occurs when using Positive Pedagogy. From the perspectives of those working within constructivism, contradictions between Piaget and Vygotsky may well make them irreconcilable but for the often multi-disciplinary approach taken in sport coaching this is less of a problem. Davis and Sumara's (2003) concept of CLT has offered me a pragmatic and useful means of analyzing learning in individual sport using Positive Pedagogy (see Light, 2014b).

Enactivism and the concept of embodied cognition (with various interpretations) can also be drawn on to help highlight the role of the body and movement in learning that, it has been suggested, constructivism neglects (Fenwick, 2001). Piaget and Vygotsky both pay some attention to action and physical experience but this is more evident in Dewey's belief that an individual's present experience and the learning emerging from it is a function of the interaction between his/her past experiences and the present experience (Dewey, 1938a). Dewey has had a significant influence on social constructivism and the central role that experience plays in his theory of experience can illuminate the role that the body, its senses and movement can play in learning, but there is a stronger focus on this in enactivism and embodied cognition.

3

MAKING LEARNING POSITIVE

As an athlete-centred, inquiry-based approach the pedagogical features of Positive Pedagogy promote positive experiences of practice through which athletes learn the content of the practice session, learn how to learn, and develop a positive inclination towards learning. The learning experiences Positive Pedagogy provides can also contribute towards positive social, moral and personal development (see for example Dyson 2005; Sheppard and Mandigo 2009; Light 2013b) but this is not its specific aim. To enhance the positive nature of learning that arises from the pedagogical features of Positive Pedagogy it draws on Antonovsky's (1979, 1987) salutogenic theory and SoC model and Positive Psychology (see Seligman and Csikszentmihalyi, 2000). This chapter focuses on the contribution that these two areas of work make towards making athletes' experiences of practice positive.

Antonovsky's salutogenic theory and SoC model

Antonovsky's (1979, 1987) salutogenic theory and SoC model suggest conditions from which good health and positive wellbeing originate. A medical sociologist, Antonovsky focuses on the socially constructed resources that facilitate people's achieving and maintaining good health. He developed the concept of 'salutogenesis' in reference to the origins of health by taking a positive, holistic approach that complements the holistic approach underpinning Positive Pedagogy for coaching. Salutogenesis is positive in that it emphasizes what supports health and wellbeing rather than what causes disease, or the 'lifestyle' approach that focuses on identifying risk factors that threaten good health and wellbeing (Antonovsky, 1996).

Antonovsky's work draws on the strengths–based approach used in social work. It takes a positive approach to help clients deal with adversity by being future-focused and drawing on the strengths they bring with them to solve or deal with the problems facing them (see Saleebey, 2005). Strengths-based approaches focus on the capacities, skills, knowledge and potential that individuals have to deal with challenges but do not ignore challenges or attempt to 'spin' weaknesses into strengths. Taking this strengths-based approach in coaching does not merely involve using positive language to put a positive spin on things. Coaches drawing on the strengths-based approach would work in collaboration with athletes to help them identify and develop their strengths and to do things for themselves by becoming motivated, competent and confident learners instead of being passive consumers of information. If a girls' secondary school football (soccer) team is down 10–0 at half-time, telling them they are playing well and to just keep doing their best is not taking a strengths-based approach. Indeed, the girls would be unlikely to believe the coach, which would erode trust between them. Identifying what they have done well and what they can do well and working with them as a team to formulate a plan for the second half and, perhaps, setting an achievable goal of reducing the gap by playing better as a team, would provide a far more positive experience for them.

Antonovsky focuses on what social factors contribute positively towards good health and wellbeing rather than on what prevents people from enjoying it. He is also more concerned with the affective and social dimensions of life with a focus on experience than with its cognitive aspects. His SoC model comprises three elements in life that he sees as providing the conditions for good health to emerge from and which are easily adapted to provide conditions from which positive athlete learning can unfold. They are: (a) comprehensibility, (b) manageability and (c) meaningfulness. In my development of Positive Pedagogy, I appropriated these concepts to develop an approach to coaching that produces positive experiences of learning for athletes by making practice comprehensible, manageable and meaningful. Here I explain these elements in more detail than in chapter 1 and, as applied to coaching, to suggest how they can be used to contribute towards positive learning experiences for athletes.

Comprehensibility

For Antonovsky, comprehensibility is developed through experience and refers to the extent to which things make sense for the individual in that events and situations are ordered and consistent. For learning to be comprehensible it should help athletes understand the sport and how the activities involved in practice help them improve. As is suggested in so much of the GBA literature, athletes need to know not only how to do something (whether a technique or tactical aspect of their sport) but also when, where and why to do it in the context of a competition game. This is equally applicable to performance in individual sport where the athlete should also know why s/he is doing a practice activity, how it fits into the goals of the session and the season and how it is going to help him/her improve and develop in the long term.

Like TGfU and other GBAs that emphasize conceptual understanding, Positive Pedagogy aims to foster deep understanding of the core concepts that underpin performance and which are learned through both action and language. For example, in chapter 8 on swimming, the improvement of skill in the two sessions sits upon the swimmers understanding the core concepts of swimming as reducing resistance and maximizing propulsion. This understanding is comprehensible, not only because it is rational, conscious and articulated, but because it also involves a practical, embodied understanding or practical sense (Bourdieu, 1986). This is developed through experience and engagement in a process of learning as the unfolding of knowledge that includes learning how to learn. It is evident in the emphasis placed on deep understanding of the core concepts of the manipulation of space and time in team sports when using GBAs such as Game Sense. It is also emphasized in Positive Pedagogy for individual and skill-intensive sports such as swimming (chapter 8 and Light, 2014a), running (chapter 10 and Light and Kentel, 2015) and throwing events (chapter 11).

Manageability

Manageability refers to the extent to which an individual feels s/he has the resources at hand to manage stress and challenge. Day-to-day life invariably involves having to deal with stress in varying forms and with the establishment and maintenance of good health and wellbeing shaped by our ability to manage this stress. Resources can be objects such as tools and equipment, skills, intellectual ability, social and cultural capital, connections, and so on. When using Positive Pedagogy for coaching the coach presents the athletes with challenges that are designed and managed to extend them and which may make them feel a degree of discomfort or pressure, physically, emotionally and/or cognitively. To have a positive experience of dealing with this stress the athlete must see the task as being a significant and meaningful challenge but one that s/he feels that s/he can deal with by drawing on the resources s/he has at hand.

Challenges are manageable for an athlete when they can be met by drawing on individual resources such as skill, physical capacity, intelligence or prior experience. The resources that the athlete has to draw on also include the knowledge that can be constructed through social interaction with peers within groups (including pairs) and the dialogue that social constructivism suggests is central to learning, such as in the debate of ideas (Gréhaigne et al., 2005). Here, positive experience of meeting challenges through focused and purposeful dialogue gives the athlete confidence in his/her ability to improve and to meet challenges through working with others. In Positive Pedagogy the coach aims to set challenges aimed at helping the athlete negotiate the proximal zone of development (Vygotsky, 1978) that extends him/her while encouraging him/her to feel that s/he can manage the task.

The coach can create the conditions for the athlete to be suitably challenged and see the relevance and importance of the challenge while also feeling that he/she can manage it. This means that designing and/or managing learning activities or experiences that provide an optimal level of challenge and learning are of critical importance for making learning challenging and manageable. The provision of a supportive socio-moral environment assists the coach in making challenges manageable and rewarding for the athlete(s). It does so by reducing anxiety and giving them the confidence to commit and to take some risks. This means that for a task to seem manageable the athlete should feel that s/he has the required skill and understanding, and can draw on the social resources of teammates and the coach, to meet it. The collective, social element is very important here.

Meaningfulness

In his work on culture and meaning Geertz (1973) sees meaning as being the desires, intentions, beliefs and values of the participants in the social setting being studied. Drawing on Geertz, Ortner (1999, p. 146) suggests that meaning is essentially a 'set of broad conceptions – about which the world is like, how it is put together, how human social beings should conduct themselves in it as a social complex of practices'. With his focus on health and wellbeing, Antonovsky uses the term *meaningfulness* in reference to how much the individual feels that life makes sense and that its challenges are worthy of commitment. For Antonovsky, meaningfulness promotes a positive expectation of life and the future and encourages people to see challenges as being interesting, relevant and worthy of their emotional commitment.

Meaningfulness is closely tied into comprehensibility. When activities engage athletes affectively and socially as well as physically and intellectually they are likely to be meaningful and thus encourage commitment from them. The Game Sense approach in team sport can make practice meaningful by situating learning in modified games that replicate aspects of the real game and that generate whole-person experiences of competition matches. This is more likely to give practice meaning and relevance than the repetition of technique removed from the game and particularly when brought to life through setting the appropriate level of challenge and engaging the athletes in productive dialogue.

Seeing and feeling the relevance of practice for competition in individual sports and understanding the aims and purposes of practice promotes engagement in athletes and gives meaning to tasks and experiences because the athletes understand what they are trying to achieve and why. Learning is made meaningful in practice when its comprehensibility gives meaning to the tasks and activities involved because they make sense in relation to the core concepts of the sport. For example, in team sports the core concepts are the manipulation of space and time and in swimming they are maximizing propulsion and minimizing resistance (see chapter 8). Focused on throwing the javelin, chapter 11 provides another example of how coaching can promote meaningfulness for the athlete. The first activity leads the young athletes to discover four principles of throwing in general that acts as a knowledge base they can draw on to understand the technique for throwing the javelin by linking it to these principles.

To assist in fostering comprehensibility and meaningfulness the coach should explain what each activity and session aims to achieve and why the athletes will be doing them before beginning. Of course this is only possible when the coach has thought through what s/he is doing for the session and season and why. This could involve discussions with the athlete, or athletes, before the season starts. Devoting a little time to a session or two that focus on understanding the core concepts of the sport at the beginning of the season, as suggested in chapters 8, 10 and 11, would help when trying to link technical detail to core concepts. This should not just involve cognitive processes but also the affective, emotional and corporeal learning that encourages long-term engagement with the activity (Renshaw et al., 2012). Having players know the strategy and plans for the season would add further to fostering comprehensibility.

Positive affective experiences of practice

During my early experiences of teaching Game Sense in pre-service teacher education programmes at The University of Melbourne and conducting research on it I was most impressed with the positive affective responses it generated among so many of the pre-service primary school teachers who had chosen to specialize in physical education (see Light, 2002). This was reinforced by my observations of primary school students' enjoyment and excitement during participation in the modified games taught by my students during visits to local schools where they taught games using a Game Sense approach (see Light and Tan, 2006). As a former primary school teacher and secondary school physical education teacher, joyful experiences of sport and other physical activity always produced the most satisfaction for me as a teacher and coach of young people, and as an observer of others' teaching and coaching.

The joy, excitement, enthusiasm and pleasure that can emerge from using a GBA approach suggest the positive affective experiences of learning across a range of cultural and institutional settings, different sports, ages and levels of experience that it can generate (see Mandigo et al., 2008; Fry et al., 2010; Train, 2012). Making practice fun and generating positive states such as joy, delight, pleasure and happiness could justifiably be the goal of teaching and coaching, and particularly for coaching children and young people (see Strean and Holt, 2000; Kretchmar, 2005; Train, 2012). Although Positive Pedagogy invariably generates these states to different degrees its prime focus is on creating conditions to maximize learning (improvement) and to help athletes learn how to learn.

Enjoyment

Positive experiences of practice can boost athlete motivation, confidence in competing and learning, resilience and interpersonal relationships, but do not necessarily generate visible displays of joy or look like fun. In some sports played at highly competitive levels a positive practice session can be brutally demanding and exhausting but still be positive and *enjoyable*. Although Positive Pedagogy includes speaking and thinking in positive ways, positive physical experience is of central importance and, as much as it may test the athlete(s) and involve some form of pain or discomfort in particular settings, emphasizes what they can do and how they are improving.

Introducing six-year-old girls and boys to beach sprinting in the nippers (junior surf life-saving) or athletics has radically different aims and methods than coaching an Olympic 100-metre sprinter or a professional boxer preparing for a world title fight, but should still provide positive experiences for the individual. The main aim of Positive Pedagogy is to provide positive experiences of practice that maximize learning outcomes (improvement), promote motivation and develop the athlete's ability and inclination to be an active and self-directed learner – regardless of the sport and the level it is played at. For children first learning to play sport, the focus of coaching should be on making it enjoyable while helping them to learn, with the degree of fun they are having typically being explicitly evident in happy faces, laughter, excitement and high levels of interaction. While physically and emotionally demanding practice sessions in highly professional sport may not produce much laughter, visible joy or excitement, they should still be enjoyable.

Positive wellbeing: an added extra

In addition to the ways in which positive states such as enjoyment contribute to athlete learning and improvement they can make a contribution towards developing what the Positive Psychology literature refers to as 'positive wellbeing'. Positive wellbeing is a broad and conclusive term typically used in reference to an individual's or group's state of being comfortable, happy and healthy but which includes their social, economic, medical, psychological and spiritual state. This is not a case of coaching with the specific goal of improving wellbeing but more one of it being a by-product of good pedagogy that the coach should think about and enhance where possible, particularly with younger athletes. When coaching children and young people this provides opportunity for the coach to focus on sport, contributing to the development of their positive wellbeing without detracting from their learning and athletic improvement. For athletes working at the elite level this is likely to be less important but the nature of the pedagogy will usually make a contribution to wellbeing – even when the coach does not focus on it.

The physical education and youth sport literature makes much reference to positive states that can contribute to developing positive wellbeing but with varying interpretations of them and views on their importance in youth sport and physical education (see Light, 2003; Kretchmar, 2005; Garn and Cothran, 2006; Strean and Holt, 2000; Pringle, 2010; Train, 2012). For example, fun is a contested term in the physical education literature (see Griffin et al., 1993) with two broadly different views on its importance based upon different perceptions of what it is.

Kretchmar (2005) argues that physical education teachers should have the 'lofty' affective goal of ensuring that students experience delight because, in tandem with providing the understanding that TGfU emphasizes, it would enable teachers of games to provide meaningful experiences for them. Strean and Holt (2000) suggest that fun exerts a positive influence on long-term participation in sport and physical education but that it is a 'subset' of enjoyment as a broader concept of positive affective experience. Scanlan and Simons (1992, p. 202) describe enjoyment as 'a positive affective response to the sport that reflects generalised feelings such as pleasure, liking and fun' but which is 'more general than a specific emotion such as excitement'. This is a useful term for including the range of positive states that athletes, from young children to the most elite, experience. It can be used to describe engagement in practice that is demanding and taxing but with no external indicators of the athletes 'having fun', yet is positive.

Strean and Holt (2000) go as far as to suggest that providing young people with opportunities for having safe and challenging fun with friends is important enough to be the *raison d'être* of youth sport. Ask any parent what they want for their children and they will invariably say that they want them to be happy, and this should be a core aim of any education system, but teaching for happiness is typically seen as being a soft option in schools (Erriker, 2009). Others see fun as a short-term experience of little significance for learning and dismiss it as an inappropriate outcome for physical education (see Garn and Cothran, 2006) but physical education teachers and their students consistently rate having fun as their top priority. It is also one of the main reasons why children and young people choose to participate in sport (O'Reilly et al., 2001; Garn and Cothran, 2006; Light, 2016).

Happiness has a wide variety of meanings ranging from a superficial view reflected in Placek's (1983) criticism of physical education teachers whose main aim is to keep their students 'busy, happy, and good' at the expense of learning, to a broader view of it being central to the development of positive wellbeing (see Diener, 2000) and effective learning (McGeown et al., 2015). Physical education and sport can make a significant contribution towards the development of positive wellbeing for young people as an important aspect of the schooling experience and something that should be valued for what it is. It can also contribute to other aspects of schooling and to development of young people into mature members of their community and society. Indeed, Dewey (1938a) emphasizes how education should provide students with experiences in the short term that are immediately valuable for the individual but which also enable students to contribute to society in the long term.

Happiness in children and young people has an important influence on their health, wellbeing and personal development that includes having a sense of belonging, having satisfying social networks, having personal confidence, being prepared to take on challenges and being resilient. Happy children and young people learn better, display more emotional literacy and are better behaved (Erriker, 2009). Positive experiences of practice also make a valuable contribution to improving team and individual performance at any level of sport.

Positive Psychology

Positive Psychology sets out to redress a traditional preoccupation of psychology with pathologies and repairing the 'worst aspects' of life by taking a positive approach that promotes its positive qualities (Seligman and Csikszentmihalyi, 2000). Focused on wellbeing and satisfaction in the past, on happiness and the experience of 'flow' in the present and on hope and optimism in the future (Jackson and Csikszentmihalyi, 1999), it aims to build 'thriving individuals, finding and nurturing talent and making, normal life more fulfilling' (Seligman and Csikszentmihalyi, 2000, p. 5).

In Positive Psychology the concept of flow refers to a state of being absorbed in the experience of action through intense concentration, as the athlete is 'lost' in the flow of experience to provide optimal (non-conscious) learning. This suggests an holistic conception of athlete experience in sport when they are extended to a point where mind and body are united. The Japanese concept of *mushin* offers another holistic conception of being lost in the flow as a state in which the person performing an action experiences a state of mind–body unity (see Light, 2014c; Light and Kentel, 2015; Suzuki, 1959). Positive Psychology uses the concept of flow to describe a psychologically positive state that generates learning. In Positive Pedagogy, I have drawn on the Japanese concept of *mushin* to suggest a similar state in which the person performing an action or actions experiences a state of mind–body unity (see Light, 2014c; Light and Kentel, 2015; Suzuki, 1959). *Mushin* is a state that expert performers across a range of cultural activities from *ikebana* (flower arrangement), *shodō* (calligraphy) and *budō* (martial arts) strive to achieve and which Suzuki (1959) suggests translates into English as 'no mind'.

Flow has been proposed as a way of explaining the experiences possible when participating in sport and practice that provides appropriate levels of challenge (Jackson and Csikszentmihalyi, 1999; Kretchmar, 2005; Harvey et al., 2014). GBA can provide the conditions that generate experiences of flow for athletes in team sports (Lloyd and Smith, 2010), with sports that require a connection with nature such as snowboarding, sailing and surfing also providing ideal conditions for the athletes to experience flow (see Light, 2016).

Positive Pedagogy does not specifically focus on promoting happiness or developing wellbeing but all five elements of Seligman's (2012) PERMA model are evident in Positive Pedagogy, which suggests how it can contribute to positive wellbeing. Below I list the five elements of the PERMA model for positive wellbeing and briefly suggest how Positive Pedagogy meets the expectations of these elements:

1. *Positive emotions.* Positive Pedagogy generates positive emotions such as joy or delight, deep engagement in learning, the building of relationships and a sense of belonging to the group, team or club that the learner is involved in (see Kretchmar, 2005; Light, 2003).
2. *Engagement.* By making the relevance of practice to performance clear, Positive Pedagogy can give meaning to the tasks involved in learning by making them

relevant and comprehensible which is needed to foster engagement (Antonovsky, 1979). Empowering athletes to shape practice to achieve their performance/learning goals also enhances engagement.

3. *Relations.* Positive Pedagogy emphasizes dialogue between athletes and between the athlete(s) and the development of collaborative relationships that are facilitated by the inquiry-based approach it adopts. This all builds trusting and productive relationships in the team, squad or group and/or between the athlete and coach.

4. *Meaning.* In Positive Pedagogy learning is made comprehensible (Antonovsky, 1979) which, in turn, gives meaning to the tasks and activities involved because they make sense in relation to the core concepts of the sport and the aims of the session and season.

5. *Achievement.* Positive Pedagogy provides opportunities for achievement through providing appropriate levels of challenge in practice that extend the athlete but enable him/her to succeed by drawing on resources such as his/her skills and/or the contributions of athletes s/he is practising with.

Positive Pedagogy does not deny what the athlete cannot do or has not been able to do but does emphasize what s/he *can* do or is capable of doing and how s/he can draw on the resources available to meet learning challenges.

Diener (2000) proposes four conditions that are required for people to experience positive wellbeing that have significance and relevance for athlete learning in sport. Briefly, these are that happy people, (1) have supportive social networks within which they are respected and respect others, (2) have long-term goals they work towards achieving, (3) feel a sense of mastery or competence in something, and (4) have the discipline to sustain a positive outlook on and approach to life. The first three of these correspond with the literature on youth sport that identifies what makes playing sport a positive experience. Although the focus of research on participation in youth sport tends to concentrate on barriers and what makes young people drop out, it does identify the more positive aspects of sport for them. More recent research that focuses on the positive aspects of participation in sport adds to this knowledge (see Cope and Pearce, 2013; Light et al., 2013). It identifies the central importance of the social environment, friendships and interpersonal relations with peers, coaches and other people in sports clubs, the importance of feeling competent or having a degree of mastery, and of learning to set and achieve goals (see Allen, 2003; Kirk, 2005b; Fraser-Thomas et al., 2005).

The first three factors that Diener (2000) suggests are needed to lead happy lives have also been very evident in studies I have been involved in on children's and young people's experiences of sport over the past decade (see Light, 2016). For example, in a study on nine- to twelve-year-old children in a swimming club the twenty participants seemed to be very happy in their club with the factors contributing to this happiness aligning with Diener's factors. They enjoyed a supportive social environment and good friendships with children in their squads, in other squads in the same club, and sometimes in other clubs, as well as having positive relationships with coaches and parents in the club. They felt they had a place in the club and their squad with the relevance and meaning of swimming in their lives assisted by significant family involvement in the club. They also felt respected and expressed respect for others, including older swimmers, parents and the coaches. All had short-term goals, with the more serious swimmers committed to regular interclub competition having long-term goals in competition. Similar factors contributing to happiness among children and young people in sport were evident in other studies I have conducted on children's and young people's sport and in studies reported on in the literature on youth sport and physical education.

Discussion

The athlete-centred and inquiry-based nature of Positive Pedagogy encourages positive experiences of learning for athletes that contribute towards maximizing learning outcomes (improvement), promote motivation and developing the athlete's ability and inclination to be an active and self-directed learner. It is not focused on personal, social or moral development but this can be a secondary, incidental learning outcome that coaches can enhance if they choose to, which would be appropriate when coaching children and young people. Experiencing positive states such as joy and delight that Positive Pedagogy can generate is also not its explicit aim but typically emerges from a GBA or Positive Pedagogy session and particularly with younger athletes. When coaching children and young people their experience of fun is typically evident in happy faces, laughter, excitement and high levels of interaction.

Positive states enhance learning in schools (Erriker, 2009; McGeown et al., 2015) and in athletic performance (see Tabeian et al., 2015). The concept of *enjoyment* is useful here because it provides a way of conceptualizing and under-standing how positive, whole-person experiences contribute to improved perfor-mance without being visibly joyful. Psychology refers to mental states as related to the mind but there are holistic conceptions of states that people experience, such as the concept of mindfulness as used in Buddhism, that better capture the notion of positive 'states' I refer to in sport. It would be too easy to dispense with the con-tribution that these positive states make towards improving performance and to think that they only matter for children and young people. While physically and emotionally demanding practice sessions in highly professional sport may not pro-duce much laughter, visible joy or excitement, they can, and should, be enjoyable to get the best out of the athlete.

Antonovsky's work aligns well with the positive experiences that Positive Pedagogy strives to provide as does its holistic approach that focuses on the affective and social dimensions of life. His focus on experience rather than on the cognitive aspects of life also complements both the pedagogy I suggest and the perspectives on human learning that underpin it and which are outlined in the previous chapter. The three conditions he suggests contribute to good health and wellbeing interact and can be applied to coaching to promote positive physical, affective and social experiences of learning in sport at any level. The appropriation of Antonovsky's work for Positive Pedagogy makes a strong contribution towards making any practice, at any level, positive but without necessarily being overtly enjoyable.

My use of Positive Psychology is also aimed at enhancing positive wellbeing but its focus is on thought, language and behaviour linked to the mind. Positive states assist in learning (Erriker, 2009) and the positive disposition that Positive Psychology can promote is helpful in all coaching regardless of age, experience or level of competition. Its integration with Positive Pedagogy assists with developing a more positive outlook and attitude for any athlete but is probably more important when used in youth sport where making practice fun, pleasurable and delightful is of prime importance.

Antonovsky's work and Positive Psychology is not only useful for assisting in making learning positive but also encourages questioning the idea that sport is somehow separate from society and day-to-day life. It does this by highlighting the significance of what is learned in sport for life outside sport and the significance of what is learned outside sport for learning in sport. This is well illustrated by the resurgence of the New Zealand All Blacks rugby team from a slump in form in 2004 to winning the 2011 Rugby World Cup under the coaching of Sir Graham Henry. Henry (2013) encouraged the team to re-embrace its history and culture, which included understanding the meaning of the *haka* and how it related to the team's identity. This holistic approach included recognizing the links between life outside and inside the All Blacks as one of the most successful international sports teams of all time and is captured in the catch cry, *Better people make better All Blacks.*

PART II

Pedagogical features of Positive Pedagogy

4

DESIGNING AND MANAGING LEARNING EXPERIENCES

Of the tasks facing coaches in taking up athlete-centred, inquiry-based approaches such as Positive Pedagogy the design and management of learning experiences and questioning are typically the most challenging (Pill, 2011; Light, 2013a). Designing the learning activities to be used is the first step in setting up a Positive Pedagogy coaching session with the coach having done most of his/her work well before the session starts. The central role that modified practice games play in GBAs such as Game Sense sets them apart from traditional coaching, which breaks the game up into component parts to be worked on separate to the game environment. These two approaches sit upon quite different assumptions about knowledge and how we acquire it. The learning theory outlined in chapter 2 emphasizes the role that experience plays in learning and this is why GBA and Positive Pedagogy place experience at the centre of learning.

Learning through experience

According to Dewey (1916/1997), learning occurs through experience in two ways, which are through: (1) engagement with the physical learning activity and (2) reflection upon this experience as a second experience.

The physical experience

Learning through the experience of playing the modified games used in GBA involves players adapting to the demands of a dynamic physical environment and making a wide range of decisions and largely occurs at a non-conscious level of cognition. When coaching team sports corporeal knowledge is developed through participation in modified games designed to facilitate or encourage particular learning outcomes through the constraints inherent in the modified game and the opportunities that these constraints offer. Drawing on Merleau-Ponty (1962), Yakhlef (2010) suggests that learning through practice is corporeal, pre-discursive and pre-social in nature. He argues that it involves a process of absorbing new competencies and knowledge into our bodies that then transform our ways of perceiving and acting. This learning is very powerful because it bypasses the scrutiny of the conscious mind (Bourdieu, 1990) or as Davis, Sumara and Luce-Kapler (2000) suggest, we know more than we know we know.

This corporeal learning takes time meaning that practice games or activities do not produce corporeal learning in one session but it is instead an ongoing and interconnected process. Drawing on Dewey (1938a), we can conceptualize how athletes have a continuum of experience in their sport that shapes the experience of the session and the learning emerging from it with the coach providing direction for experience and learning. That is to say that the athlete's present experience of a practice game or activity is a function of the interaction between his/her past experiences and the present learning experience of the game or activity and with the environment.

The ways in which the GBA coach manages the physical learning environment in a practice session can be illustrated with the manipulation of court shape and size in volleyball. When coaching volleyball the coach could use a narrow, long space, which restricts scoring across the court but opens up space for scoring deep in the court. For defensive shots in volleyball it also offers the opportunity to gain time to recover by returning the ball deep and high into the rear of the court. In practice games and competition matches, developing knowledge is enacted and visible as knowledge-in-action but cannot necessarily be articulated by the athlete. It is this knowledge, expressed in action, that is the real marker of learning and the end aim of Game Sense and Positive Pedagogy coaching used in any sport (Light and Fawns, 2003).

Positive Pedagogy is underpinned by an holistic conception of learning and experience that rejects the dualistic separation of mind from body and the overlooking of the body in which the mind is privileged and bodily activity is seen to intrude on learning (Dewey, 1916/1997). As I have suggested in *Game Sense* (Light, 2013a) and in chapter 2, work on embodied cognition in enactivism (see Varela et al., 1991) provides a useful way of understanding how the body itself learns. It suggests that the aim of developing thinking players (see den Duyn, 1997) in Game Sense should not be restricted to thinking as a conscious and rational process, such as that which occurs during the articulated, collaborative reflection on action in Positive Pedagogy and GBA. Instead, coaches should also consider corporeal learning, embodied cognition/learning and the notion of the thinking body (Light and Fawns, 2001; Cuddy-Keane, 2010). The idea that the body itself thinks challenges what Dewey (1916/1997) sees as the evils of dualism that restrict thinking to a dis-embodied mind and which sees movement as interfering with learning, as captured in Rodin's bronze sculpture, The Thinker.

The Japanese concept of *mushin*, which figures strongly in martial arts training, provides another way of conceptualizing the body's role in learning and the relationship between mind and body in action. Reflecting the monist ontology underpinning Japanese cultural life and recognizing how difficult concepts are to translate, Suzuki (1959) suggests that *mushin* means 'no mind' in English. As is so often the case, cultural concepts do not lend themselves to precise translation but this does reflect the way in which reaching a state of *mushin* involves removing the *interference* of the conscious mind. It is a state reached after extensive training in which the interference of the conscious mind is removed to allow for purity of action and response in which the mind and body function as one (Light and Kentel, 2015). From this perspective, learning is seen to be a process of reducing the gap between the intent of the mind and the body's ability to enact this intent in a process of uniting them in the purity of action. Expert players in team sports with a sense of the game often display the same unity of mind and body in at-action decision-making that suggests a merging of perception, thought and action (see Light, Harvey et al., 2014).

The Game Sense approach aims to contextualize practice by replicating aspects of the dynamic physical context of team sport. This is done to facilitate the transfer of learning in practice to the competition game and to make practice meaningful while keeping it focused on the competition match rather than 'training to train' (Jones, 2015). The context in most individual sports that are typically technique-intensive, such as swimming and athletics, is not as important as it is in team games but experience is also at the centre of learning in Positive Pedagogy, as applied to individual sports. As Dewey (1916/1997, p. 156) argues, 'The material of thinking is not thought but action'.

As with team sports when using GBA, the coach designs an experience that focuses on improving a particular aspect of performance or a skill that involves meeting challenges generated by constraints and the opportunities for solutions that the experience offers. Typically, it uses a constraint that creates a problem to be solved by the athlete. Initially this is through intellectual and physical adaptation, as suggested in psychological constructivism (see Piaget, 1958) and CLT (Davis and Sumara, 2003) but is enhanced by reflection and social interaction with learning seen as a process of discovery. This not only refers to the discovery of knowledge (articulated and enacted) but also to the discovery of problem solving skills because they cannot be taught but must, instead, be discovered through active learning (Piaget, 1958).

In chapter 8 the coaching of the second kick in butterfly provides a good example of this. In it swimmers are asked to compensate for the constraints of swimming butterfly using only one arm which is aimed at having them understand the role of the second kick and to help them improve its contribution to the stroke. In this exercise the constraint imposed by one-arm butterfly provides an opportunity to compensate with the effective execution and timing of the second kick.

Reflection upon experience

The second way in which learning is structured around experience in Positive Pedagogy is through reflection upon it and discussion about it that Dewey (1916/1997) suggests is, in fact, a second experience. Reflecting upon, and talking about, initial experience brings it to consciousness through language and dialogue in particular. This dialogue can be between the coach and individual athletes or groups of athletes, and/or between athletes such as in the collaborative debate of ideas about changing the baton in the 4 × 100 track relay discussed in chapter 10. In this example the four young girls in the relay team work as a team of four but split into pairs at each of the three changeover points to provide two perspectives for the discussion. The two girls practising the changeover provide an internal reflective perspective (largely based upon how it felt and on the interaction between the incoming runner and the receiver) with the other two providing an external perspective (how it looked) for the debate of ideas. In this example, the coach participated in these discussions to facilitate interaction and the construction of knowledge in the early stages but gradually withdrew as the girls developed their knowledge of the technique in action and the ability to reflect and engage in dialogue that generates understanding. A fuller discussion on dialogue and reflection follows in chapter 5 with a focus on questioning but this example of coaching the relay baton changeover illustrates the central role that experience plays in Positive Pedagogy for coaching.

The rest of this chapter focuses on (1) designing learning experiences and (2) managing learning.

Designing the learning experience

In their presentation at the 2008 TGfU International conference in Vancouver, Rod Thorpe and David Bunker emphasized the importance of 'getting the game right' when taking a TGfU approach in reference to the design of the modified games and the modifications needed to optimize learning. Learning through the pedagogy of Positive Pedagogy arises from the interplay between conscious, rational and non-conscious, embodied learning as a 'conversation' in learning between the body, expressed in action, and the mind, expressed in speech (Light and Fawns, 2003). This involves implicit, corporeal learning through processes of adaptation to the constraints of the practice activity, some of which is brought to consciousness through the use of language in individual or collective reflection after and on action.

The dialogue and the development of ideas and conceptual understanding that athletes articulate are features of Positive Pedagogy for coaching but can lead coaches to lose sight of the central aim of coaching which is to improve knowledge-in-action (Schön, 1983; Light and Fawns, 2003). Despite the range of positive secondary learning that a Positive Pedagogy approach can generate (see Light, 2014b), the main goal is to improve performance, at whatever level the coach is working. In the development of Game Sense in Australia, Rod Thorpe identified how many team sport coaches were already using games for learning but he offered structure for the use of games which included questioning to enhance learning through games (Light, 2004, 2013). In Positive Pedagogy questioning is also of central importance but it is the experience of learning through participation in the practice activity that is *the* most important for learning and it is knowledge-in-action that is the most important measure of learning.

Some scholars involved in the development of contemporary TGfU and tactical games (TG) have drawn on information processing theory from cognitive psychology to explain how learning occurs in GBA (see Griffin and Patton, 2005). They propose that there are two distinct stages of learning to play games, which are the development of 'declarative knowledge' and 'procedural knowledge' (see Thomas and Thomas, 1994). Declarative knowledge involves knowing *that* something is the case, such as knowing that Canberra is the capital of Australia. It is consciously known and can thus be verbalized. Procedural knowledge involves knowing *how* to do something such as how to surf or speak a second language without necessarily being able to explain how to do it and is largely learned implicitly. According to information processing theory, declarative knowledge always precedes procedural knowledge and this has influenced conceptions of learning in TGfU (see Griffin and Patton, 2005) but this dichotomy has been challenged by some, such as researchers working on language learning. This encourages questioning the information processing explanation of learning in and through GBA as being reductionist and too linear. Certainly, it does fit well with the constructivist perspective on learning that underpins this book. From a social constructivist perspective, Kiraly (2000) suggests that language translators' training should be focused on *doing* (procedural knowledge) prior to learning about (declarative knowledge) translation with Alvio (2005) arguing for balanced interaction between the explicit (declarative) and implicit (procedural) aspects of translator training.

In sport, the information processing analogy between learning and a computer (input-process-output) is appealing to some but is limited in its ability to capture the complexity of learning to play a game well, throw a javelin or develop a feel for the water in the breaststroke. The conception of learning as being a linear process with declarative knowledge always preceding procedural knowledge fails to recognize the ongoing interaction between learning by doing and learning by reflecting and talking which seems to be largely due to the implicit nature of embodied learning and the difficulty involved in precisely identifying it or measuring it (see Alvio, 2005). In Positive Pedagogy approaches to coaching team sports such as TGfU and Game Sense, athletes can articulate knowledge about action and doing through reflection and dialogue prior to visible or explicit enactment of it in their doing but this overlooks the contribution that the ongoing 'conversation' between action and speech makes towards learning (Light and Fawns, 2003).

In regard to games teaching, the embodied learning occurring through playing practice games and the conscious learning occurring through reflection and dialogue operates as a learning conversation between the mind expressed in speech and the body expressed in action (Light and Fawns, 2003). This learning conversation recognizes the interaction between bodily experience and language and the interaction that Alvio (2005) suggests there is between the development of declarative and procedural knowledge that leads to the development of knowledge-in-action. As important as language and questioning are in Positive Pedagogy the coach's main aim is to enhance learning through experience with the end aim being the construction of knowledge that is enacted. This means that the experience of doing is of prime importance and should be the main focus.

Designing an appropriate activity is the starting point from which the coach observes learning and modifies the activities used to maintain a level of challenge that optimizes active learning (Light, 2013a). In coaching team games the tools at hand include (1) varying the size, shape and dimensions of the playing space, (2) varying the number of players and/or the ratio of players (eg. 5 V 3 or 6 V 2) and (3) changing the rules of the game and changing the equipment such as the type and number of balls used. For individual sports there is more variability but coaching will typically involve placing some sort of constraint on the athlete that presents a problem s/he has to find a solution for or to create awareness. This can be done individually through interaction with the coach or collectively with other athletes in the group. In designing the learning activity the coach needs to consider his/her athlete's existing knowledge, skills, experience and dispositions towards learning. This is to enable him/her to set challenges that extend athletes and engage them enough to learn but which are achievable with the help of the coach and the other athletes involved in the session. In this way (as suggested in chapter 3) the coach and fellow athletes can be seen as resources to be drawn on to meet the challenge of the activity or exercise.

Often the challenge of designing an appropriate learning activity can be circumvented by merely drawing on commonly used activities but adopting Positive Pedagogy. This is what I have done in the examples provided for swim coaching in chapter 8 where I use common 'drills' that place a constraint on the swimmers to encourage them to non-consciously adapt and, over time, embed movement patterns in the body. Constraints-led theory sees such constraints as boundaries that shape the emergence of intended behaviour with the interaction of different constraints forcing learners to seek stable and effective movement patterns (Davids, 2010). The use of constraints I suggest in this book should not be confused with constraints-led theory as it has different aims and sits upon different epistemology.

Underpinned by a social constructivist perspective on learning, Positive Pedagogy can be used to enhance learning as a social process of interpretation and adaptation and to empower the athlete to learn as illustrated in chapter 8. This is done through the use of reflection, dialogue and other interaction, facilitated through questioning. For example, in the swimming session in chapter 8 I draw on my experience of coaching junior swimmers that was aimed at helping them understanding the reason for the second kick in butterfly, improve it and be able to effectively work it into their stroke. The constraint I used here was having them perform one-armed butterfly but with learning enhanced through reflection on action and dialogue between coach and swimmers and between swimmers, prompted by questioning. One-arm butterfly reduces the thrust provided by the arms when the head is up to take a breath, which is when the second kick is performed. This makes it difficult to breathe and when I stopped them solving this problem by breathing to the side I hoped it would point them towards compensating for the reduction in propulsion by working on the timing and execution of the second kick.

When changing coaching practice from the more common instruction and demonstration of technique to the active learning involved in the Positive Pedagogy approach coaches should change slowly by gradually loosening the reigns according to how well the athletes adapt. This is not only to enable the coach to deal with a new way of doing things but also for the athletes to adapt to a very different approach to learning. The athletes should take more initial responsibility for the analysis of learning/performance in practice games and the appropriate adjustments required to maintain optimal levels of engagement.

In education, student engagement refers to learning that involves curiosity, interest, commitment and passion. It recognizes the intellectual, emotional and physical commitment needed to maximize learning and the links between non-cognitive factors such as motivation, interest, curiosity, responsibility, determination, perseverance and so on, and cognitive learning such as improved academic performance, test scores and information recall (Newmann, 1992). Athletes who have adapted to the empowerment and increased responsibility provided in Positive Pedagogy are often involved in the design and/or the modification of practice games by the coach as an important part of the learning process. This empowerment is actually the central mode of learning in the inventing games, or student-designed games, approach (see Hastie, 2010).

Managing learning

There are an increasing amount of resources now available for ideas on basic practice games that coaches in team sports can draw on for start-up games but very little is available for coaches of individual sports. This places more pressure on them to be creative but, paradoxically, this need for creativity occurs in sports that typically have strong traditions of mechanistic coaching that emphasize direct instruction and learning as a process of reducing variation from an ideal form of technique. In this way they promote conformity over creativity. I would, however, like to note here that, despite the athlete-centred and inquiry-based nature of Positive Pedagogy, there is still a place for direct instruction and coach demonstrations of skill with direct instruction evident in some of the practical chapters in Part III – but it does not dominate the session(s).

In the Applications section of this book I have included some activities that some colleagues and I have used for coaching individual sports such as swimming, running, throwing, croquet, karate and gymnastics. These examples and discussions may help coaches come up with ideas for designing learning activities but the observation skills, understanding of learning and the adjustments required provide what is probably the biggest challenge for coaches.

Once the coaching session has begun coaches need to be able to identify how learning is progressing and respond by making appropriate modifications to the nature and demands of the learning activities used and focus on achieving and maintaining levels of challenge that promote engagement. An experienced Positive Pedagogy coach is constantly watching, listening to and developing a sense of athlete progress in learning and thinking about how s/he can tweak or fine tune the task(s) to keep the athlete engaged. This requires having similar observational and analytical skills to those required for watching the athlete in competition but consider learning as well as performance. This ability to analyze progress, identify areas in need of attention and get a feel for the athlete's learning is developed over time through reflective practice and productive interaction with athletes and is a marker of an experienced coach.

A good coach never stops learning with the role of a facilitator of learning in place of being a director disposing him/her towards being a co-participant in learning and being a reflective practitioner (Schön, 1983; Davis and Sumara, 1997). An attitude of openness to learning can assist in the development of analytic and observational skills 'developed from the cycles of game play followed by discussion, debate, dialogue with learners, where learners devise action plans and then test these out, refining them over time' (Harvey and Robertson, 2015, p. 24).

Most coaches will know their athletes' abilities and dispositions well enough to be able to design activities of appropriate difficulty that extend them while allowing them to succeed as a starting point but will initially be less able to analyze learning and understand the nature and progress of that learning. While analytic skills and experience are very important for assessing learning and adjusting the tasks and degree of challenge it is more important for the coach to *understand*, not only the progress of learning, but also the athlete's experience of learning as the subjective dimensions of learning and participation in practice.

Subjective understanding of athlete learning

When managing learning through experience it is important for the coach to get the right balance between challenge and success to optimize engagement and learning. Experienced coaches will have a feel for the pace or flow of the session and of athlete engagement as indicators of getting the demands of the activity right, but coaches also need to develop more detailed observational skills and understanding of the athlete(s) to tune the demands of the activity to get it 'humming'. Observation of progress can be combined with understanding developed through discussion between the athletes and coach and between the athletes to help the coach understand their level of engagement in the activity. Observation and the use of any observational instrument is one source of information about performance but the coach requires a more thorough understanding of the athlete's performance to make managing learning as effective as possible. The Positive Pedagogy approach to coaching is humanistic and holistic, which means it requires knowing athletes as individuals and being sensitive to their experiences of the practice sessions.

The coach has to listen, look and get a feel for the athlete's experience of learning. S/he has to listen to (not just hear) what they have to say, watch closely during the practice and develop a sense of empathy for the athlete(s) that can be developed though interaction between the coach and athletes as research on high school swimming in France suggests (Lémonie et al., 2015). Indeed, attentive listening is an important skill for any coach to develop, whether they use Positive Pedagogy or not. Burton and Raedeke (2008) emphasize the importance of listening to athletes to understand them by being an empathetic listener. They suggest that 'empathetic listening' (p. 26) involves considering the intent of the speaker, their feelings, the meaning it seems to have for them and their feelings when they speak as well as watching and considering body language and using his/her heart to empathize with the athlete's feelings to understand.

Positive Pedagogy is an holistic, humanistic approach that considers athletes to be complex, thinking, feeling people that the coach needs to understand, rather than objects to be manipulated and/or measured. A good coach needs to care about his/her players for them to achieve their potential (Jones, 2009) and be able to not only understand them, but to empathize with them to get the most from them and help them 'be their best' (Jowett et al., 2012). This is of central importance in Positive Pedagogy for managing learning. GBAs such as Game Sense offer a range of tools for making adjustments to manage learning such as changing the size of the space used, the number of players and the ratio of defenders to attackers, but there is no such clearly identified box of tools for coaching individual sport.

The importance of 'feel'

One effective way of managing progress in Positive Pedagogy for individual sports is to focus on athlete 'feel' as many examples used in the Applications section do. This requires a significant shift from analyzing performance or learning from an objective, external point of view to gaining a subjective understanding of performance from an internal perspective. From assessing children's 'fundamental' skills to the use of computers for sport performance analysis and game performance assessment instruments such as the GPAI (game performance analysis instrument – see Griffin et al., 1997) used in GBA, assessment and analysis is achieved from an external and objective perspective.

Some writing in sport coaching recognizes and accounts for the subjective aspects of athlete participation and the importance of coaches understanding their athletes from a subjective perspective but, given the significance of the sensuous, affective and emotional nature of whole-person participation in sport, it needs more attention. Recent innovative work in France, with some published in English, focuses on understanding the subjective experiences of athletes in team sports (see Mouchet, 2005, 2008, 2014; Light, Harvey et al., 2014). Mouchet (2014) suggests that, in team sports, there is a paradox between the subjective nature of experiences of players on the field and the rationalistic, reductionist and often critical approach of many coaches.

If the practice activity is too difficult, frustration, a lack of success and sense of achievement and positive intrinsic feedback will diminish motivation and learning.

The coach will then need to make some changes to the activity to make it possible for the athletes to begin to taste success while keeping the task challenging. Skilful use of questioning is of central importance here to help the athlete move from what s/he can do to realize his/her potential for learning as explained by Vygotsky's (1978) notion of the zone of proximal development (ZPD). If the activity is too easy it will not motivate athletes(s) to strive for success and will not require engagement and commitment to the task from which learning emerges. Establishing and then maintaining appropriate levels of challenge requires the ability to analyze and understand learning and being able to adjust the difficulty of the task. For coaches less experienced with the Positive Pedagogy approach this means that the coach should have preplanned ideas for adjusting the demands of the activities up or down.

Owing to the significant differences between it and directive coaching, Positive Pedagogy takes time for the coach and the athletes to adjust to, understand and embrace. However, once athletes adapt to being empowered to learn and to taking responsibility for their learning they can be asked for suggestions about when and what modifications are needed to make the activity better in terms of enjoyment and improving learning. Indeed, athletes that have adapted to this approach will not wait to be asked for input into modifying the activity when they feel it is necessary and this is very valuable for any coach genuinely interested in maximizing athlete engagement and learning.

5

QUESTIONING FOR LEARNING

With Stephen Harvey

Questioning forms a key feature of athlete/student-centred approaches to coaching and teaching but presents a significant challenge for practitioners (Wright and Forrest, 2007; McNeill et al., 2008; Forrest, 2014). In Positive Pedagogy the prime aims of asking questions are to stimulate thinking and promote interaction between athletes and between the coach and athlete(s) from which learning emerges (see Vygotsky, 1978; Fosnot, 1996). This means that coaches must do more than ask simple yes/no questions. They need to employ questioning that is open-ended, stimulates thinking, fosters curiosity and promotes interaction between the coach and athletes and between athletes.

This chapter begins by discussing why coaches need to ask questions and what the aim of questioning is in Positive Pedagogy. Just as athletes need to know *why* and *when* they should take particular action or perform a skill and not just *how*, coaches need to know why they are asking questions. After suggesting why coaches need to ask questions I then discuss what questions to ask and when to ask them.

Why ask questions?

The general education literature recognizes the importance of questioning for developing problem-solving ability (see Sullivan and Clarke, 1991) and critical thinking (see Yang et al., 2005) as learning outcomes that are also of importance in athlete development. Whether coaching in team or individual sports and focusing on skill execution or the tactical elements of a sport, questions are not asked just to get an answer for the coach. They are asked to promote the thinking, reflection and productive interaction from which learning emerges. When athletes are asked a question they have to think to answer it but the thinking required for a yes or no answer is unlikely to make a significant contribution to learning.

When taking a Positive Pedagogy approach the coach asks questions to promote deep thinking and reflection, at an individual and/or collective level, to help athletes engage intellectually in the practice session. This requires questions that stimulate thinking about the problem at hand and which the athlete draws on his/her prior experience and existing knowledge and verbal interaction with others such as teammates and the coach to answer. This use of questioning in a Positive Pedagogy approach is aimed at developing understanding and facilitating the construction of new knowledge through reflection upon action and dialogue and not on getting the 'correct' answer. Questioning that generates this thinking, reflection upon action and purposeful dialogue, links embodied, implicit learning through participation in physical practice with conscious, rational thinking occurring through the use of language. This dialogue brings experience to consciousness to enhance what we learn through first-hand experience with Dewey (1916/1997) suggesting that we learn through the experience itself and through the second experience of reflecting upon it. As discussed in more detail in the preceding chapter, although articulated knowledge may appear to develop before enacted knowledge, this does not necessarily reflect how learning is progressing. Instead, 'absorbing' knowledge through experience interacts with collective and/or individual reflection as a 'conversation' between the body, expressed in action, and the mind, expressed through language (Dewey, 1916/1997; Light and Fawns, 2003). Good questioning can also generate the curiosity and collaboration required to encourage the formulation of solutions to be tested and evaluated, whether in relation to technique such as streamlining off the wall in swimming or to complex tactical problems in team sport.

Coaches adopting a more traditional approach typically communicate through monologue to provide direct instruction and feedback, and by using demonstrations (Williams and Hodges, 2005). Social constructivist and enactivist views of learning emphasize the central role that interaction plays in learning, which includes that between learners (including athletes) and between teacher and learner (see Fernandez-Balboa, 1995; Barker et al., 2013; Lémonie et al., 2015). This is supported by studies that identify how over-emphasizing instruction in sport coaching and physical education limits learners' opportunities for developing decision-making and problem-solving skills (Ford et al., 2010).

Positive Pedagogy is an holistic approach to learning that sees learners as whole beings and rejects the dualistic separation of mind from body and knower from what is known that obfuscates the intellectual dimensions of sport (Light and Fawns, 2001). Part of this problem lies in long-established and limiting views of learning as occurring only in formal education settings with the body under control and expressed in language or writing (Davis et al., 2000). Work on embodied cognition (Varela et al., 1991) and the notion of the thinking body (Light and Fawns, 2001) challenges these restrictive ideas on learning to highlight the folly of attempting to separate mind from body in sport. In a challenge to the cognitive approach in psychology and an objective view on learning, enactivism (Varela et al., 1991) sees the mind as being inseparable from bodily experience and the world as something that is brought forth through experience (see chapter 2).

Questioning is a key tool in athlete-centred coaching for empowering athletes to take responsibility for their own learning and to learn how to learn as they develop into independent learners (Light, 2014b). A study on the influence of Game Sense on elite-level rugby coaches found that the New Zealand coaches believed the athlete-centred approach and the use of questioning empowered players and promoted strong interpersonal relations as something they valued highly (Evans, 2012, 2014).

More traditional approaches, where the coach operates as the expert who transfers objective knowledge to his/her athletes, encourage them to become reliant on him/her while discouraging them from taking responsibility or being accountable for their own learning and performance. Athlete-centred approaches such as Positive Pedagogy encourage athletes to learn how to learn and to become more independent learners who are reflective and can work with teammates and other athletes to identify and solve problems as independent learners.

Good questioning can generate curiosity and the desire of learners to find answers to the problems posed by the learning activities set by the teacher/coach. Consequently, learners are encouraged to collectively develop ideas and experiment in practice as something that requires them to think, reflect and evaluate their own learning/progress. Effective questioning should encourage athletes to reflect upon their performance to allow them to best solve problems and make correct decisions (Oslin and Mitchell, 2006). Good questions should not limit the possible responses but, instead, expand them to help learners develop their critical thinking skills (Wright and Forrest, 2007).

The Zone of Proximal Development

As Harvey and Light (2015) suggest, Vygotsky's (1978) Zone of Proximal Development (ZPD) provides a useful way of thinking about how questioning enhances learning due to the way in which it emphasizes the coach's guidance and encouragement of verbal interaction for learning. The ZPD refers to the gap between the learner's 'actual developmental level as determined by independent problem solving' and the higher level of 'potential development through problem solving' that can be realized 'under adult guidance or in collaboration with more capable peers' (Vygotsky, 1978, p. 86). Vygotsky's focus here is on children and young learners but the 'adult' would include the coach, regardless of the age or experience of the athletes. Vygotsky suggests that the skills and understandings that exist within a learner's ZPD emerge from interactions with knowledgeable others such as peers and/or adults and that the most effective teaching (or coaching) aims at the ZPD instead of at the learner's level of independent performance to produce gains in their development with a focus on how the person in a teaching role assists and enhances learning.

Vygotsky emphasizes the role of language in learning such as in the dialogue between learners, and between learners and the teacher/coach. From a constructivist perspective, scaffolding on existing knowledge can assist learning within the ZPD and is developed through effective questioning by the teacher and productive dialogue with other athletes. These discussions are typically guided by core concepts and stimulated by appropriately timed and expressed questions from the coach. As athlete understanding improves, the coach gradually withdraws support and assistance after which the learners will be able to hold the debate of ideas session on their own with limited prompting and probing of the teacher/coach required (Wood et al., 1976).

This process is illustrated in chapter 10 with the example of coaching a primary school girls' 4 × 100 track relay team. In this example I began with direct technical instruction but moved towards an inquiry-based approach by encouraging purposeful dialogue that I initially guided and prompted. As the four girls learned to learn through reflection and dialogue I gradually stepped away from the discussions. This recounting of my own experience of coaching using Positive Pedagogy provides a good example of how questioning can be used to focus on the ZPD and assist learners (athletes) in realizing their potential for learning (improving) through purposeful dialogue that is stimulated by appropriate questioning (Harvey and Light, 2015). Although the coaching began with direct instruction, learning occurred through reflection and interaction that was strongly guided by coach questioning in the first few weeks of the intervention in a process of guided 'problem solving under adult guidance' (Vygotsky, 1978, p. 86). This suggests the importance of questioning and dialogue in helping athletes move from what they already know and can do to realizing their learning potential while also showing how an inquiry-based approach to coaching can be used when focusing tightly on technique.

What questions to ask

By structuring opportunities for questioning and the debate of ideas (Gréhaigne et al., 2005) the coach can guide and facilitate the improvement of the athletes' problem-solving capabilities through their interaction with each other. As research on teachers and young people in sport suggests, interaction between students/athletes and between the coach/teacher and students/athletes makes a significant contribution towards learning and the development of the coach's empathy for the athlete as suggested in enactivism (see Barker et al., 2013; Lémonie et al., 2015). This not only assists learning, but is also very helpful for establishing an ethic of care that Jones (2009) suggests assists in helping athletes reach their potential in performance. With the use of skilful questioning the coach can prompt and probe to stimulate the athlete's exploration of specific aspects of their performance with understanding emerging from these reflective episodes that is enacted in competition. Harvey and Robertson (2015) suggest that coaches who are developing their questioning skills should begin with broad, general questions to get the dialogue started and then gradually make the questions more specific to and focused on the aims of the session.

Moving beyond simplistic questioning

Simply asking questions will not necessarily stimulate the thinking and social interaction from which learning emerges. Teachers and coaches across a range of settings ask questions but as research in education suggests, it is largely limited to asking surface-level questions (Kracl, 2012). For example, a pilot study of thirty-eight elementary and high school social studies teachers indicated that most of the questions they asked were at the literal level of comprehension (93 percent), with less than 7 percent being interpretive (Daines, 1986). Research on nursing teachers (Sellappah et al., 1998) and pre-service physical education teachers (McNeill et al., 2008) reported similar findings. Seventy-six percent of pre-service teachers in McNeill et al.'s study asked low-order questions involving knowledge recall with only 6.7 percent of their questions being open-ended or divergent and capable of developing tactical awareness and critical thinking. Low-order recall questions do not stimulate participants to think at a deeper level or elaborate on their responses (Peterson and Taylor, 2012) or encourage substantive debate, discussion and dialogue between the participants (Harvey and Light, 2015).

Promoting thinking and interaction

Kagan (2005) suggests a useful categorization of questions into those that are skinny or fat, high consensus or low consensus, and review or true. Skinny questions are those that require a yes/no type of answer and little thinking on the part of the student. Fat questions are those that require more evaluation, synthesis and evaluation on behalf of the learner. Like skinny questions, review questions simply ask learners to recall information, whereas true questions ask for more thought and detail in the answer such as where the coach asks what tactics might be effective in a particular situation.

When coaching team sports this might include freezing play such as in a small-sided game like a 5 V 5 passing game in basketball where the aim is to complete five passes without losing possession. At a point where both teams are in one corner of the space (half or quarter court) the coach could stop play by asking the players to freeze. S/he could then ask the team in possession questions such as, 'Look around you – where is the space? How can you use this space to get more passes completed?' or 'Is there a better way you could use the space available to you?' When they move the receivers to where the space is to offer passing options the coach could then ask the defending team, 'How can you respond to this?' When asking these questions the coach may well have an expectation of what the answers will be but must always be open to different ideas and suggestions.

The idea of skinny and fat questions aligns well with high- and low-consensus questions. High-consensus questions are those for which most of the group would provide the same or similar response, with low-consensus questions generating divergent thinking and responses. A Positive Pedagogy approach to coaching generally requires using fat, low-consensus, true questions to generate a range of possibilities but when focusing on technique in sports such as swimming (see chapter 8) this may change a little. Coaching technique-intensive sports, or focusing on skill in team games (chapter 7), usually requires a narrower range of possibilities and fewer opportunities for divergent thinking. In these cases coaches are likely to use what

Mosston and Ashworth (1986) refer to as a guided discovery teaching style in which the coach gives athletes problems to solve that lead towards the discovery of predetermined knowledge. This approach tends to involve more convergent thinking than the divergent thinking that is encouraged when focusing on the tactical aspects of a team sport.

Convergent thinking should not, however, be universally dismissed as being unhelpful for problem solving. It can be used as a tool in creative problem solving by encouraging the use of critical thinking to solve a problem through which the athlete draws on standards and probabilities to make judgements during the creative problem-solving process. As Cropley (2006) suggests, while creative thinking involves the development of new ideas generated through divergent thinking, the evaluation of the novel ideas occurs through convergent thinking and the use of knowledge as a source of ideas, which suggests pathways to solutions and provides criteria of effectiveness and novelty.

In coaching focused on skill or technique, questions tend to be used to guide athletes towards the discovery of a preferred way of performing a technique or skill and be more of the skinny, high-consensus, true type. This discovery is, however, still open to interpretation and adaptation by the athlete who can find more meaning and relevance for the knowledge developed than through direct instruction due to an active learning process that involves emphasizing experience and reflection upon it in and after action (Light and Wallian, 2008).

To provide an example, I draw on an activity I proposed with Nathalie Wallian for swimming (Light and Wallian, 2008) when working with young swimmers to improve their streamlining off the wall at the completion of a tumble turn by aligning the head with the body to reduce resistance. Here the coach could ask them to push off the wall to see how far they can travel without kicking or using their arms and measuring the distance travelled with cones on the side of the pool. First s/he would ask them to push off with their heads up and then with their heads down (aligned with their bodies to reduce resistance). Measuring the distance travelled provides some immediate, explicit and conscious (intrinsic) feedback, but skilful questioning that promotes reflection upon (and in) experience engages the body and its senses in learning that is far more meaningful and lasting.

The emphasis in this example should be on how it feels and how the swimmers can work it into their streamlines with discussion among the group and between the swimmers and the coach. This might involve the coach asking questions such as, 'Why do you think you travelled farther with head down than with head up?' and 'How did it feel with head down compared to head up?' The squad might then be given time to work in pairs or small groups to apply what they had learned about head alignment to their streamlines off the wall in a full tumble turn and with the use of the dolphin kick. After this the coach could call them in as a whole squad and ask questions like, 'Do you *feel* any difference in the way you are streamlining now?', 'Can you *see* any differences in the way the other swimmers are streamlining?', or 'What things were you focusing on when you were streamlining at the end of the session?'

The debate of ideas

Gréhaigne et al. (2005) provide a pre-prepared list of generic questions for small teams of learners to lead their own 'tactical timeouts' through what they termed the debate of ideas. While its initial application was for team sports such as football (soccer), basketball and rugby, this idea can be applied to striking and fielding games, net and wall sports, target games and individual sports (see Chen, 2001; Light, 2014a; Light and Kentel, 2015).

In sport coaching the use of the debate of ideas can help the coach manage multiple groups, whether in team sports or with pairs or clusters of athletes in individual sports such as in the examples provided in Part III. The debate of ideas provides opportunity for dialogue, debate and reflection during the generation of new action plans. In the debate of ideas among groups all athletes should be engaged in discussion with no one athlete dominating it, and the group should be progressing towards solving the problems to be solved and generating understanding as a group. If this is the case there is little need for the coach to intervene but if there is a need to shape the discussion then the coach should employ some open and generative questioning.

If there are multiple groups of athletes participating in debates of ideas then s/he should keep the questions brief. If the aim is to bring a quiet athlete into the discussion the coach can simply ask him/her, 'What do you think Becky? Do you have any ideas at all about how we can deal with this problem?' If the coach feels that the discussion is off track s/he can intervene by asking a question that draws attention to something the group may be neglecting. In a session on helping athletes discover the principles of throwing, the coach might ask athletes as observers or participants, 'Where do you think that the thrower is initially generating this power from?' (see chapter 11). The coach, using Positive Pedagogy, aims to facilitate discussion and purposeful dialogue by asking open generative questions such as 'Please tell me more about that' or 'What happened then?' as has been suggested as a broad approach not limited to Positive Pedagogy or GBA (Peterson and Taylor, 2012, p. 297).

The reflective toss

Questions asked by the coach during the debate of ideas should increase the level of intra-group interaction (Gréhaigne et al., 2005). The ways in which a coach uses questioning to facilitate the debate of ideas is very similar to van Zee and Minstrell's (1997) suggestions about the reflective toss. The reflective toss begins with a statement from a student (or athlete) on the game just participated in or could be his/her response to a question by the coach. In the right environment this should stimulate an initial level of dialogue as others in the group respond to the athlete's opinion or statement with the coach facilitating interaction through questions (Harvey and Light, 2015). The coach's aim here in using these questions is to 'toss' responsibility back to the learners to encourage them to reflect and to help each other by elaborating their thinking to the rest of the group.

The method suggested by van Zee and Minstrell (1997) aims to help athletes or students appreciate and understand each other's perspectives, which contributes towards building harmony and respect among the group (Forrest, 2014). It contrasts with what Forrest (2014) calls the Initiation, Response, Evaluation or IRE method of questioning, or the yes/no format of questioning that shuts down interaction between the coach and athletes and between the athletes themselves when more than one is involved. The important point here with the use of coach questioning during the debate of ideas is that it should promote interaction within the group.

In GBA small-sided games provide ideal conditions for the debate of ideas among the teams competing in the modified practice games but can be used when coaching individual sports. For example, chapter 11 provides an example of using Positive Pedagogy to help young athletes discover the core principles of throwing and apply them to throwing the javelin. It recounts coaching that put the athletes into small groups to solve the problem of finding the most efficient ways of throwing a variety of objects. This was conducted just like small-sided games with me moving between the groups to ask questions that stimulated interaction and facilitated the discovery of the core principles of throwing.

The example of using Positive Pedagogy to coach primary-school children the baton change in the 4 x 100 metre track relay provided in chapter 10 begins with direct instruction but moves to an emphasis on dialogue and reflection. This involves the incoming runner and the runner receiving the baton practising the changeover and discussing it, after which the other two runners join them for the debate of ideas focused on refining the changeover. In this example the coach initially intervened by using questioning to encourage purposeful discussion but as the runners developed independence he gradually stepped back to let them direct their own learning.

A feature of the debate of ideas and the reflective toss is how the coach steps back from determining learning to act as a facilitator of learning. The type of questions used are critical to the success of this approach with the coach offering prompts and probes to stimulate interaction and further debate and discussion, which creates an environment conducive to higher-order thinking.

When to ask questions

The balance between talking and doing is important for maintaining motivation and engagement as well as for maximizing learning. I have found with teaching undergraduate pre-service teachers who try to adopt GBAs such as Game Sense that they often frustrate learners by asking too many questions, stopping the action for too long or asking questions at the wrong time with similar problems reported in the coaching literature (see Roberts, 2011). One beginning teacher in Melbourne who was developing her Game Sense approach recounted to me how a student told her that she should stop asking questions because she was being paid to tell them what to do. In coaching, Roberts (2011) identifies the same problem with young players who were frustrated by a lack of game time due to being asked too many questions by cricket coaches trying to take up a TGfU approach.

The most important consideration here is the maintenance of the 'pace' of the session and the engagement of the athlete(s) that relates to the conversation between the mind, expressed in speech, and the body, expressed in action (Light and Fawns, 2003). My use of the term engagement draws on the idea of student engagement used by Newmann (1992) to emphasize how it involves making a psychological investment and taking pride in performance rather than just doing what is asked of the athlete. Experienced coaches have a feel for the pace of the session and the progress of learning that they should draw on when making decisions about when to stop play for questioning and for the duration of their intervention. Drawing on my practical experience of coaching and teaching in workshops around the world I would suggest that it is better to ask too few questions than too many, but the timing is probably a more difficult issue.

When working with groups or teams of athletes it is common practice to ask questions at the end of an activity to step it up to a more challenging level, make it more complex or to move up to the next activity as part of the session plan that moves from simple to more complex and challenging activities. There are also opportune moments during practice sessions for intervening with a question or two for the whole group. This could involve the use of an athlete or group of athletes to demonstrate what the coach considers to be success in meeting the challenge of the activity or task that the entire group can discuss and which is stimulated by the coach's questions and which features in many of the chapters in Part III.

When coaching a group of athletes who are doing the same activities/tasks the coach would normally stop them when s/he identifies a problem occurring across most of the group. S/he can also make use of planned intervals when teaching/coaching to develop higher-order thinking during which s/he should ensure that as many athletes as possible participate in the discussion. When coaching individual sports in which the athletes are working on a task in pairs (or groups of three) the coach might call them in to share what they have learned among all in the group at an appropriate time. In this case Harvey and Light (2015) suggest that the coach should make sure that whole-group questioning is kept to a minimum and to encourage different athletes to answer questions. As I learned through coaching rugby in Japan, culture plays a big part in shaping learning and can radically change the group dynamics when asking questions. In these cases the coach has to be able to adapt to the specific cultural context. For example, in Asian settings athletes can be reluctant to speak up in front of the coach and the rest of the squad but are more likely to speak up and participate in discussion in small groups of peers (see Light, 2015).

Coaches working in individual sports can modify the use of group discussion in small-sided games by pairing athletes or having them work in groups of three by using a reciprocal teaching approach (Mosston and Ashworth, 1986) in which the athletes change roles as teacher and learner (coach/athlete). For example, in chapter 8 I recount a session in which I put swimmers in pairs to engage in reciprocal teaching, which involves dialogue. Here an extra swimmer could be added to operate as an observer of the coaching which offers a third perspective as well as more opportunity for interaction and the debate of ideas in individual sport.

Thus far, I have only dealt with issues involving the coach asking questions, but once athletes adapt to a Positive Pedagogy approach they typically ask questions of the coach and of their fellow athletes. When asked questions by athletes coaches should avoid being defensive and embrace the spirit of engaging with athletes that is helped by seeing themselves as co-participators in learning with their athletes (Davis and Sumara, 1997) even though they are guiding learning. For the coach, coaching and learning should not be seen as being mutually exclusive. Coach questioning aims to stimulate athlete thinking and interaction and questioning from athletes should be seen to do the same for the coach. Just as the coach's questions do not seek simple answers, athletes' questions should not be dismissed with yes/no responses that shut down thinking. Instead, they should be seen as invitations for dialogue, remembering that, although the coach guides and facilitates learning, s/he is participating in learning as well. This could involve using the reflective toss to engage other athletes in the group in an approach that suggests a sharing of the learning approach rather than just deflecting the question.

Conclusion

The suggestions for questioning I make in this chapter are structured around the core aims of asking questions to promote thinking and the social interaction from which learning emerges. The chapter emphasizes the importance of having a sound understanding of the role that questioning plays in Positive Pedagogy that requires understanding *why* and *when* to ask questions as well as *what* and *how* to ask athletes. This reflects the emphasis placed on conceptual understanding in Positive Pedagogy (including GBA) and on deep foundational knowledge over superficial technical knowledge. This chapter takes quite a broad approach to questioning that engages with the principles, ideas about coaching, and philosophical assumptions that underpin Positive Pedagogy, but Harvey and Light (2015) propose some more practical guidelines for asking questions that might be helpful for some coaches.

The reasonably detailed discussion on why to question, what to question and when to question provided in this chapter provides some guidance for coaches but also highlights some of the challenges involved in developing effective questioning. These challenges can tempt coaches to return to a more familiar and comfortable relationship with athletes in which the coach delivers information to passive receivers but in which athlete learning is limited. Coaches interested in developing their skill in questioning should consider and reflect upon the ideas presented in this chapter to develop their Positive Pedagogy influenced approach to coaching and read some of the emerging literature on questioning in coaching and teaching for GBA and Positive Pedagogy (see Forrest, 2014; Harvey and Light, 2015). Beyond the detail provided here for questioning, coaches need to embrace a different relationship with their athletes. This requires repositioning the coach from being the font of all knowledge (den Duyn, 1997) to someone who guides, shares and learns with his/her athletes.

6

PROMOTING INQUIRY

Positive Pedagogy for sport coaching is an athlete-centred, inquiry-based approach. There is considerable overlap between these two terms but my use of 'athlete-centred coaching' refers to coaching that places the athlete at the centre of learning, as an active learner. Additionally, it picks up the notion of a humanistic approach to coaching developed from humanistic psychology (see Maslow, 1968) within which the coach considers the athlete as a thinking, feeling person who has a life outside the sport (see Kidman, 2005). In doing so, it challenges the mechanistic reduction of humans as complex and interconnected beings to a set of separate elements such as the mind, the body or the spirit. My use of the term 'inquiry-based learning' refers to a range of inductive approaches to teaching that find their origins in Dewey's proposal for an inquiry approach to teaching science in schools well over a century ago. He challenged what he referred to as 'traditional' teaching by arguing that students should be actively engaged in their learning with the teacher adopting the role of facilitator or guide (Barrow, 2006; Dewey, 1916/1997). He suggested six steps for an inquiry approach to teaching that involves the students:

1. Sensing a perplexing situation
2. Clarifying the problem
3. Formulating a tentative solution
4. Testing the hypothesis
5. Revising with rigorous tests
6. Acting on the solution

My suggestions for taking an inquiry-based approach to coaching team games (Light, 2013a) and Positive Pedagogy for individual sports (see Light and Harvey, 2015) are based upon these steps proposed by Dewey. In the practical examples and suggestions discussed in Part III, the coach typically (but not always) creates a problem to be solved by imposing a constraint and facilitates an inquiry-based approach to solving the problem. Dewey's original ideas on an inquiry approach to teaching have more recently inspired a range of variations that include inquiry-based learning (IBL), problem-based learning (PBL – Schmidt, 1998), discovery learning (Bruner, 1961), inquiry learning (Papert, 1980), experiential learning (Boud et al., 1985) and constructivist learning (Steffe and Gale, 1995).

All these approaches sit upon constructivist epistemology and the belief that learning is a process of constructing new knowledge through the interpretation of learning experiences shaped by prior knowledge, experience and dispositions (see Bruner, 1990; Piaget, 1950). Prince and Felder's (2006) suggestions about the features of inductive approaches such as these offer another useful guide for developing coaching that takes an inquiry approach. They suggest that inductive approaches:

1. Are learner-centred and focus on student learning rather than on communicating content or knowledge;
2. Emphasize active learning as learning by doing which typically involves students discussing questions and solving problems;
3. Develop self-directed learning skills in which students take responsibility for their own learning;
4. Are based upon constructivist theories of learning, which propose that students construct their own meaning of reality and knowledge (see Dewey, 1933; Vygotsky, 1978; Bruner, 1990).

Inquiry-based approaches to teaching also commonly use collaborative or cooperative learning (see Dyson, 2001) with inquiry done in and out of formal class time and commonly conducted by working in groups. In Positive Pedagogy for sport coaching, the provision of opportunities for the formulation of solutions to problems that are tested, evaluated and modified is clearly a form of inquiry-based pedagogy that reflects the four features Prince and Felder (2006) suggest are evident in inductive approaches to teaching.

Whether in small groups, pairs or in a one-on-one situation with an athlete, the Positive Pedagogy coach adopts what Freire (1970) describes as 'problem posing' pedagogy with the coach designing and managing learning activities that present problems for the athlete(s) to solve. S/he encourages interaction (whether between members of a small group or between the coach and a single athlete) that leads to the formulation of solutions that the athlete(s) tests and reflects upon and/or evaluates in a process of structured inquiry. This reflection is enhanced through appropriate questioning that, when coaching in individual sports, will often focus on how it felt. As I suggest in chapter 4, this requires the coach developing sensitivity to indicators of subjective experience as well as considering the external, objective view of performance.

This emphasis on inquiry that involves reflection in and on action, dialogue and the collaborative formulation of ideas or suggestions to be tested is very different to traditional coaching that emphasizes the coach-to-athlete monologue of direct instruction and feedback in the pursuit of correct technical execution. It also requires, and builds, a different set of relationships between coach and athletes and between athletes. This is due to the emphasis it places on active learning and the change in the coach's role from someone who determines learning to someone who shapes, guides, and sometimes shares in, learning. It develops better understanding and trust between coach and athlete than traditional direct instruction does, but can be a little uncomfortable for athletes who are unused to this approach and who are not yet ready to open up and to trust their peers and coach.

Inquiry-based pedagogy can also involve an element of risk for the athlete that could discourage him/her from being actively involved in the process of inquiry and which can be exacerbated by anxiety over failing or making a mistake. These concerns are what make it necessary to provide a socio-moral environment that supports risk-taking and encourages athletes to see errors as constructive opportunities for learning.

Formulating, testing and evaluating solutions

In the Game Sense approach to coaching team sports, players typically play the practice game long enough to get a feel for it and identify the problem that faces them (Light, 2013a). They are then given time to discuss this as a group and develop solutions or strategies that they feel might work. This would usually involve the coach, (1) explaining the game and ensuring they understand, (2) letting them play the game to get a feel for it and to experience the challenges they need to meet, (3) stopping to ask a few questions that help identify or confirm the problem(s) to be solved, (4) encouraging them to formulate a strategy or action plan through group dialogue, (5) asking them to implement the strategy or plan in the game, and (6) stopping the game and having them critically reflect upon how it went and suggest modifications or identify if it didn't work (Light, 2013a). This last step could be conducted within the team if they were going to have the opportunity of testing it again in a practice game. If they were not to have another opportunity to test their strategy, this discussion would be conducted as a whole-team discussion in a collective reflection, evaluation and development of what they learned over the session, as a way of sharing learning.

When coaching an individual sport, a similar process should be followed but with some modifications. As explained in chapter 4, the design of the learning activity often involves imposing a constraint that presents a problem to be solved that provides opportunities for solutions to be developed. Here the coach:

1. Clearly explains the activity and asks questions to get an indication of how well the athlete understands the task;
2. Asks the athlete to do a couple of practices to get a feel for the task and asks a few questions to ensure that s/he fully understands; and
3. Then leaves the athlete or athletes to practise.

If other athletes are practising at the same time the coach would move around the individual athletes or their groups asking one or two questions to stimulate and focus thinking while monitoring their progress. If working with a single athlete in a one-on-one situation the coach could, literally, step back to provide a little distance and give the athlete time to reflect in action (Varela et al., 1991) and get a feel for the task as s/he adapts to the task at an embodied and conscious level of thinking and learning. If more than one athlete is practising and they are accustomed to being active, self-directed learners then they will likely interact whether asked to or not.

Once the athletes (or athlete) have/has a feel for the activity and the challenge to be met the coach would ask them to discuss ideas for the best way of dealing with it. Whether accustomed to the approach or not, they should be asked to work together and to critically reflect upon how they have been solving the problem. For example, in chapter 8, on coaching the second kick in butterfly, I recount coaching young swimmers in England to make them aware of, and to improve, their execution of the second kick (two kicks per stroke in butterfly) by working in pairs using a reciprocal teaching style (Mosston and Ashworth, 1986).

The constraint I used in this activity was making them do one-arm butterfly and not allowing them to breathe to the side. This was aimed at making breathing difficult and for it to become the problem to be solved. I began by asking all of the swimmers to swim two laps of the (25 metre) pool doing one-arm butterfly, after which I asked them as a group (there were only eight in the 'squad') how that felt and what particular problems it presented for them. I then adopted an inquiry-based coaching approach by asking them to form pairs to work on solving the problem of how to compensate for the reduced propulsion through discussion. After the pairs had arrived at a solution I asked them to take a reciprocal learning approach (Mosston and Ashworth, 1986) with one of them swimming and the other watching to provide an external perspective on his/her partner's performance and his/her subjective experience of it. They then switched roles. Although it was aimed at aiding the discovery of efficient technique the constraint imposed was not intended to produce a predetermined motor response. Instead, it was intended to highlight a problem that was solved through interaction and active learning that involved formulating, testing and evaluating solutions. The end result could look the same as it would when using a constraints-led approach (see Renshaw et al., 2010) but, sitting on constructivist epistemology, the learning process is perceived differently with the swimmers also learning how to learn.

Once athletes adapt to this approach they typically develop enthusiasm for meeting the challenges presented by the coach and look forward to being part of a collective effort that involves rich social interaction focused on achieving a common goal. When dividing athletes into a number of small groups or pairs the coach needs to move between the groups to ensure that there is a sharing of ideas and that all athletes are engaged in the dialogue and the collaborative process of problem solving. Some groups may not require any intervention by the coach while others may require some well-directed and generative questions to engage the quieter athletes or reduce the dominance of a particular athlete (Harvey and Light, 2015). While the more confident and experienced athletes may initially dominate proceedings, the less experienced can make valuable contributions when encouraged by the coach. It is worth noting here, and particularly with young athletes, that they are not only improving performance as the main aim of most coaching (Jones, 2006) but also learning how to draw on all of what members of the group have to offer and to listen to others.

Athletes who are new to athlete-centred, inquiry-based coaching will initially need to be encouraged by the coach to express opinions, to speak up and to think for themselves within a supportive socio-moral environment and to be able to see that mistakes are part of learning and improving as suggested by DeVries and Zan (1996) in regard to teaching informed by constructivist perspectives on learning. The development of trust and dialogue between athletes will also make a significant contribution towards cohesion in the training group or squad and towards the building of the supportive socio-moral environment discussed in the next section. Individually, it will help them develop the capacity and inclination to discuss issues at practice and to solve problems independent of the coach as reflective, thinking athletes.

Developing a supportive socio-cultural environment

The culture of teams or organizations that adopt a Positive Pedagogy approach and the feel or ambience of a practice session guided by a Positive Pedagogy approach (team or individual sports) is typically very different to sessions in which the coach takes a directive approach. This is largely due to the different sets of relationships it develops between athletes and between them and the coach and the ways in which they communicate. In coaching that takes an athlete-centred, inquiry-based approach, there are typically more equal power relationships than in traditional coaching. Relationships are also more collaborative in nature with communication occurring through dialogue in place of the top-down monologue that characterizes most directive coaching.

The ways in which coaches learn to coach comprises a complex mix of formal, non-formal, explicit and implicit learning over time. An inquiry-based approach to coaching invites the coach to adapt to the demands of the approach and develop as a reflective practitioner who is open to learning in and through practice, which can make a significant contribution to coach development (see Cushion et al., 2010; Light et al., 2015). The inquiry-based nature of Positive Pedagogy, the relationships it builds between coach and athlete(s) and its collaborative approach encourage critical reflection and being open to change and learning for the coach. Regardless of what approach coaches take, they should always be reflective and open to learning through their entire career, regardless of what level they work at or how successful they are. This is facilitated by the nature of Positive Pedagogy coaching and the relationship between coach and athletes.

Over the past decade or so research and practice in sport coaching have bene-fitted from recognition of athlete development as learning (Kirk, 2010) and the insights into coaching practice and coach development that educational theory offers (Jones, 2006). The way in which a Positive Pedagogy approach brings the coach closer to his/her athletes and encourages dialogue between them facilitates coach learning while s/he guides athlete learning. In regard to teaching, Davis and Sumara (1997) conceptualize this as being a co-participant in learning but this does not detract from the work of the coach in enhancing improvement in performance. Coaches who adopt an open-minded and collaborative relationship with their athletes and who are critically reflective will constantly be making small adjust-ments, and, sometimes, larger ones, in their coaching as they adjust to particular athletes and contexts and as they develop their coaching. This occurs as they come to know more about their athletes as people and become more attuned to what their athletes do, say and feel.

With an open, collaborative disposition they can also learn about the content of their coaching whether it is a tactical or technical aspect of the sport. Most coaches see being respected by their athletes as one of the most important indicators of being a good coach (see Potrac et al., 2002; Light and Evans, 2013; Evans, 2014) but this should not be restricted to respect for the superior knowledge they hold, their experience, displaying the moral qualities they expect of their athletes, or their ability to make the hard decisions. A coach who openly demonstrates his/her inclination to learn and improve through critical reflection upon his/her athletes' responses and learning should gain respect from them for their honesty and humility.

Stepping back from centre stage where the coach directs all the action and determines all learning towards adopting a more equal, collaborative set of rela-tionships with athletes typically creates anxiety for the coach, who can feel that his/her importance has been reduced. This can be exacerbated by his/her sensitivity to the views and opinions of outsiders and a widely held view, promoted by mass media, of a good coach being a strong leader who is knowledgeable and explicitly in control. This is well illustrated in a study I conducted with some leading Australian Game Sense coaches (Light, 2004). One participant who held a high-level position in football (soccer) coach education told me how he would tell coaches that, to improve team performance, they must use Game Sense but when the club com-mittee comes to watch they should do drills because they look neat and with the coach clearly in control s/he would look like a good coach to them.

Some coaches may feel disempowered by taking more equal and collaborative relationships with their athletes and worry about looking or feeling weak or not 'earning their money' but it actually requires and develops more strength and confidence as a coach. The bluster of a coach barking instructions at athletes with an unquestioned belief in what s/he tells his/her athletes to do always being right can intimidate athletes, disempower them and discourage them from asking ques-tions. It can make them docile learners who can't think for themselves. From one perspective, this may make the coach look strong, confident and knowledgeable, but from another perspective, not being open to being questioned or engaging in dialogue suggests that the coach is not grounded and actually lacks deep confidence. Shouting and being dominant does not necessarily equate to being a strong coach or a strong person. Many coaches do not like being asked questions because they don't have the answers.

It is far too easy to follow well-established patterns and drills that are never questioned or critically considered and guided by a mechanistic view of the athletes as objects to be manipulated but never listened to or considered as subjective beings. In this approach there is no need for dialogue or for the coach to be tuned in and sensitive to how the athletes feel. There is no emphasis placed on the athletes actually understanding what they are doing or why they are doing it. Opening up to athletes' questions and a dialogue with them may initially be intimidating for coaches unused to doing this but the pressure it places on them and the critical reflection it encourages will make them a better and more knowledgeable coach. They may worry about being caught out without the 'correct' answers to athlete questions but as they develop skill in working with their athletes they will not only help the athletes learn but will learn themselves. This does not devalue the coach's position in any way but, instead, develops a more honest and trusting coach–athlete relationship that benefits both athlete and coach development. The coach is still 'in charge' but this is less explicit with this being a far more productive form of leadership than treating athletes as objects and striving to be an unapproachable autocrat. Initially, 'stepping off centre stage' takes a lot of work, reflection and critical thinking and represents a real challenge for most coaches but it is worth it with this repositioning of the coach of pivotal importance in building a supportive and encouraging environment.

In a traditional, directive and coach-centred session athletes can hide as passive learners, not engage intellectually and avoid being noticed; but in a Positive Pedagogy approach the coach asks them to reflect, participate in dialogue and express and share opinions and feelings. A Positive Pedagogy coach encourages athletes to be active, curious and confident learners, to speak up, think of ideas that they share with the coach and fellow athletes, to experiment and be creative. The athletes' inclination to do this will vary from one institutional setting to another and from one culture to another but in most cases athletes are not inclined to speak up and be active learners unless they are learning in a socio-moral environment that supports them.

In reference to constructivist-informed teaching, DeVries and Zan (1996) suggest the need for a socio-moral environment that supports students and encourages them to engage in inquiry-based learning. In Positive Pedagogy coaching the coach asks athletes to speak up and articulate ideas, make suggestions for solving tactical and/or technical problems, voice opinions and comment on other athletes' ideas. In doing so, we ask them to take risks and open themselves up during discussions when they suggest ideas and articulate reflections upon their experiences. This is asking much of athletes of any age and any level of performance who have learned what they consciously know through traditional coaching as passive learners. It is even more problematic when they have been learners who avoid responsibility for learning and performance by doing only what they are told to do to shift responsibility for results and learning on to the coach.

In Positive Pedagogy the coach encourages active learning, social interaction, critical reflection, collaboration, problem solving and creativity, which necessarily involves taking some risks. To get athletes to be actively engaged, take risks and speak up freely coaches have to build the supportive environment that provides a space where they feel secure enough to take these risks. Changing the socio-cultural environment of the group, squad or team and/or the culture of the club or school will take time and effort but is relatively easy to maintain and build on over time. Developing this environment in a team or squad is also strongly influenced by the tone of the organization within which it operates such as the sports club or school.

Learning from errors

Even individual sports tend to have a very social dimension because they are typically coached in a club or school setting with a number of athletes training and competing together in a team or squad (see Kirk and MacPhail, 2003). The importance of team cohesion and the development of a sense of team for team sports is obvious, but in sports such as swimming and athletics the sense of team and mutual support is equally as important (see Light, 2010). Just as is the case in team sports such as basketball, rugby or football, a sense of belonging and support from teammates is important for athletes participating in individual sports. Building a positive team, squad or club culture is an important task for coaches in any sport (Martens, 2004) and this can take a considerable amount of time when starting afresh but, once established, they can reproduce their values, beliefs, meanings and behaviours as different athletes pass through them.

Trust and good relationships are important for any coaching context but are of particular importance for coaches using a Positive Pedagogy approach. DeVries and Zan (1996) emphasize the importance of students adopting a positive perspective on errors by understanding that errors and mistakes provide opportunities for learning, which is equally important for athletes. With good coaching, mistakes become constructive errors from which valuable learning emerges when, assisted by the coach, athletes critically reflect upon them and engage in productive dialogue with peers or in a one-on-one situation with the coach. This is something that is particularly important for the coach when s/he asks the athlete to experiment, take risks and/or be creative. It is also far better for athletes to make mistakes (tactical or technical) during practice than in competition.

Creativity

Creativity is an important asset in many sports and particularly in team sports but can also be a useful capacity for athletes in individual sports. It cannot be directly coached or taught but can be fostered by creating appropriate physical and socio-moral environments from which it can emerge. The inquiry-based nature of Positive Pedagogy encourages the productive interaction and opportunities for experimentation that can foster the development of creativity (Light and Light, 2016). It can motivate athletes of all ages and excite children and young people by empowering them to actively take charge of their learning and work together in creating ideas, improvising, creating new strategies and/or new ways of performing skills.

Just as it takes time for a team or individual athlete to adapt to the Positive Pedagogy coaching approach it takes time to establish a supportive socio-cultural environment. It is easy for academics to speak of learner empowerment but athletes who fear being embarrassed or humiliated if they make mistakes are unlikely to be interested in being empowered and are probably happier to just do as they are told. For these children and young people they can avoid responsibility for their own learning because if anything goes wrong they can blame it on the coach or teacher.

You cannot develop creativity by telling the athlete what to do and when. To foster creativity the coach should create appropriate physical learning environments through which s/he structures experiences and provides opportunities for creativity to emerge. Creativity cannot be taught but it can be fostered and encouraged. Some psychologists suggest that curiosity and creativity are naturally occurring in children but that they are suppressed as they pass through the schooling process (Lin and Reifel, 1999). This is because, after years of being told what to do and how to do it in school, young people asking *why?* is replaced by them asking *how?* (Beghetto and Plucker, 2006).

Creativity is important in most sports and should be encouraged in coaching. From a broader social perspective coaching should not contribute towards the decline of human creativity. Even when focused on the details of technical execution coaches should look for opportunities to encourage curiosity, inquiry and learning how to learn as demonstrated in some of the chapters in Part III. For example, in individual sports where the coach is focusing on technique, s/he could group athletes into pairs or groups of three to experiment with ways of overcoming the constraints imposed upon athletes by the coach or in improving technical execution such as outlined in the examples provided in Part III.

Generally recognized as the most influential thinker in education during the twentieth century, Dewey (1938a) makes a distinction between experience that he describes as being 'educative' and experience that is 'miseducative' that is useful for thinking about how Positive Pedagogy can provide opportunity for developing creativity. For Dewey (1938a), educative experience expands possibilities for human learning and growth in the future while miseducative experience restricts possibilities and growth in the future. From this perspective, repetitive skill drills with no opportunity to engage in reflection and dialogue are miseducative. On the other hand, Positive Pedagogy is educative because it enhances the possibilities for human development, including creativity. Coaches cannot directly teach creativity but they can develop environments that foster its emergence and development while contributing towards the pursuit of fuller humanity (Freire, 1970).

While it is possible to argue for teaching skill and technique by using direct instruction there can be no doubt that creativity cannot be taught. Indeed, as Kirk (2005a) points out in writing on TGfU, the traditional focus of teachers on the drilling of technique in games is largely driven by the hidden curriculum of social control and is focused on class control and safety more than on developing skilful games players. Developing creativity in any sport requires an open and inquiring disposition on the part of the coach with a view of his/her role as being a co-learner and guide instead of an instructor who tells athletes how to be creative.

Discussion

The notion of athlete-centred coaching has attracted considerable interest from academics, practitioners and national governing bodies. It has a range of interpretations but typically involves focusing on the athlete as a person and promoting active learning through using learner-centred pedagogy. For example, Sport and Recreation New Zealand (SPARC) suggest that athlete-centred coaching 'promotes *learning* through athlete *ownership, awareness* and *responsibility*. It describes a way of coaching that encourages coaches to increase the awareness and responsibility of the athlete by asking questions as opposed to giving instructions' (emphasis in original – SPARC, n.d., p. 1).

Athlete-centred approaches to coaching team games and Positive Pedagogy are also inquiry-based, as is the problem-based learning (PBL) that Jones and Turner (2006) suggest coaches could use to develop holistic coaching. Inquiry-based approaches typically present particular challenges for coaches unused to the changes these involve when shifting from coach-centred pedagogy. The inquiry-based nature of Positive Pedagogy and GBA is probably the feature that most distinguishes them from 'traditional' coaching approaches that tend to emphasize direct instruction and which are underpinned by the assumption that coaching involves the transmission of objective knowledge. The central role that experience plays in learning and the emphasis placed on questioning are core features of Positive Pedagogy, because it is an inquiry-based pedagogical approach.

Significant attention has been paid to questioning as one of the challenges facing coaches when attempting to adopt GBA (see Wright and Forrest, 2007; Roberts, 2011; Harvey and Light, 2015) and it is equally challenging when using a Positive Pedagogy approach to coaching individual sports. Designing and managing learning experiences are also very challenging but have received far less specific attention in the literature (for exceptions see Turner, 2014; Harvey and Robertson, 2015). Both these features of Positive Pedagogy coaching reflect its inquiry-based approach with questions asked to stimulate thinking and interaction between athletes and between athletes and the coach, which is critical for an inquiry-based approach to coaching.

PART III

Applications

7

INTRODUCTION TO APPLICATIONS

Part III presents nine practical examples of how Positive Pedagogy can be used across a range of sports and contexts to ground the ideas developed in the book in practice. It draws on my experiences of coaching in different countries and settings, and on those of four others who I invited to contribute to this section. The aim of this part of the book is not to tell or show coaches what to do. Its aim is to provide insights into real-life experiences of coaches working in different sports and activities and how they have interpreted and applied Positive Pedagogy in their coaching. This includes the experiences of the two colleagues and two Ph.D. students I invited to share their experiences of, and ideas on, adopting Positive Pedagogy for their coaching as coaches and teachers new to the approach.

Rather than being instructive, the examples provided are reflective, first-hand accounts of coaching that adopts Positive Pedagogy, and which reflect the openness and reflective attitude to coaching practice promoted in this book. The examples of applications presented in this section of the book are by no means intended to be prescriptive or to provide a step-by-step model for its implementation. The aim of each chapter in Part III is to provide insights into actual experiences of coaching and teaching that can generate thinking about how the reader could apply this pedagogy to his/her own coaching or how it could influence their practice. Like Positive Pedagogy, the intent of these chapters is to promote curiosity, thinking and reflection.

Skill in team games

The fixation of many coaches on developing skill as their prime focus in team sports can make it difficult for them to accept GBAs as being effective because of the ways in which they appear to devalue the importance of skill. The same problem exists with physical education teachers who have spent their careers focused on skill in the belief that it must be learned to enable students to play any games – modified or not. During the resurgence of interest in TGfU over the 1990s, this belief in the prime importance of skill manifested in a 'technique versus tactics' debate in the literature on games teaching (see Turner and Martineck, 1992). The terms 'skill' and 'technique' are often used interchangeably but Thorpe (1990) suggests that there is an important distinction between them. For him, technique is a way of efficiently performing a movement, such as passing a ball, outside the game while skill is technique performed effectively within the context of a game.

Around the turn of the twenty-first century the unhelpful oppositional relationship between technique and tactics began to give way to a more holistic focus on the game as a whole (see Griffin et al., 1997; Kirk and MacPhail, 2002). This continuing development has since seen growing recognition of the complexity of team games and learning to play them that includes paying attention to the interaction of tactical knowledge, skill, awareness, decision-making and other elements of game play in whatever aspect of the game is being worked on. This means that all practice should be contextualized to some extent.

Despite these positive developments the place of skills in GBA continues to present an ongoing problem for many coaches and teachers with the biggest problem being a reluctance to recognize the complexity of play in team games and the folly of trying to reduce coaching to the repetition of de-contextualized skill drills. Skills are undeniably important in team sport but are seen in GBA as being inseparable from other elements of play with a need to be learned and developed in context. Rather than just focusing on how to execute a skill the Game Sense coach helps his/her players in team sports learn when, where and why. This does not mean that coaches should not, or cannot, spend time working on skill because there will be times when a particular skill may need some specific attention. However, this does not mean that the coach has to suddenly drop GBA pedagogy to revert to skill drill. Instead, s/he should retain the integrity of his/her coaching but narrow the focus of the coaching session.

In the tactical games approach (see Griffin et al., 1997), breaking from modified games to focus specifically on technique is planned into the learning process in a game–practice–game pattern. In TGfU it is also commonly suggested that, if skill is holding up the progress of the game, then the teacher or coach should either stop the game for some focused practice on the skill or modify the skill demands of the game to enable learning to develop. Indeed, in my first workshop with Rod Thorpe in 1996 this is precisely what he suggested. Here I offer what could be seen as a compromise between these two responses. I suggest narrowing the focus of the coaching and learning objectives to the particular skill that needs attention but maintaining the need for, and development of, awareness and decision-making. When New Zealander Robbie Deans was coach of the Wallabies (the Australian national rugby team) I was fortunate enough to watch a training session with a small group of local coaches. At the completion of the session Deans told us that all practice activities always had to develop awareness and decision-making, which is something that made a lot of sense to me and still does.

Before moving on to provide two practical examples I briefly discuss the role of skill in a technical, coach-centred approach and a Game Sense approach after which I suggest how Positive Pedagogy can be applied to coaching skill in team sport.

The place of skills in the technical and game based approach

Technical approaches to coaching skill typically see competence in performing core skills as being fundamental to learning to play. Coaches adopting a technical approach believe that the players have to develop competence in core skills before they can participate in practice games. This reflects a view of skill being an entity that is separate to the game with an idealized form of it commonly referred to as its 'textbook' version developed through drill, repetition and coach feedback to reduce errors (Williams and Hodges, 2005). With this approach, technique is practised out of context until the coach feels the players are ready to move into practice games or game-like activities. Skill is learned first then gradually contextualized. The focus is on skill execution – skill first and then the practice game.

While there is variation between the various forms of GBA coaching, they are all informed by a conceptualization of the game as a whole and complex entity with all aspects of play interrelated. From this perspective, skill is one important part of the game as a complex phenomenon with decisions about skill execution relevant to the specific situation and good technique being what works in the game. It is learned in context within modified games or activities that demand and develop a degree of awareness and decision-making within which players adapt to increasing tactical and technical demands of the games or activities. In this approach skills enable the game to be played and developed. The focus of GBA is on the game.

A Positive Pedagogy approach to coaching skills for team sports

Coaching specific skills in team sports should maintain most of the features of GBA such as Game Sense but will have reduced complexity and typically take more of a guided-discovery approach than a problem-solving approach (Mosston and Ashworth, 1986). A Positive Pedagogy approach to coaching skill would ensure that, no matter how tightly focused the session is on skill, the activity or game must require and develop awareness and decision-making. From Thorpe's (1990) perspective, this is coaching a skill rather than technique. As tight as the focus might be on a particular skill the coach should not abandon his/her focus on learning in context and on active learning. Instead, the coach should narrow the focus of the session and use game-like activities such as the two quite simple examples I provide in this chapter to reduce, but not eliminate, the complexity of the sport.

Football (soccer) dribbling

It is a long time since I last coached full time but I have been fortunate enough to have had the opportunity to coach a range of team sports across a wide range of cultural and institutional settings and primarily through workshops for teachers, coaches, academics and university students (see Light, 2015). Whenever I do a session on football and ask how the participants were taught to dribble the answer is always that they were taught by dribbling around cones. This is a classic example of Dewey's (1938a) contention that skills learned out of context are useful only in that particular setting. The ubiquitous dribble around the cones drill teaches players to master the task of dribbling around fixed cones but there is little reason to believe that it transfers to competition games. It is also invariably boring.

To focus on the skill of dribbling in a way that is more likely to contribute to better game play I offer the example of a training activity called 'dribbling in traffic' (Light, 2013a, p. 120). This activity focuses on the skill of dribbling in a situation that replicates some of the 'real game' conditions in which it needs to be executed by requiring and developing awareness and low-level decision-making. The GBA coach has a toolbox of ways in which s/he can adjust the level of challenge for players that includes varying the size and shape of the space used, the number of players involved and the ratio of attackers to defenders in modified games (see Light, 2015). With this in mind the coach determines the space available and the number of players per space with a number of small-sided games that suits the number of players in the team. S/he then provides each player with one ball and asks them to dribble around the space, exploring as much of it as possible but avoiding making contact with other players, losing the ball or letting it go out of the marked space.

After giving the players enough time to get a feel for the activity the coach calls in the team to ask a few questions aimed at encouraging them to focus on technique, perception/awareness and making decisions about how to maintain control of the ball by seeing and using space. For example, the coach could ask (from Light, 2013a, p. 120), 'What can you do to avoid bumping into others in the grid?', 'Where is the best point to focus your vision so that you can control the ball yet be aware of spaces in your peripheral vision?', 'What parts of your feet can you use to change the direction of the ball quickly?' and 'What can you do to stay in control of the ball and be able to change direction quickly?' If needed, the coach can also provide some instruction about ball manipulation technique.

After this intervention the players return to their grids to focus more on the aspects of dribbling that were discussed or explained during the break in which the coach needs to be aware of how much time is spent in talking in relation to doing to maintain engagement. At this point the coach could also adjust the level of challenge up or down to suit the skill of the players and the pressure s/he wants to put on them. This could involve making the grid smaller to make it harder to find space or making it bigger to make it easier to find space. To provide a cognitive challenge, the coach could change the shape of the grid from a square to a long narrow space, to a triangle (with space at one end) or an 'L' shaped grid with each space providing different challenges within which the same skill is performed and developed.

This is a very simple activity but, when compared to dribbling around the cones, provides opportunities for learning to dribble that are far more like those encountered in the real match and, therefore, more likely to contribute towards improving skill execution in competition matches. The coach can use instruction about technique in this approach but learning is still athlete-centred. The players reflect upon action/experience through dialogue between them and the coach in the example provided here but it is also possible for the coach to encourage dialogue between players within each small-sided 'game'. For young players in particular, instead of standing in line waiting for their turn to dribble this activity has all players moving and learning at once. There is no waiting in line and no sense of surveillance.

Rugby passing

The second example of using Positive Pedagogy focuses on coaching the skill of passing in rugby and also draws on a practical example from my book *Game Sense: Pedagogy for Performance, Participation and Enjoyment* (Light, 2013a).

The coach begins by setting up grids or spaces of appropriate size for the number of players and their abilities. For example, younger players may need to be closer together because they are not strong enough or skilful enough to make long passes. Usually I begin with a 20 x 10–15 metre grid with four to five groups of three to four players and one ball each. If these are your own players you will know their ability well and be able to take this into account when setting up but still need to be prepared to tweak conditions as the session progresses.

At each grid all players form a line across the grid to run down to the other end (20 metres). Before they start the coach can outline and demonstrate a few technical aspects of the pass, depending upon what type of pass s/he wants to focus on. Former Japan and Australia rugby coach and current England coach Eddie Jones adopted a Game Sense approach as head coach of Japan for the 2015 Rugby World Cup. He recommends keeping initial instruction in passing simple by emphasizing only the need to have the fingers pointing in the direction of the receiver's hands (where they will be) upon release (Jones, 2015). In my experience of using this activity with less experienced participants it has been useful to encourage the receiver to sprint a couple of steps to ensure that s/he is in front of the receiver and to maintain alignment.

Owing to the fact that I tend to coach or teach less experienced participants who I do not know, I typically begin this activity like a more traditional practice drill; I have each group running and passing to the other end of the grid where they wait for the other groups to arrive before setting off to the end they came from. At the moment when all groups have completed their run there is opportunity for the coach to ask a few general questions depending upon the age, experience and skill level of the team. These might include 'What can you do as a receiver to take the ball at pace and accelerate onto it?', 'When you have the ball in hand where should you pass it to help the receiver hit it at pace?' and 'When you receive the ball what can you do to give your receivers depth to run onto the ball and maintain forward momentum?'

Next, I would usually introduce the need for awareness and decision-making to contextualize the act of passing. The activity begins in the same way but when each group arrives at the other end of the grid they do not wait. Instead, they immediately turn around to return by running at the oncoming groups. This presents a situation in which, although each group is running and passing as they had been during the first stage of the activity, they have to deal with the interference of other teams coming at them from the opposite direction. This requires awareness of what is going on around them and making decisions about the timing and speed of passes, and the possibility of evading an oncoming player with ball in hand based on this. To keep the same width of the passes but increase the cognitive demands of the activity on the players, and the adaptation of skill execution to the interference of the other groups, the coach can shorten the length of the grid to, say, 15 metres. This increases the number of times the groups have to negotiate oncoming groups and reduces the time between these situations in which they have to make 'at-action' decisions (Light, Harvey et al., 2014).

At any time s/he sees fit, the coach can stop the players at each grid or as a whole team (if more than one grid is being used) to ask questions or make suggestions about the technical aspects of passing in relation to the conditions of the activity and the interrelated issues of when, why and how to pass. To step up the pressure and learning at the end of this stage the coach could ask the players to reduce the time the ball is held in hand (hot potato) as much as possible and, after a few runs, ask them what strategies they used to meet this challenge, what type of pass this required and what technique might be involved. For example, s/he might ask 'How did having to unload the ball immediately change the task for you?' or 'What ideas or strategies did you use as an individual to deal with receivers having to unload the ball so quickly?' When using this activity in workshops over the past few years where technique was letting the players down I would either reduce the demands of the activity or intervene with some brief instruction.

When I have used this activity I typically increase the complexity of the activity and the demands placed upon passing skill by introducing passing patterns such as a cut-out pass (skipping one teammate) and an inside pass from the receiver back to the player who was 'cut out'. Any other passing pattern could be introduced here, such as a pass and loop. Typically, working with groups of four players, I would ask them to continue to keep the time with ball in hand to a minimum and complete one sequence of the pattern I asked for. This would begin free of interference by waiting at the end of the grid for all groups to arrive before setting off but when they appeared to be comfortable and competent in an unopposed situation I would have them return in the opposite direction without waiting as was done in stage two. When the players have adapted to this challenge the coach could ask them to see how many sequences they could complete in a set time or number of 'laps'.

Discussion

In all the activities for coaching skill in football and rugby described in this chapter the coach maintains characteristics of the Game Sense approach that typically involve managing the demands of the activities based upon the players' progress and engagement and asking questions. This typically involves modifying the size, dimensions and shape of the playing space or grid, the number of players and the difficulty of the skill being performed to maximize learning and enjoyment. The coach can also use direct instruction when needed and particularly when focusing on the technical aspects of the skill. With this approach, technical instruction is provided when it is needed as the demands the activities place on the skill increase. This shows the relevance of the technique for passing as a skill performed in a game-like situation to the players. It also highlights how passing and catching in games are skills that are relational, complex and interrelated (MacPhail et al., 2008). Passing has no function without catching.

The approach I outline here develops the skill of passing within a context that is similar enough to the real game to transfer but with a focus on it as a skill and on its technical aspects. It can stand alone as a replacement for a skill drill or be built upon to increase in complexity. For example, the dribbling-in-traffic activity could lead into the 'pass and run five' activity (Light, 2013, p. 123). In this activity the players work in pairs in a larger space where they have to pass to their partner and then run 5 metres to receive the pass and return immediately to their partner who has also run 5 metres, while other pairs in the same grid are doing the same.

Compared to practice games used in GBA that are aimed at developing tactical knowledge and complex decision-making, both examples in this chapter have a narrow focus on the specific skills of dribbling in football and passing in rugby. This enables the coach to focus more on the technical aspects of the skill while keeping the execution of the skill contextualized and, therefore, transferable to competition matches. This means that while allowing for a tight focus on skill this Positive Pedagogy approach maintains the integrity of GBAs as holistic approaches to coaching that focus on the game as a whole through positive learning experiences by the athletes.

8

SWIMMING

Although there is a tactical dimension to competitive swimming, technique is of pivotal importance but the traditional, mechanistic approach is not the only way to coach. Learning to swim efficiently is more complex than traditional coaching approaches suggest and there is much to gain from the use of pedagogy informed by views of human learning that account for its complexity and of learning as an holistic process (Light and Wallian, 2008). The development of swimming technique is not merely a process through which the swimmer reproduces standardized, 'correct' movements, because it involves interpretation, reinterpretation and adaptation (Light and Wallian, 2008). Learning in swimming unfolds from the personal interpretation of technique and whole-person experience of it by the swimmer within a, literally, fluid environment. Dewey's work has had a significant influence on the development of constructivism with him suggesting that learning (education) involves an 'unfolding from within' (1916/1997, p. 68) with similar language and conceptions of learning characterizing contemporary approaches to learning that recognize, and strive to account for, its complexity (see Davis and Sumara, 1997).

Despite official rules set by the international swimming organization (FINA) that limit variation in the different strokes and the ongoing development of the most bio-mechanically efficient movements in swimming, techniques are not completely standardized and uniform due to individual interpretation and reinterpretation by swimmers (Light and Wallian, 2008). Learning technique in swimming is not merely a process of reproducing a 'correct' model but, instead, one of interpretation and adaptation on an individual basis that can benefit from teaching and coaching approaches that move beyond the limitations of direct instruction. It is these aspects of swimming that require coaching that can account for the complexity of learning to swim fast and which eschews a view of it as a non-problematic, linear process of replication.

This chapter outlines two examples of how Positive Pedagogy can be applied to coaching swimming technique by drawing on learning activities that I developed from watching and talking to experienced swim coaches. Both examples aim to develop an understanding of the two fundamental concepts of swimming, which are: (a) maximizing thrust/propulsion and (b) reducing resistance. When swimmers develop an understanding of these two fundamental principles they can draw on this knowledge base to interpret instruction on technique and adapt it to their ways of swimming. The two examples provided in this chapter aim to enhance embodied and reflective understanding of how performance of the technique influences propulsion and/or resistance as part of the complex act of swimming. This understanding of these two principles is not limited to the conscious knowledge expressed through articulation but includes the corporeal learning and feel for them developed through experience.

In these two examples, understanding and knowledge-in-action is developed through a 'conversation' between the non-reflective learning arising from experiences of engagement *in* action and the conscious, reflective learning *about* action (Light and Fawns, 2003). Non-reflective learning occurs through adaptation to the (enabling) constraints (Davis and Sumara, 1997) imposed on the swimmers by the training activities with rational, conscious learning occurring more through the swimmers' individual and/or collective reflection upon and during experience.

The first example draws on my experience of working with a small group of swimmers in Leeds, England, aged twelve to sixteen, in a practical demonstration of Positive Pedagogy coaching for swimming at a post-graduate summer school on sport pedagogy. It provides an example of how coaches can use standard drills for learning activities in a Positive Pedagogy approach suggested in chapter 4 to help the swimmers feel, think about, and understand the purpose of the second kick in butterfly and to improve its effectiveness. The second example also uses a standard drill used to develop feel for the water in breaststroke. It is informed by my observations of coaches in the UK and Australia using these drills and the insights in personal experience that some of my studies on young swimmers conducted across different cultural settings have provided for me (see Light and Lémonie, 2012; Light et al., 2013; Light, 2016). It is also informed by my own personal experience of developing feel in breaststroke. When thinking through my ideas on Positive Pedagogy and the development of feel in swimming I asked an experienced breaststroker to coach me using the activities outlined and discussed in the second example to give me a subjective understanding.

Developing the second kick in butterfly

This example draws from my experience of working with six competitive age-group swimmers in England aged twelve to sixteen as part of a postgraduate summer school on sport and physical education pedagogy. As one of the presenters I delivered a one-hour lecture on my athlete-centred approach to coaching individual sports that I was developing but had not yet named Positive Pedagogy. I then conducted a ninety-minute demonstration using swimming as an example that was followed by a one-hour tutorial for discussion. I was able to use my connections with the local swimming club to invite six age-group swimmers, aged twelve to sixteen years, who had qualified for the national age-group championships.

I chose swimming and a focus on improving the second kick in butterfly as a very technical aspect of the stroke to highlight the ways in which athlete-centred pedagogy could be used in technique-intensive sports. The aim of the session was to develop awareness of this part of the kick and to assist the swimmers in understanding how it fits into the whole stroke.

After a warm up I asked the swimmers to swim one-armed butterfly but to breathe facing forward rather than to the side, as is sometimes done to make breathing easier. I did this to help accentuate the relationship between the second kick and breathing. After they had swum a few laps I stopped them to ask how it felt and what particular difficulties they felt arose from only being able to use one arm. I asked questions such as 'How did that feel compared to normal 'fly?' and 'Can you identify any particular problem or difficulty that it seemed to create for you?'

After a few more questions from me one of the male swimmers said that he was swallowing a little water, after which I asked the others whether or not they experienced the same problem with general agreement in their responses. This allowed me to focus some questions on breathing by asking 'How do you think you can compensate for the lack of propulsion that is creating problems with breathing?' The answer came almost immediately from one of the girls, who suggested that kicking more effectively could compensate for the reduction in propulsion created by only being able to use one arm. I then asked how many kicks were usually performed per stroke, to which two swimmers answered that there were two. Following this I asked which one would be more appropriate with only tentative responses offered that I did not follow up on because I wanted them to discover this through experience and reflection.

Next I asked the swimmers to work in pairs to discuss the issue at hand, formulate ideas for improving their kick to provide enough propulsion to make breathing easier and try it out in the water. When they had done this I asked them to then do some reciprocal teaching (Mosston and Ashworth, 1986), which involved one coaching the other and then changing roles (reciprocating). This provided them with the experience of doing, watching their partner, thinking about it as they 'coached' their partner and talking about it. One from each pair then demonstrated their technique to the group doing one-arm butterfly, after which we discussed it with the six swimmers drawing on objective (watching) and subjective (doing) perspectives. This then expanded what could be seen as distributed thinking/cognition (Bruner, 1990) across the entire group, emphasizing the social nature of learning and the greater capacity for learning in a group than at an individual level.

After this I asked them to spend five minutes practising the kicking technique that we had collectively agreed was most efficient but with the removal of the constraint of only being able to use one arm which allowed them to work the technique into the full stroke. Comments from the postgraduate students watching suggested that they could see a positive change in the way that the swimmers swam butterfly over the one-hour duration of the demonstration. Some of the swimmers said that they *felt* an improvement over the session with one thirteen-year-old boy, who was a national finalist in the 100-metre butterfly, telling his father that he had discovered something very important. His father told me later that his son had been very excited and stimulated by being asked to think and problem solve in swimming, having someone care about him and having someone interested in what he thinks. He felt a sense of liberation and empowerment.

Clearly one such session is unlikely to make a lasting difference to the technique of the swimmers and this approach is relatively time-consuming, but it would typically be done early in the season and only need to be done once. If in subsequent practice sessions the coach were to help the swimmers make connections with the conceptual understandings and the linking of technique to them they had learned in a session like this, it could help them develop their technique in more demanding training while they adapt the technique to how they swim in race conditions.

Developing feel for the water in breaststroke

Developing a *feel* for the water is an important aspect of learning to swim fast but is a vague concept that is difficult to pin down or measure. It is also an aspect of performance that, although evident in other sports such as equestrian sports and surfing (Dashper, 2012; Fitzsimons and Light, 2016), has been overlooked in the coaching and physical education pedagogy literature. Coaching feel in swimming 'moves beyond technique and into the realm of the phenomenon of the swimmer's connection with the water' (Light, 2008a, p. 142). It involves the swimmer's adaptation to moving through, and connection with, a fluid environment.

As feel cannot be taught using direct instruction, coaches typically provide particular experiences through which the swimmer learns by doing and reflecting in action or even by experiencing a state of *mindfulness* in which the body and its sensations are central to learning if encouraged to think about what they are doing. In Buddhist traditions the concept of mindfulness refers to a state of awareness of the individual's being and doing (Cohen, 2010) and has been appropriated to circumvent some of the limitations of Western dualism (see for example Varela et al., 1991; Seligman and Csikszentmihalyi, 2000). It is a concept that is widely used in Positive Psychology and interpreted from a psychological perspective that Cohen describes as it having been 'psychologicalized'. Referred to as 'drills' by most coaches, activities used to enhance feel for the water do so by imposing constraints that encourage the swimmer to find ways of compensating for them and which intensify the experience and awareness of contact with the water. This is much like the use of enabling or liberating constraints to establish a balance between structure and freedom for learning as proposed by Davis, Sumara and Luce-Kapler (2000).

Coaches use these drills because they work, but rarely do they talk about how or why they work with their swimmers or ask them to describe or reflect upon how they felt. Learning to improve feel through performing these drills occurs mostly at a non-conscious level through performance of them over time during which the swimmer adapts to the demands of the task. To develop feel of the water in the hands, fingers and forearms in breaststroke, coaches typically have their swimmers perform two types of 'sculling' as two halves of the breaststroke pull, and usually without a kick (but it can be used to develop feel in all strokes). These are the front, or outward, scull, in which the swimmer propels him/herself by using only the first part of the stroke from the 'catch' (out-sweep), in which the swimmer first catches the water, and the inward scull (in-sweep) as the second part of the stroke. The front scull is also used more generally to help younger swimmers develop feel for the water for all strokes. Sometimes the swimmer is allowed to use a small flutter kick but more often no kick at all is allowed. The swimmer might also be allowed to use a 'pull buoy' (leg float), which is a flotation device they clamp between their legs to keep their body level in the water. This is done to emphasize the experience of sculling by making it the sole means of moving forward through the water.

Sculling helps develop a sensitivity to contact between the forearms and hands/fingers and the water and improve efficiency in getting hold of the water. In this activity the swimmer solves the problem of moving through the water by exploring the most efficient ways to perform in response to the constraints imposed, leading to improving feel for catching and using the water. This promotes awareness of, and sensitivity to, contact with the water by the hands, fingers and the edges of the forearms. Unless the coach specifically tells the swimmer to focus on an aspect of the scull (which would be unusual), s/he solves this problem as a process of adaptation involving reflection *in* action that can involve a state of mindfulness (Varela et al., 1991) and which often occurs at a non-conscious level.

Through performing this training activity the swimmer typically adapts to the demands of sculling without conscious reflection and with learning emerging from this response to the constraints imposed. For most swim coaches using such activities to develop feel in their swimmers, their pedagogy does not go beyond setting the task and having the swimmer perform the drill. Using Positive Pedagogy to maximize learning through the scull could begin by asking swimmers to use a pull buoy and do the out-sweep action with fists closed, asking him/her where s/he can feel the water and what s/he can do to best catch it and use it to move forward. Examples of questions the coach could use here would be, 'How did that feel?' or 'How can you get hold of the most water with your fist closed?' Questions will vary with the age of the swimmers and experience and the time available but typically encourage them to reflect upon action.

Learning from reflection *on* (after) action can be enhanced by verbally encouraging athletes to reflect *in* action, which would involve a degree of mindfulness. In this example of learning through the scull with fists closed this could involve asking swimmers to do the fist-closed scull and think about 'How can you catch the most water with your fists closed?' If more focus is needed the coach could say, 'When you scull I would like you to experiment with the angle of your fist and forearm to see how you can catch the most water'. Rotating the fists to a 'palm out' position close to 180 degrees for the catch and the outward movement will enable the swimmer to move forward most efficiently. Having elbows up high in the water facilitates this and is something the coach could draw attention to by asking the swimmers to think about this while sculling. In striving to catch water with a closed fist the swimmer will invariably raise his/her elbows without being asked to but, as this may figure in the debate of ideas, it is something the coach should draw attention to while the swimmers are in the water. Instead of just telling them what to do s/he could ask, 'When you were sculling with your fists turned out where were your elbows?' as a lead-in to asking, 'Why do you think your elbows were up? How do you think this helps catch more water?... This time think about where your elbows are and why this might be'.

The swimmers might then be allowed to half-open their fists and be asked questions about where they can feel water pressure and so on, with the coach using similar questioning and prompting as suggested above. The next stage could involve sculling with hands completely open and reflecting on how different it feels and why, compared and contrasted with the more constrained previous versions of the scull (fists half-open). Here the coach should probably intervene briefly to suggest that in breaststroke with the hands open, the hands should be outward-facing but at around a 45-degree angle for maximum efficiency. S/he could explain why but younger swimmers would likely struggle to feel the difference. Finally, the swimmers would swim normal breaststroke while focusing on their contact with the water as reflecting-in-action or achieving a state of mindfulness (Valera et al., 1991) as an awareness of their body in action. Although this approach focuses on one part of the stroke it links the scull with the full stroke used in breaststroke while linking technical aspects of swimming with feel.

This exercise provides for learning feel at an embodied level while also offering the opportunity for the coach to enhance this learning by bringing experience to consciousness for rational consideration and representation through language through dialogue. The constraints that the activities suggested in this chapter impose are aimed at having the swimmer explore and discover possibilities as *enabling constraints* (Davis et al., 2000). The pedagogy used and the use of language, and questioning in particular, brings this learning experience to a conscious level for discussion, debate and the formulation of ideas, but there is a limit to which the non-rational learning(s) can be rendered rational and consciously knowable.

Discussion

The suggestions I make for coaching in this chapter provide opportunities for learning through doing, individual and collective reflection upon experience and verbalizing understanding through the structuring of social interaction. The coach provides an experience designed to present particular problems or challenges that are initially met at a non-conscious level. S/he then asks questions that, although they may be designed to lead to the discovery of predetermined learning, can still be liberatory (Freire, 1970) and facilitate experiencing the joy of discovery. The use of questions by the coach and the dialogue they promote bring some of the embodied, non-conscious learning that occurs as the swimmer adapts to the constraints imposed to consciousness for rational consideration. They also show how dialogue can enhance learning in swimming as opposed to an almost universal monologue of direct instruction that dominates swim coaching.

The activities and questioning suggested in this chapter link learning to the core concepts of (1) reducing resistance and (2) increasing propulsion in swimming that Fosnot (1996) calls the 'big ideas' used in constructivist-informed teaching. Understanding the importance of these two concepts and how all technique relates to them can liberate swimmers and empower them to interpret what the coach tells them and to understand why technique is executed in a certain way rather than taking on the role of the 'dumb machine' (Light and Fawns, 2001).

The pedagogy I set out in this chapter aims to improve swimming performance as a complex process of learning that cannot be reduced to the repetition of discrete components. Although the first example (second kick in butterfly) focuses on a specific aspect of technique it is inseparable from the whole stroke and the experience of swimming as a phenomenon that includes the swimmer and his/her connection with the water (physical context). Coaching in the way suggested here gives this part of the stroke meaning for the learner. The second example focuses on feel as a less tangible aspect of swimming that cannot be taught through direct instruction. To help me understand how this learning unfolds from the activities I describe in the second example, I asked an experienced and successful junior breaststroker to coach me for a couple of sessions. I am not a highly experienced swimmer but really felt a difference between how I was doing breaststroke before and after the two sessions. It also helped me to reflect in action and be mindful of my body and its movement while performing breaststroke. Swimmers who have 'feel' are what triple Olympic gold medalist in the men's 100-metre freestyle, Pieter van den Hoogenband, describes as 'natural' swimmers who disturb the water less and create less 'splash' (Jeffery, 2012, p. 36).

The approach I suggest in this chapter fosters the learner's capacity and inclination to interpret and 'work through' (Dewey, 1916/1997) the challenges the coach sets while promoting their development into independent learners. It provides positive learning experiences that, while enhancing learning, contribute to the development of an enjoyment of learning and learning how to learn. Teaching technique in any sport is likely to involve more of a guided discovery teaching style than a more open problem-solving style (Mosston and Ashworth, 1986) but it is complex because learning involves more than conscious cognition and repetition. It involves swimmers interpreting and adapting technique to their way of swimming in different ways through experience, reflection and dialogue rather than mechanical reproduction of one 'correct' model.

9

CROQUET

With Jenny Clarke

In this chapter I present a practical example of Positive Pedagogy for coaching by recounting my own experiences of coaching croquet to older athletes in a croquet workshop. In this example I wanted to encourage the athletes to learn to use intrinsic feedback as a way of discovering the best stance and grip for playing a wide range of strokes. The example draws on my experience of coaching a group of twenty athletes in their sixties and seventies at a regional croquet workshop delivered at a New Zealand croquet club to focus on the most basic aspect of croquet, which is hitting a ball cleanly. While the tactical nuances of croquet, and golf croquet, are typically developed over a series of episodes of experience, reflection and experimentation, by far the most critical and rarely mastered aspect of the game is the simple ability to strike a ball cleanly and with moderate power (McCullough and Mulliner, 1987). Tactical training in croquet has long been delivered through lectures and lessons learned through errors during match play but, more recently, approaches using Game Sense have been used to provide game-like experiences to facilitate both technical and tactical learning (Clarke, 2016). Technical coaching in croquet is almost exclusively delivered through a demonstrate-and-replicate pedagogy where the individual aspects of coaching tend to be correctional with a focus on what is done incorrectly and fixing mistakes. The Positive Pedagogy approach generates dialogue within the player, between players, and between the player and coach. This encourages curiosity about players' own technique with the focus clearly placed on what is done well and, perhaps most critically, building on the existing skills and knowledge of the player.

The literature in GBA confirms the capacity of this pedagogy to generate positive outcomes such as positive affective experience (see Harvey et al., 2009), improving relationships (Chen and Light, 2006) and developing tactical knowledge (Bohler, 2009). Positive Pedagogy is an extension of the pedagogical features of Game Sense (Light, 2013a) and TGfU (Teaching Games for Understanding, Bunker and

Thorpe, 1982), developed to include individual sports, that appears to work with children and young people as suggested by the limited literature on it (see Light and Kentel, 2015; Light, 2014a). However, there is little literature on its application to older athletes.

As I illustrate here, it is also an ideal pedagogy for teaching older athletes as a group that has been largely ignored in the GBA literature and has received limited attention in the broader literature on sport coaching.

Background

All of the participants in the workshop were over sixty years old, many in their late seventies and early eighties, and all had come to the workshop having only ever experienced direct coach-centred coaching – many from me in previous coaching sessions. Despite very positive feedback in sessions I had conducted in the past it was evident to me that the participants' knowledge retention was poor, even when technical drills were employed and the aspects of poor technique were explained to them. During the workshops I had always noticed how many of them quickly reverted to old habits, and was frustrated with not seeing any significant improvement over these sessions. Another challenging factor of croquet coaching is that it is generally delivered in a one-off half-day or full-day workshop.

I was unsure of what I could do to improve learning until I read Light's (2013) book *Game Sense: Pedagogy for Performance, Participation and Enjoyment*. This had a huge influence on my thinking about coaching as an academic and as a practising coach. It gave me a new way of looking at coaching that was exciting and motivating but which presented me with the problem identified by the under-graduates in the introduction to this book: How can I use Game Sense to teach an individual sport? I was aware of the TGfU and Game Sense game classification that suggests croquet is a target game but was still faced with the problem of using Game Sense for a skill-intensive sport until I read Light's (2014a) publication on coaching swimming. In particular, the emphasis placed on 'feel' when coaching breaststroke resonated with my experiences as a croquet player and coach helping players understand what a 'good' stroke is.

In the workshop with the senior athletes my aim was to encourage them to want to learn (curiosity, motivation and agency), provide the tools for them to learn (developing feel, games-based approaches and collaborative learner-centred development) and, where possible, begin to establish a 'community of learners'. My use of the term 'community of learners' refers to the idea of learning as a shared endeavour and with all participants having active roles in socio-cultural activity (Rogoff, 1994). It refers to a group of people who share values and beliefs and who actively engage in learning with, and from, each other. This was all to happen in one day, which seemed a huge challenge to me but, as I will try to show in this chapter, is possible when using a Positive Pedagogy approach.

Hitting a ball 'hard'

This example of a Positive Pedagogy activity created the setting for the whole workshop by challenging the athletes to hit balls harder and harder. While sheer power is rarely required in social and club-level competition, I used this activity to encourage the athletes to explore aspects of their technique, such as their stance (foot position), grip (where and how they held the mallet) and mechanics of the swing that would also benefit their more gentle strokes. Once an athlete can hit a ball hard while maintaining balance and control it is much easier to make a gentle stroke by transferring what is learned when hitting the ball hard to hitting the ball more softly. The idea here was to exaggerate the normal demands of a gentle stroke by challenging the athletes to meet the demands of a hard hit and to focus on using feel to enhance learning as Light did in his study on swimming (2014a). To shift the focus from accuracy and target acquisition, I gave the athletes a larger target area to hit the ball into. The target area was marked out with colourful beanbags, which were used to create lines at 10 metres and 12 metres away. The athletes were instructed to simply hit a ball into this area. There were plenty of balls and with assistants returning the balls to the players they were able to hit many balls.

I began with a comparatively short distance to the target area that I thought would provide challenge but allow for all to taste success. The players were pro-gressively challenged to hit the ball longer distances; however, beginning with the shorter starting distance made it easy for all players to successfully achieve the goal set while providing a positive physiological and psychological warm-up activity that gave the players confidence. While this activity was proceeding, I moved among the group asking questions such as 'Are you comfortable hitting a ball this far? Do you feel stable? Can you feel good contact when you hit your ball?'

After everyone had had a few shots, I gradually moved the target zone farther away. From about 15 metres, some players began to miss-hit strokes. I watched several try, pause and watch other players, and then have another attempt. After they had had some time to contemplate the challenge facing them they typically called me over to talk or to ask for help. Here I asked questions to encourage them to explore options for changing their own technique with a focus on feel, such as 'How does it feel now? What do you think is going wrong here? Do you feel stable now?' We would also pause to look at particular players' techniques from time to time. Typically, this simple activity generated curiosity and very lively conversations that attracted nearby players, who would join in and share their reflections with us. Common responses to my questions would include 'My wrist felt uncomfortable', or 'I didn't feel I hit it with the middle of the mallet', or even 'I nearly fell over when I had to hit it that hard!' A lot of comments also reflected attempts to provide answers, which parroted comments from other coaches, such as 'I was standing too close' or 'I was standing too far back'. I tended to probe further into these stock responses by asking questions that focused on how the stroke felt, such as 'What makes you feel that's the case?' This question would more often than not be answered with responses about their kinaesthetic experience, with a focus on how the execution of the stroke felt. Typically they commented on how they hadn't made clean contact. Following the inquiry-based approach as espoused by Dewey (1916/1997) a century ago, this involved discovering a 'perplexing problem', clarifying the problem, coming up with possible solutions and testing them (see also chapter 6).

After having identified a problem, the next step for the athletes was to find possible solutions. I encouraged the athletes to experiment with the areas where they felt something was not ideal with their technique and to discuss their ideas with a partner if they thought that would help. One of the particular challenges of working with older participants is that many have additional constraints imposed on them due to injury and age-related physical decline. This means that a one-size-fits-all approach can not only be unhelpful for promoting improvement but that it can also lead to discomfort and loss of motivation. On the other hand, Positive Pedagogy encourages athletes to explore individually, and collectively, to find solutions for themselves and at a pace of learning that suits them (see chapter 12 on the kayak roll) and emphasized the need to experiment.

One of the examples of where the athletes experimented was changing from having one foot next to the other with a small gap for the mallet to swing between them to strike the ball forward to having a staggered stance, with one foot up to half a step in front of the other. Players who experimented with having one foot farther forward tended to find it improved their balance, providing a wider base of support for the backward-forward swinging motion, which enabled them to better maintain their balance when driving the mallet forcefully into a ball. Others experimented with the three main grips (McCullough and Mulliner, 1987) and with varying how high up the mallet shaft their hands were. A few also tried standing closer to or farther from their ball, but with their attention mostly focused on feeling a clean impact in the stroke as feedback on how well they had performed the strike. I also made suggestions to individual players about what changes they might try, such as feeling the mallet pause at the top of the swing before bringing the hands forward. These were delivered by way of suggestions about what actions to try, then followed up with questions about how the action felt and how it compared to previous attempts. The focus of the entire session was on improving striking technique by developing the athletes' feel for individual technique and building on that individual performance.

Through gradually increasing the challenge and, for some players, finding a shorter 'maximum' distance to concentrate on, the players began to understand their individual swings better, and all showed improvement towards a more stable and repeatable technique. In the group discussion that followed the session, improvements in understanding were evident in comments such as 'I put one foot half a step in front of the other, and felt more balanced even hitting the ball really hard' and '[A player] next to me was using standard grip, so I tried it and the shots felt much more solid to me'. I also noticed a lot of players nodding in agreement when others spoke of what they had felt when striking the ball and the confidence they had gained. By this time the focus of reflections and dialogue was on how strokes felt and how the changes they had all tried and tested contributed to them feeling clean contact with the ball.

This session led onto practise of 'jump' strokes – hitting the ball firmly into the ground to cause it to jump up and over an obstruction. With the confidence, balance and power developed from the first session, players all quickly mastered this often-challenging stroke, showing immediate benefits from being challenged to 'discover' how to hit a ball hard and apply what they learned to this task.

From my perspective as a coach, the real successes of using Positive Pedagogy were the individual improvements in performance it generated and the confidence the players gained in terms of both being able to perform skills and in their ability to learn. The interaction and experimentation by players were evidence of curiosity and a sense of agency in developing technique, both of which were the real goals of this one-off workshop.

Discussion

Brookfield's (1995) four lenses for reflection offer a useful way of understanding why the approach I took worked so well. The four lenses are literature, student, peer and self. The literature is discussed throughout this reflective article with the other three being present in the workshop as the practitioner (self), the participants (student) and a peer (an assistant coach and observer).

I gained a lot of pleasure from the session, having decided to follow Light's (2014a) suggestions for focusing on developing feel. I also wanted to support the athletes to each improve their own technique and gain skills to get the most out of their own styles of play. Of all the workshops I have delivered with adult athletes, in this session the participants all most appeared to be most enjoying themselves, understanding what was being asked of them and feeling a sense of growing confidence and success. The questions I was asked, the participants' answers, and the discussion generated from my own questions suggested to me that the players were rapidly gaining the skills to use internal feedback to understand their own play. Having chosen to implement a new approach to coaching, I also felt a strong sense of relief and satisfaction at the success of this session because I had taken a risk by using an athlete-centred approach to teach older athletes who were more used to being coached through direct instruction, being passive learners who receive knowledge, and trying to copy technique that is demonstrated to them.

The response from the participants was very positive, with the discussions throughout the workshop suggesting an increasing attention to, and use of, internal feedback, and many very enthusiastic and grateful comments, including one from a participant who said, 'I really enjoyed myself…while I had come along today, I had been thinking of not playing any more…the two sessions I had with a friend had been very con-fusing. …I now understand what I am doing'. Another participant was particularly enthusiastic about her ability to develop her own technique as she has a chronic back injury, which meant that she could not use a traditional 'correct' technique.

The final view is from the lense of a peer acting as an impartial observer and has always been important to me. From my perspective as a coach I was very pleased with the session but wanted to know if my own observations were supported by those of a peer. The observer was an international coach with many years of experience in coaching from beginner to elite players. He enjoyed the session and said that he was surprised at how well it worked. As a well-known coach, many of the players spoke with him following the session, with him describing them as being very positive and enthusiastic about the session and their comments reflecting increased confidence in their own abilities from the session.

Dewey (1938a) suggests we learn through engagement with a learning environment rather than through instruction. He reminds us that we must ensure experiences are educative, and need to foster an enthusiasm for learning, rather than simply providing unguided experiences. The three requirements for effective Positive Pedagogy are (1) a well-designed and managed learning activity, (2) effective and open questions to encourage cognitive engagement and (3) an inquiry-based approach that provides opportunities for designing strategies and trying strategies and solutions within a supportive learning environment. The activity I describe in this chapter provides these elements and offers progressions and alternatives to suit the needs of the athletes.

The questioning I used encouraged creativity and seemed to foster confidence in the athletes' ability to discover their own solutions to technical challenges and focused on feeling the sensation of a clean hit. The level of the activities appeared well matched to the players' abilities and experience as they exhibited and reported many of the elements of *flow* described by Csikszentmihalyi (1990). There are a number of examples of how to use Positive Pedagogy for coaching young people in this section of the book but there are none that involve older athletes, which reflects a general neglect of research interest in them. Using Positive Pedagogy for coaching older athletes was daunting for me, with the concern that a lifetime of direct coaching for the athletes would lead them to expect a fully structured, carefully timed workshop as in the previous years. Additionally, the athletes were well conditioned to being passive learners. They were used to sitting quietly, listening to 'experts' dole out wisdom and demonstrations of perfect technique developed through their past croquet and other sporting and educational experiences.

The response from the participants could not have been more positive for me! The progression of the shooting-based activity created a positive atmosphere where individuals interacted to find solutions to an increasing challenge and discussed their ideas and the outcomes of their experiments. As the day proceeded with other Positive Pedagogy and Game Sense activities, people delighted in discovering, testing and refining tactics and skills. The feedback following the session was very enthusiastic.

The Positive Pedagogy approach I used in this workshop enabled the participants to work together, engaging physically and cognitively, and gain feedback from each other, enabling the coaching ratio of one to twenty to work effectively. The enthusiasm and understanding shown by participants strongly suggests that using

Positive Pedagogy to coach a target sport such as croquet could be effective, even with an older group of participants.

Conclusion and reflection

Despite these being older participants with a long history of being coached through a direct, coach-centred approach, the participants I coached in the day-long croquet workshop enthusiastically embraced an athlete-centred and inquiry-based coaching approach. The design of engaging and effective activities and learning experiences is critical to the success of Positive Pedagogy (Light, 2014a; Light and Harvey, 2015). Engaging athletes both cognitively and physically supports deeper learning and enables coaching to be effective with a high athlete-to-coach ratio. This offers promising ground for further advances in coaching target sports through games-based approaches, teaching athletes across a range of ages and past experiences. Further work is needed to provide broader evidence of the efficacy of this pedagogical approach in the sporting context of croquet but, as a practising coach and academic who has only begun to work with Positive Pedagogy, this was a very reassuring and motivating experience for me.

10

RUNNING

In this chapter I present two examples of how Positive Pedagogy can be used for coaching aspects of running. The first example focuses on helping children understand and improve the use of their arms in beach sprinting, with the second example drawing on my experience of coaching baton changing in the 4 x 100 metre track relay to eleven- and twelve-year-old girls in an Australian primary school.

Although there is a tactical dimension to running that is particularly important over longer distances there is a clear need for athletes to develop technical proficiency. This may require some direct instruction but, even with a strong focus on learning technique, coaches can take an holistic and humanistic approach for helping athletes of any age to learn technique. I outline an approach here that is guided by Positive Pedagogy as an ongoing 'conversation' between pre-reflective and reflective learning, between speech and action (Light and Fawns, 2003) and aimed at developing knowledge-in-action (Schön, 1983).

Using the arms in running

This example of applying Positive Pedagogy outlines an activity for helping primary school–aged children understand and improve the important contribution arm movement makes towards sprinting. The learning activities used involve placing a constraint on running that creates a problem to be solved through reflection in and on action, dialogue and collective inquiry. This activity focuses on developing children's awareness and understanding of the role that the arms play in sprinting and improving it. I have also used this activity when helping a primary school teacher in physical education classes, but this chapter draws on my role as a coach (age-group manager) for beach sprinting in a Sydney junior surf lifesaving (nippers) programme (see Light, 2006 and Light, 2016 for some insight into the nippers).

When coaching a group of eight- to ten-year-old 'nippers' in the beach sprint I asked them to run holding a ball or a rubber relay baton in both hands. If you do this exercise yourself you will appreciate how this impedes sprinting. After a couple of runs with this constraint imposed I would ask them to reflect upon the experience by asking questions such as 'How did that feel?' and 'Why do you think that restricted your running so much?' to focus their attention on the feeling of running without the drive provided by the arms.

The next step was to remove the constraint to allow the nippers to compare and contrast running when not using the arms and running with free use of their arms. Here I would ask questions such as 'Did that feel any better?' and 'How did that compare to not being able to use your arms?' to which the group would respond by expressing their enjoyment of being able to run freely. I would then typically ask, 'Have you learned anything about running by running without using your arms and then using them?' to which, invariably, the answer was that they learned how important the arms are for sprinting. Unlike some other examples in Part III, the use of this constraint was not intended to demand a solution to a problem. Instead, it was aimed at creating awareness of the role that arm movement plays in sprinting.

In the next part of the session I playfully encouraged the group to have a little fun in discovering or confirming what the most efficient use of the arms is in terms of the magnitude of movement to get the best drive. I would ask questions like 'Now we know how important the arms are for sprinting but what do you think is the best way to use them?' to which there would be a range of answers such as 'Move your arms really fast' or 'Put a lot of power into your arms', which I would encourage discussion of as I narrowed the focus to the question of what the optimum range of movement might be. Sometimes I asked, 'Do you think that bigger arm movements would help you run faster?' and suggested that we should test that idea by running with 'really big' or 'huge' arm movements to see how it worked.

Reflection upon this exaggeration would typically bring the group to the conclusion that really big arm movements were not efficient because they threw out the timing of their arm and leg movements. I would often start this collective reflection by asking how it felt. For example, I would ask, 'We know that our arm movement is important for running as fast as we can so maybe using bigger movement will help run faster? What do you think?' After one run through I would ask them whether or not it seemed effective and then ask them to suggest why it did not work, using questions to encourage thinking about the relationship between stride and arm drive. I would then ask them to go to the other extreme by asking them to run with very small but rapid movements of the arms by suggesting, playfully, 'Well, big arm movements did not work for us but I wonder if using small but very fast arms would work?' I would then go through the same process of a couple of short sprints and collective reflection on how small but fast arms worked.

After taking the use of the arms in sprinting to extremes I would then ask the group to do a couple of sprints using their arms in the way that they felt was most efficient. We would then regroup for reflection upon how this felt and to discuss what they thought was the best range of movement and why. This sometimes included having one of the nippers with good technique demonstrate for the rest of the group to comment on or analyze his/her technique.

This approach involved providing the nippers with a particular experience designed to produce preferred learning, having them reflecting upon it and engaging in dialogue with each other and the coach. Through this process I focused on how it felt as I have done in other activities in this section of the book, such as the second activity in chapter 8 on swimming. I would ask them whether or not they felt it was effective and why. This approach does not preclude direct instruction and in the latter stages of these sessions I would tell them what the range of arm movement should be, but the lasting learning that this approach encourages emerges from the conversation between reflective bodily experience and the mind expressed as speech (Light and Fawns, 2003) in a process of discovery. This approach to coaching sprinting technique can provide comprehensive, holistic understanding of the principles of running and provide a foundation from which young athletes can interpret information provided by the coach and apply it in their learning. When young athletes are empowered to learn and can connect the details of technique to core concepts they can work through the application of technical information to perform as relatively independent learners as they adapt it to their ways of running. In fact, the understanding of how the arms contribute to speed and power learned from the approach I describe here was very helpful for later instruction on starts, where the drive of the arm opposite the driving leg and the first few pumps of the arms are critical for success.

Relay baton changeover

There is an important tactical dimension to exchanging the baton in the 4×100 metre track relay due to the 20-metre distance within which each exchange must be completed but here I concentrate on structuring learning how to perform the techniques required for efficient changeovers using Positive Pedagogy. I draw on my experience of coaching a senior girls' primary school 4×100 metre relay team in an Australian primary school over a five-week period, during which we trained twice a week for sixty minutes a session.

The first training session adopted a directive approach through which I outlined and demonstrated baton-changing techniques, explaining the reasons for them and giving the runners time to practice. Throughout the practice sessions I emphasized our aim of trying to get the baton travelling around the track as fast as possible and at a consistent pace as the 'big idea' underpinning the session (Fosnot, 1996). From the next session on I moved gradually towards an athlete-centred approach, session by session. First, all four runners and I discussed and agreed on the points at which the baton should be exchanged at each of the three changeovers, taking into account how we could use this to give our faster runners more of the 400 metres to run. We then proceeded to the first changeover where the first and second runners practised and the other two (the third and fourth runners) watched, as observers.

Their observation was guided by predetermined key points I had suggested such as the speed of the incoming runner, the point at which the receiver begins to run, whether or not the receiver is making her hand a good target and the effectiveness of the baton-to-hand placement in avoiding the need for readjustment.

At each changeover I sought the subjective perspective on experience of the two practising as a shared experience and the objective view from the other two runners who were acting as observers. After each exchange I asked the receiver how it felt and how she thought that the incoming runner could help make it a better change-over. This included asking questions such as 'How did that feel?' and, when noting a problem, 'What can you both do to solve that problem?' I would then ask the incoming runner what she thought the receiver could do to make it easier to make an exchange that was smooth and maintained the speed of the baton. For example, I would ask questions such as, 'Were you happy with that changeover?' and 'That looked a lot better – what did you do differently?' Next I would involve the two observers by asking for their opinions on the exchange and for any suggestions they might have to improve the changeover by asking questions such as, 'How did that look to you?' and 'How do you think they can improve that part of the change-over?' For coaches taking up this approach or something similar they need to keep the appropriate balance between doing and talking as discussed in chapters 4 and 5. I then moved on to the next changeover to repeat this process of doing, reflecting, talking, developing solutions and trying them out as the runners refined their technique and worked through the learning process while developing a sound understanding of how this contributed to getting the baton around the track as quickly and smoothly as possible.

I would ask the incoming runner how she thought the change went and whether or not there was something the receiver could change to make it more efficient with an emphasis on a smooth transfer that facilitated keeping the baton moving. The third and fourth runners were then asked for comments and suggestions as observers. After the four girls agreed to some adjustments or changes the first and second runners tried again. This was repeated at each changeover point with under-standing and technique improving among all four runners in the team as they adapted their technique.

The girls were initially a little hesitant to engage in dialogue but this changed as they adapted to the more athlete-centred approach and the increased engagement that it generates. Within two weeks they did not have to be asked by me but, instead, automatically engaged in discussion, analysis and the debate of ideas (Gréhaigne et al., 2005). Through participation in activities, reflection, dialogue and inquiry the girls progressively adapted the baton-change techniques to their existing knowledge and experience. As the coach I was initially central to the progress of learning due to the ways in which I initially instructed the girls how to perform the technique and how I subsequently encouraged and facilitated interaction and reflection. However, as the girls developed knowledge of the skills they learned how to learn and shifted towards becoming more active learners with my involvement gradually reduced.

After a month of learning through Positive Pedagogy the girls were able to coach themselves, collectively discuss performance, identify problems, and generate solutions without being asked to do so. The team qualified through three levels of competition in the PSSA (Public Schools Sport Association) to compete at the New South Wales state athletics championships for schools. Watching from the stand I was pleased that they qualified for the final but felt that they performed below their normal standard in the heats and had a few ideas on what to work on. Before walking back to speak with me about their performance in the heat, the girls gathered to discuss their performance. When they completed their discussion and came to speak with me I asked them what they had been talking about with the answer being that they were talking about how to improve their performance. I then asked them what conclusions they had arrived at to which they had identified the same problems that I had and had arrived at a similar solution I had thought about.

Over five weeks of learning in this way the four girls had moved from relying completely on me for instruction to becoming independent learners as I retreated to the point where I was almost redundant by the time they competed in the state championships five weeks after our first training session. This is how Vygotsky (1978) and others (see Wood et al., 1976) suggest the teacher or mentor should help the learner bridge the gap between what s/he can already do and what is possible to learn through his concept of the zone of proximal development (ZPD). The ZPD refers to the 'potential development through problem solving' of the learner that can be realized 'under adult guidance or in collaboration with more capable peers' (p. 86) who withdraw as learning progresses. Over five weeks my pedagogy moved from direct instruction to an athlete-centred approach, with the four girls moving from being dependent upon me for information to being independent, confident and active learners.

In the approach I describe here there were basic, predetermined techniques that I initially taught through direct instruction but real learning (as a process of transformation) occurred over time through processes of reflection in and on action, dialogue and inquiry that involved me moving from coach-centred to athlete-centred pedagogy. This Positive Pedagogy views learning as a social and shared process with building a supportive environment among the runners essential in this process due to the way in which it fosters collaboration and a focus on team, rather than individual, performance.

Discussion

When applying Positive Pedagogy to individual sports, typically there seems to be more variation between the different sports, athletes and the goals of the activity, session or season than between team sports. In the first example presented in this chapter, on coaching children in the use of the arms in beach sprinting, I imposed a constraint but it was not aimed at creating a problem for the young athletes to solve as was the case in chapter 8 on swimming. The constraint of not being able to use the arms in beach sprinting was aimed at highlighting and developing awareness of how important the arms are in sprinting. Once established, I used exaggeration (huge arms and fast arms) as experiences for the nippers to reflect upon and to steer them towards discovering the most effective range of arm movement. Later in this session I did revert to some direct instruction to get them not only driving their lead arms forward and up (fingers level with shoulder) but also having their recovering arm pulling back with equal power and range of movement in a push–pull action. However, this built upon their previous experience and learning to make it relevant and meaningful for them.

In the five weeks of coaching senior primary school girls in the 4 x 100 changeover I did not use any constraint at all. There was no particular physical experience designed to foster particular learning. Instead, I focused on the technique needed in the relay and began with direct instruction for the first session in which I explained the technique I wanted them to do. However, from the next session on I increasingly adopted a Positive Pedagogy approach as learning about the technique and how to become active, inquiring learners progressed. Over five weeks they moved from relying on me for information to being so confident in their ability to learn as a group that I was close to being unneeded at the NSW state championships. In both the nippers beach sprint sessions each Sunday morning over summer and the five weeks of coaching the girls' relay team, the young athletes not only learned efficiently but also enjoyed the experience and had positive attitudes towards learning that came from more than winning competition races.

With both examples I present in this chapter I suspect that some coaches might be concerned with the time I seem to have spent and which might not seem feasible or possible for them to find. With this in mind I would like to make it clear that I am not suggesting taking the same approach every session. I did the session described on using the arms in beach sprints for the nippers at the beginning of the season to provide understanding that the young athletes could draw on over the rest of the season and linked technique in subsequent sessions to this understanding. In regard to the girls' relay team, I felt that the progress the girls made over five weeks was a highly valuable return for the time spent. Initially, progress was a little slow, but after two weeks of this approach the pace of learning, the motivation and the confidence to learn as a group made learning rapid and enjoyable for the girls and for me.

11

JAVELIN

This chapter focuses on coaching or teaching the basic throwing technique for javelin. Although the example I use here draws on my experiences of teaching undergraduate pre-service teachers the ideas are clearly applicable, and adaptable, to coaching contexts. The chapter draws on a unit of work I developed for pre-service teachers at the University of Melbourne (Australia) on throwing. It used an experiential, inquiry-based pedagogical approach aimed at having students understand the core principles of throwing as a basis for teaching them how to throw the javelin. As part of a physical education teacher education programme the sessions were aimed at showing the pre-service teachers one way of adopting an inquiry-based approach to teaching throwing events in physical education.

The first session focused on developing an experience-based, comprehensive understanding of four principles of throwing that would inform learning the basics of how to throw the javelin. The knowledge and skill developed in the sessions discussed here could also form the basis for teaching other throwing events in athletics such as the javelin, shot put and discus, as well as throwing as a skill in team sports such as softball, cricket and handball. The pedagogical approach I took emphasized experience and was athlete-centred and inquiry-based in nature. In school settings this unit would be aimed at students in their first few years of secondary school (junior high school).

This unit of work focused on the 'root movements' of throwing upon which the ensuing, more detailed, teaching of technique was based and with an aim of maximizing release velocity. This understanding of how power is generated is developed through experience, reflection and dialogue, with an emphasis on how it feels, and provides the core knowledge that the students or athletes can draw on to develop into independent learners. Along with social interaction with peers, it provides some of the resources that learners can draw on to meet the challenges involved in learning or improving throwing technique in javelin or other throwing events. Drawing on Antonovsky's (1979) ideas, this helps make the challenge of the tasks involved comprehensible and manageable for athletes, which contributes towards making learning positive.

The root movements of throwing

The three factors that most influence the distance a projectile travels in throwing events are: (1) speed of release, (2) angle of release and (3) height of release. In this chapter I focus on using Positive Pedagogy to facilitate learning how to maximize release velocity by understanding and then applying four core principles of throwing, which are:

1. Movement that shifts weight from back to front
2. Movement of joints involved from flexion to extension
3. Conservation of momentum from the rotation of larger body mass (lower body) through to the smaller body mass (upper body)
4. Upward movement

When teaching pre-service teachers I would divide the class into small groups of four or five, with each group given an object to throw but one of unusual shape or dimensions that was not something normally thrown. Before the class I would walk into the storeroom and look about for a variety of objects that looked like they would present an interesting challenge to throw. For example, in one session I asked groups to throw large cones (like those used in road works), plastic cricket bats and plastic cricket stumps, light plastic balls with holes in them and heavy medicine balls which were excellent for learning how to generate power from the ground up through rotation. The task set for each group was to work together to devise the best way of throwing the object as far as possible by reaching maximum release velocity at the appropriate angle of release. Their task was to answer the two questions, 'What is the best way to reach maximum release velocity to throw this object as far as possible?' and 'What is the best angle of release?'

Ensuring safe practice, I asked each group to collaborate in coming up with some ideas for throwing their object as far as possible through discussion between themselves, proposing techniques and testing them. I set out marker cones every 10 metres to give a rough idea of distance thrown that they could use to compare throws if needed. I walked around the groups watching, listening and asking questions to promote thinking about developing the most efficient way of throwing their particular object. For each group I would only make passing comments and ask questions that I did not necessarily expect an answer for unless I felt some form of intervention was required.

Next I would stop the class and call all students in to ask one or two members of a group that seemed to be making good progress to demonstrate the ideas they had developed. I would ask the rest of the class for input on whether or not they thought it was successful and, if so, why it was successful and what the particular student seemed to be doing well. The sorts of questions that I asked of the student performing the throw or of the class watching were very open and included 'Why do you think that throw was so successful?', 'What did you do to maximize the speed of release?' and 'Was there anything in particular you were focusing on when you threw?'

In this part of the lesson I would ask for ideas on identifying some 'big ideas' for throwing, drawing on some of the more specific ideas on technique to ask questions that I hoped would lead to identifying any of the predetermined principles of throwing. For example, when one student suggested something along the lines of saying that 'twisting the hips' was important for being able to throw a long way, I would ask something like, 'What does that do?' or 'How does it help generate power?' to which students would typically say something about producing power. I would then ask, 'And where is the power coming from?' or 'Where does the thrower first begin to develop this power?' This was aimed at helping the throwers discover that the initial generation of power from the larger muscles of the lower body originates from the pivot on the balls of the rear then front foot. For a class of younger students that does not initially identify the role of the rotation of the hips in throwing, the teacher/coach could ask all the students to throw a ball while keeping their hips intentionally locked in place and then by using the hips and asking how this changed the results (distance) and how it felt.

I would then ask the groups to rotate and move on to finding the most efficient way to throw a different object. I would ask them to take with them what they had learned about throwing up to this point and apply it to throwing their new object and to take note of any significant aspects of throwing that they felt helped. I asked them to focus on how they were using their bodies to generate maximum speed of release and to continue focusing on identifying a few big ideas about how to maximize release velocity. The number of rotations taken would depend upon time available and the progress of learning but at least two are needed to provide an opportunity to apply ideas and techniques from throwing one object to another. It is also helpful if these objects are as different as possible.

When the rotations were completed I would call in the whole class to reflect upon their experiences as individuals and groups in a whole-class (team) discussion. This discussion was aimed at having the class identify any key ways in which we could use our bodies to maximize release velocity and, therefore, distance thrown. I would also ask about release angle but, invariably, this was discovered very quickly. In this discussion I used questioning to highlight ideas that aligned with the four core principles identified earlier in this chapter. For example, if a student suggested the need to move the throwing arm from flexion to extension I would ask him/her, 'What about the legs? Does this apply to the joints in the thrower's legs as well?'

If all goes well and the session develops as planned, skilful questioning should provoke identification of all of the four principles of throwing but this was not always the case for me. This final stage of the session/lesson sometimes tested my ability to stay with questions that generate thinking and interaction and avoiding narrowing the questions to the point of them asking for yes/no answers. The important thing here is to keep the focus on students answering the core question of 'How can we maximize release velocity?' In my experience of teaching this unit I sometimes had to use questioning that was quite focused and which sought a predetermined answer as a deductive question that seems opposed to the typically inductive questioning typically used in GBA. However, as I have suggested in chapter 5, deductive questioning has a place in an inquiry-based approach. For example, the evaluation of novel ideas developed through divergent thinking occurs through convergent thinking and the use of knowledge as a source of ideas that suggests pathways to solutions (Cropley, 2006).

Throwing the javelin

The example of teaching javelin I provide here follows on from the session above but any other throwing event could be taught or coached by drawing on this knowledge of throwing developed through the session discussed above. The session/lesson would begin with a review of what the students knew about the principles of throwing because this is what they would be asked to draw on when learning how to throw the javelin.

When applying these principles to the javelin the teacher or coach can continue with an inquiry-based approach or take a more instructional approach but one that is still influenced by the inquiry-based approach and which connects technical instruction to the students' understanding of the four principles of throwing. Coaches or teachers continuing with a more inquiry-based approach would typically set challenges and ask questions more than tell students what to do and provide opportunities for small-group problem solving. Alternatively, the teacher can take a more traditional approach in which s/he instructs on technique but asks some questions that link technical instruction to the athletes' experience and understanding of the principles of throwing for them to make sense of it. A more inquiry-based teacher might ask, 'What do we know about using body rotation for throwing?' and follow by asking, 'Do you think we could apply that to the javelin?' A teacher taking a more instructional approach might focus on the technical details of how to maximize release velocity through body rotation but ask them to think back to what, and how, they learned about rotation of the body in throwing to point out how this relates to technique.

Looking at throwing the javelin from a technical perspective, the athlete uses his/her whole body to sling the javelin as the summation of forces that begin from the ground and work up through the body as energy is transferred from large body mass to smaller body mass and, ultimately, into the javelin (Silvester, 2003). Within this movement the rapid transfer of the body's momentum into the braced left side of the body is the most critical aspect of technique (Gorski, 2003). Ideally, this is done without losing any speed or momentum from the 'soft' right-leg touchdown (for a right-handed thrower) to the braced left side during the throwing crossover. The momentum is then transferred up the body segments into the release of the javelin from the hand. This technical process can easily be (and should be) linked to the students' basic understanding of the principles of generating and conserving momentum through rotational forces, movement from flexion to extension of the joints involved and moving from low to high, which relates to releasing the javelin from a high position. This basic knowledge can inform the learner's interpretation of the coach's technical instruction and empower him/her to make sense of it and to be able to reflect in and on action.

According to Gorski (2003), the javelin throw should give an impression of an explosive, horizontal movement. Much as I propose in this book, he also suggests that coaches and athletes should base the refinement of technique upon an understanding of what he calls 'key concepts'. For Sylvester, the six concepts are:

- Maintained or increased momentum from the run-up into the throw
- Backward lean as the legs 'run away' from the upper body
- Initiation of the throw from the legs
- Separation of the hip and shoulder axes
- Firm bracing from the left side
- Delayed arm strike

These are different to the core principles of throwing I propose but this is because they are more technical and specific to the javelin yet can clearly be grounded in the broader principles I propose when coaching older or more experienced athletes.

In the classes that I taught I tended to continue with an inquiry-based pedagogical approach but with a tighter focus on technique as the learning progressed and moved towards more technical detail. I would begin the lesson by saying that technique for throwing the javelin is aimed at maximizing the release velocity – as it had been in the more general session on throwing. I would ask the students to answer the core question of 'How can we achieve maximum release velocity when throwing the javelin by drawing on what we already know about throwing?' As might be expected, the first suggestion was often to run up quickly to maximize the speed of the javelin before beginning the throwing action but I would initially limit this to three or four steps because inexperienced students can get lost on a long run-up and a short run-up encouraged them to accelerate harder. I would then use some direct instruction in regard to technical details they needed to know before they could begin practising.

I introduced some techniques such as how to hold the javelin when running (with choices on grip) and would tell them that they needed a couple of cross-over steps to open up the hips in preparation for delivery, during which they had to 'overtake' the javelin (withdrawal) in preparation for delivery. I would do a brief demonstration and ask them why they thought the cross-over steps were necessary to which there were usually quite quick answers related to facilitating the generation of rotational forces. I would then, again, set up small groups of three or four to practise throwing with the short run-up and focus on a couple of key technical points that peers in the group would comment on and discuss with the thrower.

Given the potential for serious injury with the javelin, this included me controlling when the javelins were thrown and fetched for the next throw.

At the end of this part of the session I would call all students in to discuss group progress and arrive at a clear understanding of the basic technical points they should focus on when throwing the javelin (how) and ask them why. This was aimed at reinforcing technical learning for the specific skill of throwing the javelin. It was also aimed at highlighting how their knowledge of the four principles of throwing had helped them learn to throw the javelin while suggesting how they could use this core knowledge when learning to throw most other projectiles.

Discussion

Like some other chapters in this section of the book, the process for teaching young people how to throw the javelin is likely to seem time consuming and possibly unnecessary. Some readers may well ask, 'Wouldn't it be quicker to just get straight into the second part without wasting so much time and effort in the first part?' or 'What busy teacher or coach has time to spend on the first part of the unit?'

It would certainly be quicker to start with the session focused on throwing the javelin but this first part of the unit is an investment made by the teacher or coach in the future learning of the young athletes' ability to learn as a long-term goal in addition to the short-term goal of improving throwing performance. This is not too removed from Dewey's (1938a) contention that all education should not only have a short-term goal focused on the individual learning but also have a long-term and more collectively focused goal of making a contribution to society. Like the TGfU approach to games teaching, the approach I suggest here emphasizes conceptual understanding. It provides a base of knowledge and understanding that students or young athletes can draw on when learning in other throwing events such as discus and shot put. It does not need to be repeated but can continue to be drawn on in future teaching or coaching. As I suggest with the examples provided in chapter 8 on swimming, this could be done at the beginning of a season in athletics clubs or at the beginning of a term's work on throwing in a school setting. The experiential nature of learning these principles should allow the students or young athletes to draw on this knowledge and experience for other throwing activities and some activities beyond throwing; for example, teaching punching technique in karate with the emphasis on generating power from the lower body (*kahanshin*), as chapter 15 explores in detail.

In karate and other Japanese martial arts power is produced from the lower half of the body as something that has cultural and biological roots and which often presents a problem for Western practitioners who tend to want to generate power from the upper body (*jōhanshin*). In *gyakuzuki* (reverse punch) the punch is delivered from the rear hand with power initially generated from the ground, through hip rotation and a minuscule lag between hip and shoulder rotation as it passes through the upper body and into contact. This could usefully be taught using the same principles as throwing with the exception of the principle of upward movement.

When teaching *kizamizuki* (front punch) the movement from the ground through to contact is much smaller than *gyakuzuki* but an understanding of three of the principles of throwing could help in learning to strike efficiently by using the entire body and not just the front arm and shoulder.

Even when taking a more instructional approach, if the teacher or coach can help the athletes or students learn by helping them understand *why* the technique is performed as it is and linking it to their understanding of the four principles of throwing used in this example, this can make a useful contribution towards developing young athletes as thinking, inquiring learners who can take responsibility for their learning instead of being completely reliant upon their coach or teacher whenever they have a problem with their skill execution.

12

TEACHING KAYAK ROLLING THROUGH FEEL AND FLOW

With Chris North

Reflection forms a central role in enhancing learning in Positive Pedagogy with frequent reference made to the work of Schön (1987) in this book. This is something I relate to strongly because of how I emphasize reflection when I am teaching in outdoor education. I also note how Schön sees the teacher's roles in constructing learning experiences as involving a focus on the level of risk involved, the freedom provided for learning, and the kinds of coaching/teaching athletes and students will need for learning. This chapter draws on my own experiences of using an approach that aligns very well with Positive Pedagogy to help kayakers learn to roll a kayak. In it I focus on (1) the role of the teacher/coach in managing risk (mainly emotional), (2) providing enough freedom for the athletes/students to learn at their own pace and have opportunities for exploration and discovery, and (3) the role of reflection.

Physical context, flow and learning

Water provides an interesting medium for exploring the use of Positive Pedagogy because movement experiences in a fluid environment are very different to those in land-based activities. Water-based activities and sports such as surfing, sailing and kayaking that are undertaken in the natural environment involve different types of connections with the water and development of a feel for it. As suggested in chapter 8 and elsewhere (Light and Wallian, 2008) swimming should also be seen as a phenomenon that extends beyond the limitations of the body of the swimmer to include the connection with, and immersion in, the fluid environment that is part of the experience of swimming. Writing and research on surfing that explores the nature of its experience as a phenomenon is limited but it does encourage understanding surfing a wave as a phenomenon made up of the surfer and the wave as a dynamic and fluid environment (Stranger, 2011; Fitzsimons and Light,

2016). The individual player cannot be separated from the game in team sports when viewed from an holistic perspective (Light, Harvey et al., 2014; Light et al., 2015). Likewise, when viewed from the same perspective as surfing, in kayaking and sailing the person cannot be separated from his/her fluid environment. There is a whole-person, sensual dimension to water sports such as surfing (including body surfing) as activities in which pleasure and aesthetics are of central importance (Stranger, 2011). As important as technique may be there is far more to the experience of kayaking. As Fitzsimons and Light (2016) suggest, this highlights 'the need for more attention to be paid to the phenomenological nature of experience in surfing and the meanings it holds for children and young people'.

In kayaking the kayaker does not have the same immersion in the water as in swimming or surfing but s/he is connected to it through the paddle and kayak. This engagement with the water regulates the nature and experience of movement. Rolling a kayak involves exerting force on the water in such a way so that a relatively solid object (the kayak and kayaker) can rise almost magically out of the water but this generation of force is itself fluid and smooth. It requires more than a particular set of technical movements. It requires interaction by the kayaker with the water, a smoothness of action and the development of *flow* (Csikszentmihalyi, 1990). The kayak roll is a complex skill which, when performed by experts, appears to be effortless and one smooth and graceful, yet powerful, movement. Although it comprises a number of technical aspects the focus of teaching and learning when using Positive Pedagogy should be on it as one whole, smooth movement with the kayaker/learner being able to link technical instruction to the roll as a whole and fluid movement as what Fosnot (1996) calls the 'big idea'. When I teach the roll I focus on how it should feel because the movements involved in kayak rolling should be easy, light, flowing and graceful. When unsuccessful, the kayak roll attempt can feel heavy, uncoordinated and cumbersome but when it is performed with flow and grace the experience is like hitting the sweet spot in cricket or baseball – it is pleasurable.

The progression

First I describe a progression and some of the challenges for myself as a teacher in those progressions. Second I look at how technology has allowed detailed 'reflection on action', with a view to enhancing 'reflection in action' (Schön, 1987). In this situation I rely heavily on peers and technology to provide external perspectives on the learning of the kayak roll. Boud, Cohen and Sampson (2001) provide a framework for working with peer teaching, a key aspect of which is that peer teaching is not a sudden 'add-on' but rather that peer teaching is integral to most aspects of the practical learning sessions. By integrating the peer teaching with the rest of the session the peers and learners (although both are inevitably learning through this process) are able to develop rapport, trust and a better understanding of the learner's needs. This form of peer teaching has the advantage that, unlike the teacher or coach, the peers face the same challenges in the same context, they talk with each other in the same language and there is less risk of embarrassment in asking what they may think would be a silly question (Boud et al., 2001). The peer provides formative evaluation for the kayaker, which benefits both the peer and the kayaker in the process of learning (Ploegh et al., 2009). I describe this in more detail below, before which I outline the steps involved in this progression.

GENERAL STEPS IN THE KAYAK ROLLING PROGRESSION

1.   Confidence activities – performing increasingly complex tasks while upside down in the kayak
2.   Wet exit – getting out of the kayak while upside down
3.   Sideways body movements – hip and head movements provide cues to correct movements
4.   Rotational movements – twisting up in preparation and releasing like a loaded spring
5.   Adding the paddle – ensuring that beginning and ending movements are maintained while using the paddle

---

Learning to roll a kayak usually begins with a range of familiarization exercises that are not only aimed at reducing any fears or anxiety but also at helping the kayaker begin to get a feel for the activity and the connection between kayak, kayaker and water. These activities build confidence in performing simple tasks while under water which can be a source of anxiety for some people. I usually begin by asking the students to divide into pairs with one as the kayaker and the other as the peer and model the peer-teaching process for the kayak roll so that students can identify cues and learn the questioning techniques. An important point here is the way in which the kayakers and peers collaboratively decide on the rate at which they move through the progressions. The kayaker–peer pairs need to discuss and make important decisions about the rate of progress through the pro-gressions and the quality of the movements being learned through dialogue and reflection. Knowledge of progress from both the internal perspective (subjective) of the kayaker and the external (objective) perspective of the peer contribute to this learning.

Through the kayaker sharing reflection with the peer, they are able to evaluate the quality and extent of their learning and decide on what next steps are appro-priate. When problems arise during the progressions pairs will ask me to come over to help them work towards the next major step and I encourage this. For example, when a pair decides to complete the wet exit, they ask me over and we discuss the steps during which I use a lot of questioning to stimulate thinking and problem solving.

A peer is standing next to the kayak, ready to right the kayaker at the first tap on the kayak. The first step is generally for the kayaker to tip upside down with arms hugging the kayak and with the peer then pulling the kayaker immediately upright. The peer then asks 'How did that feel?' or 'What was that like?' Answers vary from 'Scary' to 'Great!' Once the kayakers seem comfortable with this experience I increase complexity and the time spent underwater by moving on to a wet exit (getting out of the kayak while upside down). A wet exit is deliberately not the first step as it involves getting soaked and requires that the kayaker completes several tasks while underwater. By designing the learning experiences in this way, the pairs (kayaker and peer) are given the freedom to determine the sequence of the steps and the rate of progress through these experiences. Kayakers and peers swap around based on their own goal setting and reflections.

This book emphasizes the ways in which subjective and objective perspectives on learning and performance can assist the learner/athlete and the coach. As important as the subjective understanding of learning is, the challenge with many sports is to gain a perspective from beyond ourselves to enhance our learning, which includes embodied, non-conscious learning as well as conscious, articulated learning. Embodied learning, like other learning, can develop miseducative as well as educative outcomes and not all experience is necessarily good (Dewey, 1938a). Dewey defines miseducative outcomes as ones which close off future growth opportunities (sometimes described as getting stuck in a rut), while educative outcomes allow greater scope for growth and align well with the Positive Pedagogy approach. For example, the teacher needs to be vigilant to ensure that the patterns of embodied knowing are not hindering learning. A particular action may be helpful with one particular problem-solving aspect of the rolling progression but actually hinder the final goal, which the teacher needs to keep the learners focused on.

A student may be able to 'muscle' her/his way through a particular task and appear to have achieved a learning goal but it may not contribute to learning to perform the roll in a smooth, graceful and effective way. Here the teacher will realize that any success achieved through this technique will be ultimately miseducative. As such, the teacher needs to intervene and make some suggestions while asking the kayaker to reflect upon his/her experiences of these different approaches and relate them to the goal of performing the roll as one smooth and fluid movement. The questions asked should stimulate thinking about how it felt and in what way aspects of technique performed contribute towards, or detract from, achieving the end goal. When I teach the roll this also normally involves changing the language used by the students by moving from 'power' words to 'graceful' words and from rigid movements to flexible or fluid movements that allow the kayak roll to be completed as one smooth, graceful yet powerful movement. This language presents an opportunity for both the kayaker and the peer to discuss and reflect on the kayaker's action and how it felt. The benefits are that the kayaker can access the external perspective of the peer to challenge or support their own internal and subjective perspectives.

The kayak roll involves a number of tasks, which must be completed simultaneously in order to successfully roll the kayak. These steps are often broken down into side-to-side body movement, rotational body movements, then adding in the paddle. For example, moving the kayak from the upside-down position to the upright position using hip and back flexibility provides a good example of flow. As soon as the body becomes stiff the action becomes increasingly forced and turns into a struggle, which is not what I am after in my teaching. Once this step is flowing easily, I introduce body rotation while trying to maintain the rhythm and smoothness of the movement but link it to the prior movement as a continuation of the smooth movement. This involves setting up like a spring that is wound up tightly and is then released so that the rotation feels more like a relaxation than a forced movement. Finally, the paddle is introduced and if all steps are combined holistically, the kayaker should rise out of the water in one smooth movement.

At each step, interaction between the kayaker and a peer is crucial to learning the movement. If the introductory movements are not quite right, the kayaker and peer should identify this through their mutual understanding, developed through peer observation (objective) and discussions with their partner that are based on the teaching and learning cues and which provide some understanding of the kayaker's subjective experience of the roll as a whole movement. Is the language more about force and struggle or more about grace and ease? If the descriptors are 'muscle-based', the pair should decide to either go back a couple of steps in the progression or do more repetitions of the step they are currently working on to find flow and smoothness. Continuing on with poor technique will mean that the basis for the roll is inadequate and halt progress at a later stage.

The role of the peer in the progression I have outlined is important for a number of reasons in addition to observing and discussing progress with the kayaker. While teaching others, the peer gains crucial insight into their own struggles with a particular aspect of the roll. These 'aha' moments support the emphasis placed on learner/athlete interaction in this book and the social nature of learning. This book consistently emphasizes the importance of trust between coach and athletes and between athletes/learners. Owing to the potential for anxiety, fear and other negative responses to being upside down in the water, developing a trusting relationship between the kayaker and the supporting peer is crucial to building confidence and supporting learning. The nature of interaction between kayaker and peer develops this trust.

Reflection (and technology)

Dialogue between the kayaker and peers and the teacher encourages the kayaker to reflect upon experience with an emphasis on how it felt and on feeling the sensation of rolling as a smooth and fluid movement. Reflection is of pivotal importance in Positive Pedagogy as a second experience that brings it to consciousness through articulation (Dewey, 1938a). Articulating the way we feel or felt when we attempt the roll or an aspect of it is a powerful form of reflection that I emphasize in the progression described in this chapter. In recent years, technology has added to our repertoire of reflective tools in teaching the roll. Many teachers now use waterproof cameras to take video footage which the kayaker can review for immediate analysis. This external perspective on experience provides an objective point of view that can help the kayaker link his/her lived experience of learning to roll to what s/he is trying to do. It also provides opportunity for the meaningful dialogue between the kayaker and peer (or coach) from which learning emerges. I have seen kayakers improve dramatically once they become aware of how they look from this external perspective.

In 2012 I developed an assignment for undergraduates as part of a kayaking course using ICT. The course was part of a physical education teacher degree and therefore had a dual outcome of students not just being able to complete the roll themselves, but also being able to teach others. The assignment task used a software package that allowed students to video and then analyze their technique in comparison to an expert. The software package provided for slowing the video, freezing frames, measuring and drawing angles and arrows and creating an audio narrative. In the early part of the course, students analyzed their own technique and created a two-minute presentation comparing themselves to an expert. Later in the course, students were given a variety of videos showing various skills and needed to evaluate these using the same ICT software.

Students commented on how they came to appreciate the finer aspects of technique through such tools because they had time to examine multiple aspects of the skill by repeatedly watching the video and making detailed notes. Indeed, as a teacher, when I first modelled the assignment, I was able to identify some weaknesses in my own performance of a simple kayaking technique. I believe that such tools are invaluable for learners of all levels. While not embodied, nor using reflection in action, reflection with ICT can enhance learning and stimulate discussion between learners. However, it is important to keep linking this self-analysis of technique to the big idea of performing a roll that feels fluid and graceful, yet effective.

Discussion and reflections

The suggestions I make for teaching the roll in kayaking in this chapter have been driven by an embodied sense of pedagogy developed over my professional career and reflect aspects of Positive Pedagogy such as learner reflection, dialogue and placing experience at the centre of learning. My recent exposure to Positive Pedagogy provided me with a clearer framework for thinking about how I teach and what I value as good pedagogy. This has encouraged me to think more about how I teach and how I can conceptualize and implement what I consider to be good pedagogy. The ideas in this book resonate with me but are not necessarily new to me. However, they provide a framework for my teaching that I am now exploring.

The progression I suggest is guided by a Positive Pedagogy approach but is a little different to some other practical examples used in Part III. While it is certainly focused on a learning experience it is not one that I designed. Like the outline provided in chapter 10 of a Positive Pedagogy approach to teaching the baton changeover in athletics, there is no modification of the activity and no constraint imposed. In outdoor education and adventure activities designing an experience is usually replaced with choosing one. For the other two features of Positive Pedagogy, my example has much in common with other examples provided in Part III of the book. It emphasizes questioning and reflection as well as adopting an inquiry-based approach aimed at helping the students experience the joy of discovery in learning how to do a kayak roll.

In the example I provide in this chapter the teacher is a facilitator of learning with little direct instruction. The focus is on learning through reflection upon experience driven by meaningful dialogue between the kayaker and his/her peer or partner over the duration of the session. When I reflect upon teaching in the way I have described in this chapter one thing that comes to mind is the need for the teacher or coach to be patient. The learning that emerges from the conversation between action and language, from reflection in action and on action, takes time and needs to be carefully managed. It also requires coach sensitivity to how learning is progressing and his/her empathy with the learners as suggested in chapter 5. Here I provide an example to illustrate this.

A student is almost successfully rolling their kayak but there are only five minutes left before the end of our session. By pushing hard for a few minutes I might be able to give them the wonderful success experience that I live for as a teacher. But I have learned that the rush to get results at the end of a lesson often results in mis-education (Dewey, 1938a). Time pressure and a focus on achieving learning typically results in shortcuts for kayakers, peers and myself as a teacher. More often than not, the student ends up either not completing the task and feeling disappointed, or completing the task but with such poor technique that it takes a lot of unlearning to correct the miseducative effects of this rush to succeed. I now give the kayakers, peers and myself as a teacher time, and cannot recommend this strongly enough. Sometimes the best learning comes from working for longer and the success tastes sweeter, not to mention how this actually results in learning as a process of transformation that leads to better skill in performing the roll.

As a teacher and outdoor adventurer with many years of experience I have found this approach has enhanced student learning. The conversations and engagement between the partners means that they take on far higher levels of responsibility for the learning process and, combined with phases of reflection, I believe this has resulted in better outcomes. Many of my students are learning to be teachers and having them take on important roles within learning and teaching can only benefit future students of theirs. As a teacher, I have sometimes found myself feeling somewhat redundant as I observe rather than take centre stage. This aspect of Positive Pedagogy does require a change in my role as a teacher. There is, however, no room for complacency for teachers because Positive Pedagogy requires a high level of observation and understanding when to step in and ask some questions and what questions to ask. The timing of this intervention can be critical for asking questions to open up the possibilities for the students who may be experiencing a 'road block' but I also need to know when to hold my tongue. My explorations of Positive Pedagogy have been educative but not always comfortable as I move to less hands-on roles. I believe that this approach can only benefit the students in my courses as they learn to be self-directing and take greater control of their learning.

13

ROCK CLIMBING

With Mohammad Shah Razak

As a sport, rock climbing only took off at the end of the nineteenth century and is thought to be founded by Walter Parry Haskett Smith in 1894 when he successfully made the first ascent (in free solo style) of the 70-foot Napes Needle in the Lake District of England. Rock climbing can be classified into many forms based on the degree of safety, ranging from bouldering as a low-risk option to the higher risk involved in free soloing where a climber climbs without a rope.

A person new to climbing might think that to climb well you need a strong upper body with powerful arms to pull yourself up the vertigo, but this is incorrect because it is a very technical sport. Indeed, rock climbing can be technically complicated but in this chapter I suggest developing an understanding of the centre of gravity and being able to shift it to make climbing more efficient as a key to climbing. In it I draw on past experience of coaching rock climbing to primary-school children in which I focused on them developing awareness of their centre of gravity and being able to shift it to climb better and as the big idea that helps the climber make sense of more detailed technique. The climber's continuous development of good climbing techniques depends upon having a sound practical understanding of this key concept.

More often than not, coaching in rock climbing is overly technical and almost exclusively reliant upon direct instruction. The rock climbing I have been involved in teaching was part of my duties as a physical education teacher in Singapore, which led me to think about alternatives to the direct instruction of technical detail. With my recent reading about Game Sense, suggestions for a similar approach to coaching individual sport (Light, 2014a) and Positive Pedagogy (Light and Harvey, 2015), I recognized similarities with what I had been developing for rock climbing. Reflecting on these experiences I recognized how I was moving towards an holistic and humanistic approach, which I provide an example of here, while making a few suggestions for improvement as a type of critical reflection informed by my understanding of Positive Pedagogy.

In this chapter, I recount coaching rock climbing and suggest how Positive Pedagogy could be used to improve it. Focused on helping children develop an awareness and understanding of the importance of balance while climbing, this example draws specifically on my experience of coaching ten- to fifteen-year-old climbers in a Singapore primary school. It is an approach that is characterized by the three pedagogical features of Positive Pedagogy with a particular focus on the effective use of questioning to stimulate the athletes' (or students') thinking and interaction with each other and the coach because this was what I emphasized as a coach before becoming acquainted with Positive Pedagogy (see Light, 2008b).

Shifting the centre of gravity for efficient climbing

Awareness of the body's centre of gravity and ability to shift it to climb efficiently is a core concern in rock climbing and forms the main focus of the coaching I recount and comment on in this chapter. In all our movements, we have a centre of balance (gravity) but it is not usually something we are consciously aware of or reflect on. The focus I place on developing awareness of where the body's balance is while in movement and on using it to make climbing more efficient is similar to chapter 15 on keeping balance, posture and a low centre of gravity when moving quickly in karate to attack with a reverse punch. The activity I describe here focuses on developing this awareness, or sensory feel, for the climber's centre of balance. It tries to develop awareness of where it is and how it changes in relation to movement during climbing for the climber to appreciate the importance of his/her own centre of gravity, which is approximately the middle of the body, around your belly (Horst, 2016).

Activity 1

This activity is done on a climbing wall that has a vertical face but with a concrete 'footpath' that joins the wall at a 60-degree angle and which is very close to the ground. Having this 'footpath' at a 60-degree angle pushes body weight forward towards the wall when traversing it and allows the climbers to move without gripping the wall with their hands. In this activity I asked the young climbers to traverse but not use their hands to encourage awareness of their centre of gravity and to have them think about using it to counter the imbalance caused by not using their hands. I then used activities designed to help them to learn how to shift their centre of gravity for efficient climbing and take some load off their upper body. They were not to use their arms as an anchor on the wall while traversing (climbing sideways). This constraint encouraged them to develop awareness of their centre of gravity and use their legs to lower it as a way of regaining their balance. The climbers solved this problem by leaning forward on the 'balls' of their feet to counter the initial loss of balance and tendency to lean backwards when not using the hands. When they stood flatfooted and did not bend their knees more on the 'footpath', the gravitational force pulled them off balance. They were allowed to swing their arms to balance as they travelled to and fro on the slanted slab of concrete of about 10–15 metres in length but not to hold the wall with their hands.

After a couple of traversing practices, I called in the group to focus on identifying the problem with questions like 'What problems are you having by not being able to touch the wall?' and 'As you moved along the wall how did you feel?' With the thinking that these simple questions promoted the climbers began to identify what Dewey called a perplexing problem and focus on solving it (see chapter 3; Schön, 1992). I used questions aimed at promoting awareness of their centre of balance, much as the coach does in chapter 10 when the young beach sprinters have to run without using their arms. I asked general questions such as 'How was the climb?' and 'How did that feel not using your arms?' Upon reflection I now think I should then have asked more focused questions such as 'How did your balance feel without being able to use your arms?' and 'What were you concentrating on to make up for not being able to use your arms?' I asked these types of questions to help the climbers develop awareness of the centre of gravity and changes in balance while climbing.

My questions after the experience led them to identify and articulate problems such as, 'It felt really hard to rely only on legs' and 'I can't stay for long on the wall.' They also identified how they had adjusted to the demands of the constraint during the experience. Further questioning identified how they had actually begun to find solutions to these problems, which suggested that they had reflected *in* action. They reflected upon the solutions they had individually arrived at through adapting to the demands of the task such as, 'I had to concentrate more on my legs and focus on my steps to have good balance' and 'I had to lean forward to shift my centre of gravity to get good balance.'

I then wanted them to interact and come up with possible solutions for the problem they had identified. Our discussion of solutions drew on some of the ways they had adapted to the demands of the activity by articulating them and sharing them with the class. They arrived at solutions such as, 'You should bend your legs and put your weight on the front of your feet to get your balance.' I then asked them all to try the 'no-hands' climb again and to apply these ideas to see how well they worked. Further discussion after this led them to conclude that they needed to maintain their centre of gravity low to keep their balance to compensate for not being able to use their hands. For me, this was a successful outcome because the aim of the activity was to develop awareness of their centre of gravity and its importance for climbing.

Activity 2

Activity 2 allowed the climbers to return to using their hands on the 60-degree sloping concrete 'footpath' but with me asking them to maintain their awareness of their centre of gravity and apply it. After being able to traverse the wall using their hands I posed the questions, 'How was this climb different from the one before?', 'Were you still aware of your centre of gravity?' and 'Did being aware of your centre of gravity help you traverse better than you usually do?' There was a general sense of relief among the climbers as they articulated how important the arms are in climbing and their pleasure at being allowed to finally use them for climbing. But, as I really wanted them to apply what they had learned about awareness of how to shift their centre of balance, I asked questions like, 'What have you learned about balance and your centre of gravity in climbing?' and 'Did being aware of your centre of gravity help you?' These questions were intended to encourage them to make the connection between the use of the hands and upper body and the awareness and adjustment of their centre of gravity. I was trying to help them understand the central importance of balance and their centre of gravity as the key concept or idea and how the use of the arms and legs are related to this. Although the hands are of great importance in maintaining balance in rock climbing, the legs are used to shift and adjust the centre of gravity. The purposeful constraint imposed in Activity 1 created a problem that I helped the climbers solve by asking questions to stimulate thinking and purposeful dialogue and reflection (Harvey and Light, 2015).

Activity 3

In Activity 3, I stepped up the challenges facing the six young climbers who had been chosen to complete this highly technical climb by working on a bouldering wall which was about 4 metres tall and on which climbs are performed without ropes (although there is always an adult to 'spot' the climber using a bouldering pad). The higher vertical face makes the task more challenging for carrying the learning of awareness and shifting of the centre of gravity. The bouldering wall also has features like an 'overhang' where the wall has a rock face or slope of more than 90 degrees (i.e. slopes beyond the vertical). This means that the climbers need to overcome this challenge before they can summit on the bouldering wall. The aim of this activity was to further develop their sense of balance and ability to use what they had learned about shifting their centre of gravity on the wall. Traversing a vertical face with an 'overhang' is far more challenging than working on a 60-degree 'footpath', making awareness of their centre of gravity and ability to shift it more important.

After each of the six climbers completed their first climb of the bouldering wall, I asked them, 'How was that climb different from the previous one?' and 'How did that feel compared to the earlier traversing?' Their responses of 'It felt even harder than before!' and 'I could feel my body being pulled down even more as I tried to climb the "overhang" surface' indicated that they felt and understood the difference and where the problem was with their climbing. The aim of this exercise was to help the climbers understand the relationships between the use of their arms and legs and the shifting of the centre of gravity under the extra pressure of climbing on a vertical face with an 'overhang'. I then asked the climbers how their awareness of balance could make their climbing more efficient on the bouldering wall. The sort of questions that I now feel I should have asked are, 'Could you feel the relationship between your arms, legs and centre of gravity?', 'How can/did you use your legs and arms to efficiently shift your centre of gravity while on the "overhang" surface?' or, 'How does your centre of gravity affect your use of arms and legs?' I think that these questions would have encouraged deeper understanding among the climbers of how their arms and legs need to work in tandem to have an efficient climb.

Following their reflections on the first climb they discussed possible solutions as a group and gave pointers to each other as they 'planned their route' for their subsequent climb on the overhang. They pointed to the wall where they would perform certain manoeuvres involving their 'heel of the foot' as they traversed along the more than 90-degree angled surface. The next step was for them to experiment and test out their plans.

After spending some time climbing and experimenting with their moves and techniques, the climbers suggested that modifications to their climbing technique were needed. In response to me asking a general and open question like 'Do you have any ideas about how you can improve your climbing technique here?', the successful climbers usually suggested spreading their feet wide apart to get at least one part of the leg across the 'overhang' followed by the other leg on a foothold. This involved shifting their centre of gravity and allowed them to transfer the load to their lower body. This then allowed them to focus on using their upper body to move across the surface and shift their centre of gravity forward/backward or in a left/right direction so that it would be easier for them to pull their body over the rock surface.

By this stage of their learning progression, the climbers were already mindful of all four points of contact with the rock face (two hands and two feet) while in a climb and how they were related to the positioning of their centre of gravity. Usually, they would also be reasonably aware of the need to place the movement of their centre of gravity at the centre of their manoeuvres on the wall so that they would not overload their hands and arms. During discussion on these points and in response to my questions such as 'What is key to a good climb?' and 'How can we climb efficiently?', typically they would suggest that 'Your centre of gravity is important in climbing' or 'I can feel my centre of gravity when I am moving.' Sometimes, I would also use my better climbers who showed good climbing technique to demonstrate on the wall for the rest to observe, discuss, comment on and analyze their technique and how it related to the core concepts I was focusing on.

Discussion

Reflecting on experience and engaging with the coach and other climbers in dialogue as part of an inquiry-based approach for learning are characteristics of Positive Pedagogy (Light and Harvey, 2015). As has been suggested in the case of using TGfU to teach games, it is an approach that encourages learning as a conversation between reflective bodily experience and the mind expressed in speech (Light and Fawns, 2003). When teaching rock climbing I placed an emphasis on balance, the climbers' centre of gravity and how to shift it to make climbing more efficient.

I used some features of Positive Pedagogy and in writing this chapter suggest how using more of it would help in coaching rock climbing.

Positive Pedagogy can produce holistic understandings of the core climbing principles of focusing on and using the climbers' centre of balance that coaches can adapt in their coaching routine. It also provides a basis for young athletes to process information, interpret it and apply it in their learning. As young climbers become empowered learners, they could associate the details of this technique to what Fosnot (1996) termed the 'big ideas' as concepts and apply it to their ways of climbing. In fact, the understanding of balance in climbing provide a crucial platform for progression when I introduced the term 'climbing effortlessly' using balance.

The examples I provide in this chapter used a constraint to develop awareness and to create a problem to be solved. This led to a greater awareness of the climbers' centre of gravity and skill to maintain balance during climbing. This constraint encouraged the learners to experiment and discover ways of improving their performance through an inquiry-based approach to coaching. They formulated a solution that involved using their legs to lower their centre of gravity as a way of regaining their balance when they could not use their arms. They were then able to transfer this learning in the bouldering activity which enabled them to enrich their learning by building upon their previous experiences and making them more relevant and meaningful for them.

Upon recalling and reflecting upon my experiences of coaching rock climbing in Singapore I realized that my coaching of rock climbing reflected some features of Positive Pedagogy. I witnessed climbers using experience, reflecting upon it and participating in dialogue. I provided opportunities for inquiry learning to construct new knowledge in the form of articulated knowledge and embodied knowledge-in-action on the rock face. My support and interactions with them allowed the young climbers to think and discuss with purpose through positive and productive relationships among themselves and between them and me.

My recent reading on Positive Pedagogy and opportunities to be involved in teaching it to undergraduate students has helped me understand why I felt my teaching had been effective. At the same time, it has allowed me to see how I could take this learner-centred approach a little further in rock climbing while giving me ideas for coaching other individual sports. Reflecting upon my experiences of coaching rock climbing made me feel that the progress the climbers made over this short time was a reward for the time they had invested in what was basically an inquiry-based learning approach. They reflected, discussed ideas, came up with possible solutions for the problems that they had to deal with, tested them and evaluated them, and accepted the mistakes they made as part of learning. As a coach at the time, these outcomes became a source of motivation and satisfaction for me. Writing this chapter and my growing understanding of Positive Pedagogy further motivates me to develop my ability to coach using Positive Pedagogy.

14

GYMNASTICS

Enhancing thought, awareness and positive experiences

With Bianca Couto de Aguiar

> Gymnastics is quite complex and very difficult. Artistic gymnastics involves the performance of highly technical stunts that require both expertise to teach and considerable skill to perform.
>
> *(Docherty and Morton, 2008, p. 41)*

In this chapter I first reflect on the way I teach and coach gymnastics and how it has evolved as an approach that now reflects the features of Positive Pedagogy (Light and Harvey, 2015). I present two examples of my coaching that are focused on what I consider to be core concepts that are challenging for young gymnasts to develop a practical understanding of. These two concepts are (1) transference of body weight and balance using handstand as an example and (2) rotation over body parts, as highlighting the backward roll.

Developing and inquiry-based approach

Over my journey from a gymnast to a gymnastics coach and a physical education teacher I developed an awareness of the challenges involved in coaching and teaching gymnastics to children and young people. I have noticed how often the complexity of the movements; the high demand of coordination, body awareness and control; and the high number of repetitions needed to achieve mastery at such young ages lead to a loss of interest and commitment from students and young athletes. Unhappy with this I tried to find a way of engaging my students/athletes by changing the way I was teaching. I made a decision to move away from highly structured classes that relied on direct instruction to a more creative, discovery-based way of teaching gymnastics, where the goal was not achieving perfection but, instead, creating a space for students to enjoy and learn gymnastics at their own pace.

During my development of this approach I found that some of the ideas that had become the base of my teaching aligned with educational gymnastics instead of with 'traditional' (artistic/Olympic) gymnastics because it is an approach that emphasizes problem solving based on movement and promotes critical thinking (Nilges, 2002). In educational gymnastics a movement is chosen and presented through a question; for example, 'How can you transfer your body weight from one body part to another?' (Docherty and Morton, 2008, p. 42). This is then followed by a period of exploration where some movements are 'selected and rejected, modified, repeated and refined, until mastery learning is achieved' (Docherty and Morton, 2008, p. 42). Through the process of problem solving, educational gymnastics can stimulate cognitive and emotional outcomes that are not limited to physical education and can extend to other areas (Werner et al., 2012). This approach provides circumstances that enhance the acquisition of neuromuscular skills and the development of social values, such as sharing and participating in group discussions (Mauldon and Layson, 1979).

As I developed this approach I recognized that to engage the athletes/students and have them achieve better results my role as a coach and teacher needed to shift from telling them what to do to helping them understand the whole movement itself and how to use their bodies. Questioning them about what they felt when performing a movement and how they thought it should be executed became a central feature of my teaching that I felt improved their performance and commitment. Through my recent reading I realized that educational gymnastics and Positive Pedagogy were very similar due to the fact that they are both inquiry-based learning approaches. The ideas presented through this book resonate with my ideas about teaching/coaching gymnastics that were originally influenced by my interest in Teaching Games for Understanding. Positive Pedagogy 'emphasizes the holistic, social nature of learning, and the role of experience, the body and its senses in it' (Light and Harvey, 2015, p. 13) and, like educational gymnastics, it provides decision-making and problem-solving situations while creating positive emotional states such as joy and delight (see Kretchmar, 2005). The three features of Positive Pedagogy described in Part II emphasize what students and athletes can do and how they can draw on their own abilities and social resources 'to meet learning challenges through reflection and dialogue' (Light, 2014a, p. 32).

Transference of body weight and balance – handstand

In the handstand body weight is transferred from the feet (naturally made for supporting the body) to the hands to end in a fully inverted position. Besides the unnatural position the body needs to take, there is also the challenge of holding that position for a few seconds. This makes its execution extremely challenging.

Before changing my way of teaching/coaching, I used to follow a standard progression towards a handstand. It would start with the use of demonstration to guarantee the visualization of the correct form of the element, asking a student/athlete to execute a 'proper' handstand or doing it myself. After that, I would create stations where the students/athletes would repeat exercises going from deconstructed forms of a handstand to a full handstand and always using a sheet with all the details, actions and steps to follow. For example: 1 – start with arms stretched covering ears; 2 – one leg in front in a lunge; 3 – hands wide open on the ground with fingers facing forward; 4 – kick the back leg up until it reaches vertical; 5 – stretch legs and feet pointed....

Activity 1

I now present an example of how I now teach/coach a handstand using Positive Pedagogy. My focus when using Positive Pedagogy is on how students/athletes *feel* when executing a handstand in different ways. To do that, my classes feature:

1. Questioning
2. Reflection
3. Dialogue

I start by dividing the class into pairs to do a quick warm-up game that involves playing tag while doing wheelbarrow with a partner. Besides using the activity as a physiological warm up, my aim is to create a situation close enough to a handstand to provide an experience for students and athletes of transferring body weight from one extremity (feet) to the other (hands). When working with more advanced groups I ask them to place their feet on their partners' shoulders, which moves them closer to an inverted position, and push a ball with their hands through a course drawn on the floor. Here I focus more on interaction and dialogue among peers in their search for strategies and different ways to succeed in the task, and less on technical aspects of execution.

Because there are safety aspects that need to be addressed when doing a handstand, especially regarding falls (attention to head, neck and back), I use inductive questioning to indirectly give them just enough information to initiate the next task safely. I ask them questions such as 'How should we position our arms when doing a handstand?' and 'What do you think can happen if we don't do that?' These types of questions are aimed at having them focus on safety issues and stimulating their thinking about critical aspects of a handstand from a safety perspective. Older children usually can point out important actions, such as 'don't bend the arms', 'keep your hands facing forward' and 'have your fingers wide open'. This process usually leads to their answers becoming more elaborate and them developing a final image of them performing a handstand.

Even before trying to do a handstand almost all of the children have a visual representation of it. While this is helpful for learning they also need body awareness and the ability to control their bodies to execute a handstand. The most common errors they make are (1) reducing the distance between each foot in the beginning of the movement, which commonly leads to a loss of balance; (2) arching their backs too much when passing the vertical position; and (3) a lack of 'muscle tone' in their bodies to control the movement. Using Positive Pedagogy I try to create an environment where my students/athletes are active learners by designing exercises capable of generating positive experiences, helping them to identify the mistake (the problem) through reflection and interaction, letting them find ways of articulating problems and, finally, helping them focus on how they felt (how they experienced their body) when executing a handstand in different situations.

Activity 2

Here I present an example of one activity I have done to help my gymnasts understand the importance of beginning from a wide stance to establish and maintain balance through the movement. I do this by actually ensuring that they do it incorrectly to feel the imbalance that it creates to foster awareness of the relationship between the width of the stance and maintaining balance while shifting the weight placed on the feet to the hands as the body is inverted. I start by dividing the class in to three or four small groups and asking them to do handstands starting with the front foot as close as possible to the back foot as a type of exaggeration of a common error. Here I introduce this error as a type of constraint to help them be aware of it and to present it as a problem to be solved. The aim here is for them to first identify the problem by letting them practise for a while with this constraint and then asking them to discuss what the problem is within small groups. Here I would ask questions such as 'How did you feel when doing a handstand starting with your feet so close together?' or 'What problem does this seem to create for you?' I would encourage them to recall the problems they felt when doing the handstand and to think about what happened and why. These questions would lead most of the students/athletes to articulate answers such as 'It felt weird because I could not kick up my back leg properly' and 'I kept losing my balance.' However, although some children are able to describe how they felt they often cannot identify the problem. In this case they give answers such as 'I felt really "wobbly" and it was really hard to go up, but I don't know why.'

After a brief discussion I would ask them to work in their groups to find solutions for the problems that they previously identified. The goal here is to have them devise possible solutions and try them out. Later, I would ask them to share the solutions they found for the problem. It was usually interesting to see how they came up with different solutions for the same problem, such as 'We should start with a big step forward because doing that I felt more balanced and we can use the bottom leg as a spring to push the floor' or 'We should start like a hundred-metre sprinter on the blocks…it is easier to lift the back leg because it is already stretched.' Even the children who cannot identify the problem the first time and typically say how the movement feels 'unnatural' or uncomfortable to them when having to begin with a narrow stance come up with similar solutions for solving the problem. Invariably the young gymnasts will identify the problem as being the small distance between front and back leg and understand why and how this makes it difficult to execute a handstand that feels good. This follows Dewey's proposal for adopting an inquiry approach to teaching science (see Barrow, 2006; chapter 6) that begins with identifying the 'perplexing' problem and then clarifying it. This takes a lot longer than just telling them from the start but the process of discovery seems to provide deep and lasting learning.

After completing this activity I normally still don't have students/athletes doing perfect handstands but I do have students/athletes who are aware of the relationship between the width of the stance and maintaining balance through execution of the handstand and who are able to critically reflect on this element of the handstand. Being able to identify a problem when performing a handstand and find a solution for it also suggests to me that they are gaining awareness of their body during the discovery learning process. They are also motivated to be active learners in the search for possible answers to the problems they have identified and they seem to enjoy the process. Some of the children enjoy the process of discovery so much that they are outwardly happy and excited as they shout, 'Look at me! I can do a handstand now! Am I doing it? Can I show my mom and dad?' or just say, 'Can we do handstands at all sessions?'

Rotation over body parts – backward roll

Executing a backward roll seems to be a fairly easy task but my experience as a coach and educator tells me the opposite. The backward roll is a complex movement that involves losing eye contact with the floor, rolling back, moving the lower body over the hands and head, and having to use arm strength to push from the floor. This makes the execution of this element very difficult. The most common errors when executing a backward roll are keeping a flat back through the movement; not tucking the chin into the chest and keeping the legs facing up which makes the rotation harder; and not using hands to push from the floor or using hands closed into fists instead of spreading the palms and fingers wide open. I have noticed that students and athletes are easily demotivated when trying this element over and over again without success. Here I break this session up into three activities.

Activity 1

At first, most of the children feel unsure or even afraid when rolling back without seeing the floor so, much like the kayak roll described in chapter 12, I would begin with an activity to help familiarize them with the feel of the rotation movement. In this activity each gymnast has a hoop on the floor or a low, wide-diameter 'bucket' behind them and about 2 metres away from them, but they can adjust the distance to suit themselves. Each gymnast sits on the floor with their back facing the 'bucket/hoop' with a large ball about the size of a netball or basketball between their ankles. The aim is to roll backwards and place the ball in the hoop or bucket. My aim here is to create a space for reflection where students/athletes could discuss as a group and reflect individually on the best way of transporting the ball, at the same time as getting used to rolling on their back.

I would normally split the class into two groups and would apply a constraint to the game by not allowing the use of hands to transport the ball, but working in pairs would also work well as is done in several of the other chapters in Part III. After letting them play for a while, it is usually interesting to observe how, in the beginning, they often whisper to each other about what they could do to place the ball in the bucket. At this stage they tend to be hesitant to articulate and share their ideas but over the course of the activity they start to express their thoughts and propose some interesting ideas, such as 'We should start like a frog with the ball between your legs and then roll back and stretch your legs to reach the bucket.'

Activity 2

At the end of the first activity I am typically pleased with the positive outcome. Students and athletes seem to feel comfortable rolling on their back, losing their fear of losing eye contact with the ground. This exercise also creates an environment in which they engage in discussion to find options to complete the task and help each other out. After the introductory game I would do a second exercise with the aim of engaging students/athletes in identifying technical problems when executing a backward roll. I divide the class into small groups and ask them, once again, to transport a soft ball held between their ankles, but this time from one circle (drawn on the ground) to another doing a backward roll. In this exercise I want students/athletes to develop awareness of the importance of using arms and hands in a backward roll and understand how to use them and when. To do this I increase the challenge involved by not allowing them to use their hands in any part of the movement (transport the ball or pushing on the ground). I let them work in groups, and after a while I call the groups in to ask them questions such as 'What problems did you find when doing a backward roll without hands?' Most of the children don't really have any problems in doing a backward roll without using their hands due to what they have learned in the previous activity about controlling the backward roll enough to drop a ball in a bucket. Not allowing them to use their hands puts pressure on them to focus on the other technical aspects of the backward roll and to do it more efficiently. When they do identify a problem I ask questions such as 'What can we do to deal with that problem?' and 'How can you compensate for not being able to use your hands?'

Activity 3

Next I put the students/athletes in a situation that stimulates reflection and comparison between different ways of executing the same element by removing the constraint and asking them to use their hands and arms on the floor. I let them try and reflect on both options and then ask them questions such as 'How did you feel when using your hands after not being able to use them?' (much like the approach taken in chapter 10 that focuses on the use of the arms in sprinting) and 'Which one do you think helped you most to do a backward roll?' Their answers, such as 'I felt that when I used my hands to push against the floor my head didn't get stuck on the ground and the movement felt smoother', suggest to me that experiencing two ways of executing a backward roll helps them develop awareness of the movement and the role that hands play in the execution of the element.

I use Positive Pedagogy to try to encourage the exploration of solutions that suit the learner's pace of learning (see also chapters 9 and 12). My aim is to develop body awareness that will help them execute each element. At the same time, I try to create opportunities for engaging students/athletes in identifying and solving problems while exposing them to situations where they articulate and reflect on how they felt when attempting a backward roll. In Positive Pedagogy, reflection plays an important role as it recalls the experience of executing a backward roll by bringing it to consciousness for articulation and discussion (see also chapter 12).

Discussion

The use of Positive Pedagogy in gymnastics can enhance holistic learning and body awareness developed through experience, reflection and the use of the body's senses while emphasizing the social nature of the learning process. Reflecting on my own practice, I recognize that using Positive Pedagogy is challenging in the beginning. Gymnastics is a very technically demanding sport that has elements with numerous components that require mastery in a short period of time. As a teacher and coach I am expected to produce immediate results. When using Positive Pedagogy it takes some time for athletes to adapt to this approach and for its contributions to student/athlete development to become visible (Light, 2004).

The examples I share in this chapter reflect upon the coaching approach I developed before being exposed to Positive Pedagogy and which moved my pedagogy towards an inquiry-based learning approach. They also provide examples of how my coaching has further developed as a result of my understanding of Positive Pedagogy. Creating situations where students/athletes have to solve problems and reflect on their practice individually and as a group has become central to my coaching. As Light and Harvey suggest, 'the central role that dialogue, reflection and purposeful social interaction play in facilitating learning in this approach can promote deep understanding' (2015, p. 1). As a coach my aim is to help my athletes perform the elements correctly but I want them to enjoy learning and to make learning a lasting transformation for them. I want my coaching to improve performance but also foster enjoyment of learning (Light and Harvey, 2015) and this is something I think Positive Pedagogy is helping me achieve.

Looking deeper into my attempts of using Positive Pedagogy in gymnastics I feel that despite the brief exposure that my students/athletes have had to this approach they are showing significant progress in the way they develop awareness of their body during the execution of elements such as handstand and backward roll. They are also becoming curious and active learners who identify the problems they are experiencing and are engaged in the discovery of possible solutions.

I close with a little reflection on what and how I have learned as a coach. Light and Harvey suggest that 'In Positive Pedagogy, errors are seen as constructive errors that are made into positive learning experiences with the provision of opportunities for adequate reflection and analysis' (2015, p. 10). I believe that these thoughts apply not only to students/athletes and their learning process, but also to me as a teacher and coach. Developing Positive Pedagogy for coaching is a learning process for the coach and one that will take time with plenty of mistakes made along the way. But I feel that reflecting on these mistakes will create positive learning experiences for me as a coach that will help me enhance students'/athletes' thought, awareness, reflection and enjoyment at the same time as it will improve their performance.

15

KARATE

In this chapter I recount a session that I taught to a class of Western karate practitioners in which I adopted an athlete-centred approach that reflects the features of Positive Pedagogy. I spent over thirty years training in karate, earned a living as a karate instructor in Australia for eight years and trained for six years in Japan where I earned a fifth dan in the Hayashi Ha Shitō Ryū Kai system. The session I recount here was focused on improving the reverse punch (*gyakuzuki*) when attacking a moving target and reflects many of the features of Positive Pedagogy. It is strongly influenced by my engagement in karate for over thirty years with my six years in Japan being the most influential.

Gyakuzuki (reverse thrust)

Gyakuzuki (reverse punch) is the workhorse of the *karateka* (karate practitioner) and is easily the most common *waza* (technique) used to score points in tournaments. It is a straight punch delivered from the rear hand on the opposite side to the front foot with power generated from the rear foot, passing through the rotation of the hips, shoulders and arm, delivered with a snap on contact. Most *karateka* assume a stance (*tachi*) for *kumite* (sparring) or competition with the left foot forward, which means that *gyakuzuki* is most commonly delivered with the right hand. Good technique for *gyakuzuki* involves a whole-body movement that begins from the ball of the right foot to generate rotational forces, such as those discussed in chapter 11 in relation to throwing the javelin. In *gyakuzuki* power is initially generated by pushing from and rotating on the ball of the rear foot, through hip rotation and a minuscule lag before it passes through the upper body and into contact as the elbow is extended and the punch is delivered with a snapping action.

The extension of the joints in the lower body and the initial rotation of the larger body mass of the lower body generate power that passes through to the smaller mass of the upper body with teaching normally focusing on keeping a low centre of gravity by dropping the hips and snapping them to release the punch. The focus is on hip rotation, producing power from the lower body and letting it flow through the upper body. *Gyakuzuki* also involves a push–pull action in which the left side of the upper body (for a left-foot-forward stance) is actively retracted as the right side rotates around the axis of the spine. This involves retracting the left fist from a guard position to the hip to add to the powerful rotation of the hips and the release of the punch with anti-clockwise rotation of the fist. Timing is of central importance to maximize power on impact. All this occurs over a fraction of a second with the *kiai* (powerful shout) focusing all internal energy (*ki*) on the one point at the one moment. Literally, *kiai* (気合) means the meeting or joining of internal energy.

Although there are exceptions, most karate tournaments strictly limit contact to avoid injury. Contestants score points by achieving a clean score (punch or kick) that the judge considers would have been a damaging blow had it been delivered full force. Light contact to the body is typically allowed but contact to the face is prohibited and can lead to the disqualification of the striking contestant. This means that, although power is not required to score a point in a tournament using *gyakuzuki*, the competitor must demonstrate technique that strongly suggests it could have been a telling blow had it not been controlled. The approach I take in the following teaching/coaching example is based upon the assumption that producing power at impact requires good technique and that intrinsic feedback provided by how contact with the pad feels (and sounds), and extrinsic feedback provided by a training partner, can be used to give technique meaning, improve it and develop it as a skill – as technique-in-action (Thorpe, 1990).

The example I provide here for improving the performance of *gyakuzuki* is based upon the athlete learning by experiencing efficient technique through striking a contact pad and reflecting upon the power and balance that comes from efficient execution. This is similar to the approach taken for coaching croquet in chapter 9. It also involves moving towards practising *gyakuzuki* as a skill by putting it into action in a context that has elements of the competition context (Thorpe, 1990).

In the session I recount and discuss here, I began by telling the athletes what the aims of it were and what the progression of activities would be. The three activities I planned to use were (1) punching from a stationary position, (2) chasing the target to punch and (3) punching while retreating. However, the time I spent on Activity 2, which I explain in detail, did not leave me enough time for Activity 3. For all activities, the pairs swapped roles between pad holder/observer and puncher but remained as training partners to develop trust. During each activity I walked around, watching, listening and feeling progress and asking questions of different pairs with an emphasis on how it felt for both the athlete striking the pad and the one holding it. This typically involved asking whether or not it felt (and sounded) 'sharp' and powerful for both partners and how balanced and grounded the puncher felt as well as asking whether or not he/she could feel good contact with the ground on impact. At the end of each activity I called the participants in for a group discussion to share ideas and learning before explaining the next activity, having outlined the progression at the beginning of the session.

Activity 1: relating technique to impact

In karate classes *kihon* (basics) is typically practised through extended repetition working in lines and sometimes by working with a partner as an opponent but without contact. To introduce the sensation of contact as a form of feedback on technique and the focus of learning in the first activity, I put the participants in pairs with one hit pad per pair to provide feedback on the quality of punches. I provided plenty of time for the pairs to work through the required task during which the participant holding the pad offered comments on his/her partner's execution of the technique. I also suggested that they could discuss progress between partners rather than just taking the passive learner–instructor roles that Mosston and Ashworth's (1986) reciprocal teaching style can encourage.

One partner held the hit pad at solar plexus height and at a comfortable distance from which the punching participant could strike without having to move his/her feet. All participants were experienced *karateka* who had a sound understanding of how to perform *gyakuzuki*. For this warm up I asked them to focus on four aspects of performing *gyakuzuki*, which were (1) to relax and let their hips sink and keep their weight low, (2) to push from the rear foot and snap the hips as they punched, (3) to let the power flow easily from the hips through the upper body to contact with the pad, (4) to snap back into a ready position after contact and maintain focus, and (5) to try to make the punch one single, smooth but sharp movement (much like the kayak roll in chapter 12).

During the activity I reminded the participants to start from a relaxed position with their hips low to develop power from hip rotation and to focus their attention on the feel of the execution by asking questions such as 'How did that feel?', 'Did that feel strong and sharp?', 'What sort of sound did that make (and why)?', 'Could you feel the power coming from your lower body at impact?' (why or why not?), 'Did you feel contact with the ground at impact?' or 'How did it feel at impact?' I also asked the partner holding the pad what s/he felt through the pad and how it linked to what s/he saw from an observer's perspective. At the end of the activity I called the group in to share what they had discovered by asking questions, such as 'Who felt that they improved their technique?' and then 'What did you change to improve it?', 'What did you discover as a pair about improving your technique?' and 'Why do you think that worked so well?' while keeping them focused on evaluating technique according to how contact with the pad felt for both partners.

Activity 2: closing the gap and maintaining *kamae*

In Activity 2 I introduced footwork and movement by asking the pad holder to call for his/her partner to strike the pad as s/he quickly shuffled backwards and away from the striker, but while ensuring the pad was at solar plexus height and square to his/her partner. This required appropriate footwork from the attacking participant to move forward quickly into a position to strike from while maintaining balance and keeping the back straight and hips forward and then to recovering to a ready position (*kamae*). Initially all the athletes handled the challenge of moving forward to deliver the punch without significant problems. To raise the level of challenge I then asked the pad holder to move more quickly, give their partner less time to reset between strikes and to move to one side (45 degrees left or right) while moving back. This led to execution becoming more ragged with the sound of impact not as sharp and clear as it had been.

The questions that I asked pairs in this situation focused on what changes they were feeling in their technique and why with reflection based upon how cleanly they felt they hit the pad. Sometimes they were too far away from the hit pad when they struck it which led them to over-reach and inhibit the generation of power from the rotation of the hips and lower body because the back needs to be straight for this. The rapid movement I introduced had prevented some of them from experiencing the pleasurable feedback that a clean and sharp *gyakuzuki* had provided when stationary or when the target was not moving away too quickly. There was a similar problem when the target was moved quickly away from them and to one side. This sometimes led to not being able to strike the pad square on, which required quick adjustment to be directly in front of the target before releasing the punch.

From my perspective as instructor I could see that the major problem was how the participants were losing their *kamae* when required to move rapidly forward. *Kamae* (構え) literally means 'base' but refers to the balanced posture of the whole body and the mental state that cannot be separated from it. It is very different to *tachi*, which translates into English as 'stance' and only refers to the lower half of the body. Concepts are very difficult to translate in any language and even the reference I make to 'mental state' in *kamae* is misleading. This is because Japanese culture sits upon a different view of the world, which is reflected in more holistic concepts (when compared to Western cultures) such as *seishin*, which refers to life spirit, which, again, does not capture the meaning it conveys in Japanese. The reason I use the Japanese term, *kamae*, here is because it captures the essence of what was missing in the execution of *gyakuzuki* when moving quickly.

The teaching I recount here was not with Japanese practitioners but with Westerners who did not have a lived understanding of *kamae* but I felt that some understanding of it would help us progress. I called the group in to talk to them about *kamae* and how important it was for them to understand what it was and to improve it. Although *kamae* is visible, the subjective aspects of it are not visible, which made talking about the experience and reflecting upon how the puncher felt quite important. Five to ten minutes is not enough time to develop a deep understanding of what is a lived cultural concept but I felt that focusing on *feeling* it as a physical and mental base from which to deliver a strong punch would help, and it did. For this reason I asked both partners to focus on *kamae*. The pad holder was to evaluate *kamae* from an observer's perspective (as related to the quality of impact on the pad) while the puncher was to articulate to his/her partner how his/her base felt.

The focus of the activity shifted to the concept of *kamae* to maintain a base of balance from which to deliver a strong punch when moving quickly. Typical questions I asked the puncher at this point were 'That didn't sound as sharp as it did earlier – how did it feel?' or 'How well balanced and ready did you feel at impact?' When they identified any dissatisfaction with how their punching felt I would ask them, 'Why do you think it did not feel as good?' and 'Do you think you had a good base to punch from?' I would ask the participant holding the pad to offer an opinion as an observer with a focus on what sort of a base the puncher seemed to have on impact.

At the completion of the activity I called the class in to share reflections on what progress they had made in adjusting to hitting a moving target and working on punching from a good base (*kamae*). In the spirit of working collaboratively in a socio-morally supportive environment without making the participants feel the critical gaze of the whole group (see chapter 6), I asked them all to form groups of six with a pair performing the task in front of four others for comments and advice. I would not take this step unless I felt that all the participants felt comfortable with this.

Most of the participants had improved their ability to chase a target and strike cleanly and could have been further challenged to deliver a good *gyakuzuki* while retreating, using the same approach outlined above. However, I did not do this in the session I am recounting because I had not planned for the time it took to develop an understanding of *kamae* and apply it to the execution of technique on the move.

Discussion

Participation in sport at any level always involves physical, intellectual, emotional and sensuous experiences that humanistic approaches consider and account for. A batter in cricket or baseball, a tennis player, or a golfer gains pleasure and positive feedback from experiences such as hitting the ball in the 'sweet spot', which is one of the joys of many sports. While physicists may claim to be able to identify and explain the sweet spot on a baseball or cricket bat there is more to it than mere physics. Whether hitting a golf ball, kicking a football, performing a floater in surfing or scoring a clean and decisive point with *gyakuzuki* in a karate bout, these are moments of flow (Csikszentmihalyi, 1990) when everything comes together perfectly in the execution of a skill. From a Japanese cultural perspective, these are moments when mind, body and spirit unite in purity of action, unimpeded by the conscious mind as the athlete experiences *mushin* (Light, 2014c). These are unexplainable moments of release from the limits of normal human life on Earth that are possible through sport. They are also experiences that, Csikszentmihalyi argues, provide for optimal learning.

The pleasure and/or positive feedback received from striking a hit pad with a *gyakuzuki* with enough efficiency to generate the feeling that all has come together at the one precise moment provides a logical focus for teaching. It may not compare with the flow experience of hitting an effortless six in cricket, splitting the defence without being touched in rugby or executing a clean aerial in surfing, but such whole-person experiences can provide a focus for coaching and learning. This is why I have used the experience of striking a hit pad to teach technique in karate. Here I am proposing a different conceptualization of learning to execute *gyakuzuki*. In this example I used the experience of hitting a solid target as a means of learning technique, which places experience at the centre of learning. This is done to provide 'intrinsic' or kinaesthetic feedback to the learner to reflect upon *in* and *after* action that is augmented by objective feedback provided by the training partner. By articulating this experience in discussion with the training partner the two learners engage in dialogue from which mutual learning unfolds.

The focus of the session was on learning through experience and reflection upon it. The nature of karate as a Japanese cultural practice and the concepts that inform it encouraged me to take a more holistic teaching approach than the reduction of a skill to discrete component parts. In particular, the use of the concept of *kamae* encouraged me to try to foster a more holistic understanding of posture during movement and its importance for throwing a good punch on the move. This is not only a base of balance from which a punch is delivered but, instead, a whole-person state of readiness. From a Western perspective it is a physical and mental state of readiness and this seemed to help the participants I was teaching get the idea of maintaining *kamae* when chasing the target.

As I suggested earlier in this discussion, the focus on how the participants felt and asking them to develop awareness of how they use their bodies generated some reflection *in* action (Varela et al., 1991) and, it seemed to me, an element of mindfulness. By referring to mindfulness I mean more the Buddhist concept of developing awareness and being continuously present with experience than the appropriation of it in psychology and its transformation into a tool or therapy for stress relief. This was encouraged by asking the participants to be aware of their bodies, where power was coming from, and their connection with the ground.

Conclusion

On the surface, this chapter presents a way of using Positive Pedagogy to teach the execution of karate technique in action by focusing on striking a hit pad and relating it to technique. In this way it should provide some useful ideas for teaching technique in karate and other striking sports. In the discussion I have taken this a little further to reflect upon some deeper issues concerned with the humanistic and holistic nature of Positive Pedagogy. Given that I am discussing teaching technique in a Japanese martial art it seems to make sense to focus on an important Japanese cultural concept that helped me as a coach/teacher and which helped the participants begin to conceptualize what they needed to do to improve their performance. This experience also brought home to me the importance of the concept of *kamae* for all technique and skill in karate and probably for all martial arts in Japan.

CONCLUDING THOUGHTS

In this book there is no attempt to tell anyone how to coach or identify which is the best way to coach individual or team sports. Nor is there any attempt made to provide a model for coaching or a sequence of steps to be taken to be a Positive Pedagogy coach. Instead, the aim is to present a framework for an innovative approach to coaching individual sports that is positive, athlete-centred and inquiry-based. I took the same approach with Game Sense (Light, 2013a) but coaching team sports lends itself more easily to providing a structure for implementing athlete-centred coaching than coaching individual sports does. In *Positive Pedagogy for Sport Coaching: Athlete-centred coaching for individual sports*, I have adapted the core pedagogical features from Game Sense to individual sports while reducing them to three, but this book is more about ideas and a philosophical approach than offering a precise guide for coaching.

The nine chapters in Part III (Applications) reflect the variety of ways in which a coach can use Positive Pedagogy while being guided by its three pedagogical features and keeping learning positive. These examples are reflective examples of my own and four other coaches' use of Positive Pedagogy or very similar pedagogy. The chapters I have co-written with two colleagues and two Ph.D. students of mine are included to provide some insight into the use of Positive Pedagogy by coaches for whom it represents a significant change in practice. Although there is a range of sports covered from swimming to croquet to karate in Part III, there is no attempt made to cover all types of sport. Positive Pedagogy aims to develop deep understanding, curiosity, learning how to learn and creativity in athletes. In a similar way the practical chapters in Part III are aimed at stimulating thinking about how the reader might use Positive Pedagogy in his/her sport and particular context, guided by an understanding of its under-pinning principles and pedagogical features that I hope will develop from reading Parts I and II.

In this closing chapter I discuss three core themes running through the book, which are (1) the influence of context, (2) humanistic coaching and (3) holistic coaching.

The importance of context

The context within which coaching (and teaching) takes place has an immense influence on coaching and learning but is often neglected in coaching practice and in writing on coaching. It is something that is typically not considered by coaches until there is a problem that they can link to it. When I first began coaching rugby in Japan I blindly charged in using an Australian approach to coaching without considering the immense influence of culture and the related education system on learning and dispositions that all my players had come through. This created so many problems for me as coach and now forms a major focus of my research programme.

Institutional and cultural contexts exert a powerful influence on players through the ways in which they shape the knowledge and sets of dispositions embodied over long periods of participation in the practices of sport and the discourses surrounding them. They also form a powerful influence upon the beliefs of coaches about coaching and the nature of how they coach and interpret innovations that is shaped through experience as athletes and coaches in particular contexts (see Hassanin and Light, 2014). The knowledge, beliefs and values embodied through experience within a particular socio-cultural context are embedded in cultural and historical meanings with Cushion et al. (2003) suggesting that this is how experience structures coaches' 'philosophies' and 'dispositions towards coaching'. These 'philosophies' (sets of underpinning principles) are situated in 'life experiences' (Nash et al., 2008, p. 536) and expressed as the deeply held values that shape and structure coaching practice (Lyle, 2002).

The actual physical context also exerts a powerful influence upon athlete learning, as is emphasized in GBA with the location of learning within modified games or game-like activities to make learning meaningful and facilitate its transfer from practice to the competition match and not just be 'training to train' (Jones, 2015). An holistic conception of team sports that is reflected to different degrees across GBA sees them as being complex phenomena that cannot be reduced to component parts. This refers to the different, yet interacting, aspects of play such as skill, awareness, decision-making and tactical knowledge and the ways in which every player (on both sides) and his/her actions are part of a complex and dynamic phenomenon (Light, Harvey et al., 2014).

This, then, means that for practice to improve game performance by a team it has to be conducted within contexts that have some of the features of the competition game context (Light, 2013a; Jones, 2015). This is evident in chapter 7 with its focus on coaching specific skills in team sports, but while maintaining the need for awareness and decision-making as part of the context in which improvements in practice have to be evident to be meaningful. It is also very obvious in individual sports performed in water such as surfing, kayaking (see chapter 12) and swimming (see chapter 8). How effective do you think it would be to have to develop competency in swimming before being allowed in the water?

Social constructivism sees context as being central to learning because knowledge developed out of context lacks meaning and relevance and does not allow the learner to use it for undertaking authentic tasks. This is because s/he does not learn within the complex environment and its complex interrelationships within which the knowledge is to be used (Duffy and Jonassen, 1992). Just as the context of language gives words meaning, the context of the game gives meaning to skills. Dewey (1939, p. 544) extends the importance of context (as the environment) to propose that the learner (organism) and environment cannot be separated because all experience involves an 'interaction of environing conditions and an organism'. As Quay and Stolz (2014) explain, the use of the term 'environment' by Dewey should not be confused with the natural environment (although, as chapter 12 suggests, it can be very relevant) because this would limit the richness of the term and how it helps understand the notion of context. They suggest that environment for Dewey does not merely mean the surrounding physical conditions because 'there is much in the physical surroundings to which an organism is irresponsive: such conditions are no part of its *true* environment' (Dewey, cited in Quay and Stolz, 2014, 16).

For Dewey the true environment is determined by the interaction between the learner (organism) and the context (environment) but as one – not as the three separate parts of environment, organism (learner) and interaction. Dewey's notion of interaction has a deep sense of integration and does not merely refer to something done between a separate learner and his/her context. Seen in another way, a learner does not live and learn *in* an environment – s/he lives and learns *by means of* an environment (Dewey, 1938a). The context, then, is not what surrounds the athlete in practice and competition; it is what s/he interacts with (in a variety of ways) to produce the experience of learning.

In this book, Parts I and II do not specifically focus on the context within which Positive Pedagogy is used to enhance learning, but this is something that coaches do need to consider, regardless of the pedagogy used. It is also something that features in many of the chapters on the application of Positive Pedagogy. The specific socio-cultural and/or institutional contexts that coaches work in may be so familiar that they are not considered. Some recent studies that have looked into the subjective dimensions of athlete performance and coaching account for the influence of a wide range of contextual spheres of influence on decision-making during competition matches by rugby players and coaches, within and outside the match (see Light, Harvey et al., 2014; Mouchet et al., 2014).

This, and other work in France, takes an holistic approach to consider the influence of contextual factors operating at 'micro', 'meso' and 'macro' levels, reflecting Gréhaigne and colleagues' (2005) suggestions for the significance of the time between decision-making and action in sport from strategic decision-making before the match begins to tactical decisions and 'at-action' decision-making where it is difficult to separate thinking from action (see Light et al., 2014). Work on the subjective dimensions of athlete participation in sport also considers the influence that 'particular events' occurring in the match, 'local contexts' (time around the match – before and after) and 'general contexts' (seen as the players' decisional background – Mouchet et al., 2014, p. 3) have on behaviour and cognition during matches. From a Deweyan perspective, these contextual aspects shape athlete and coach behaviour and learning through interaction.

Humanistic coaching

Some of the research and writing on GBAs over the past two decades identifies them as being humanistic (see Kidman, 2005), which is a theme running through this book. Humanistic coaching refers to perspectives on coaching as responses to the long-established dehumanization and objectification of athletes that views them as objects to be worked on and fine-tuned for performance. This mechanistic approach privileges 'the technological, biophysical and scientised aspects' of coaching (Nash et al., 2008, p. 530) while ignoring what it is to be human and how this influences participation in practice and competition and learning.

This view of athlete-as-machine is readily on display with some swim coaches who write their sets, times to be met and numbers of repetitions for their athletes on the whiteboard. They communicate predominantly through a monologue of instructions at the end of sets and shouting as they pace up and down the pool with little attention paid to how their swimmers are feeling or what they think and typically not inviting any questions from the swimmers. This is not to say that all swim coaches work like this but it is a sport that lends itself to this mechanistic approach.

Humanistic coaching sees athletes as thinking, feeling humans with a life outside the sport that has an influence on how they practise and perform in competition. It also considers the influence that coaching has on their lives outside and beyond sport. Mechanistic views of team sports as being 'complicated' (see Davis et al., 2000) assume they can be broken down into discrete components that can be worked on outside the game and reassembled for the competition match and lie in contrast to alternative views of them as complex phenomena. In a similar way, mechanistic views of individual athletes break the athlete down into component parts while ignoring the fact that every human being is different and comes to practice with a unique set of embodied experiences that make his/her interpretation of coaching, and the learning that unfolds from it, unique.

The humanistic approach to coaching finds its origins in the work of social psychologists who took a humanistic approach to psychology and, most notably, that of Andrew Maslow and Carl Rogers with his subsequent ideas on the development of learner-centred teaching. Rogers (1951) suggested that, rather than one person being able to teach another directly, s/he can only facilitate their learning. Maslow (1968) rejected behaviourist explanations of learning, which he saw as being reductionist, to argue that experience should be the primary focus in the study of human learning. He emphasized choice, creativity, values and self-realization as distinctively human qualities, and believed that meaningfulness and subjectivity were more important than objectivity. His approach is based on the philosophy of existentialism and humanism and could be seen as a phenomenological approach. Developed in response to what some psychologists saw as the limitations of behaviourist and psychodynamic psychology, the humanistic approach is often called the 'third force' in psychology (Maslow, 1968).

Humanistic psychology has had a significant influence on teaching and classroom management in schools. Maslow's (1970) holistic approach to education and learning considers the entire physical, emotional, social and intellectual qualities of the learner and how they influence learning. In response to the same concerns with the objectification of athletes and the dominance of behaviourist theories of learning in sport coaching in psychology and teaching, some in coaching saw what a humanistic approach might offer coaching. As one of the early researchers to write on humanistic coaching, Lombardo (1987) called for coaches to focus on the development of the 'whole' athlete and to encourage them to reflect on the subjective experience of participation in sport. This not only suggested a shift towards identifying and accounting for affective experiences of sport but also towards recognizing and accounting for the subjective experiences of sport and for athletes as whole human beings. The notion of humanistic coaching has since influenced much thinking about coaching and particularly in regard to understanding how GBAs work and how they can be further developed (see Kidman and Lombardo, 2010).

The influence of a humanistic perspective on sport coaching in Positive Pedagogy is evident in its focus on engaging the athlete as a whole person to enhance and give meaning to learning and on how this coaching approach develops the athlete through sport for life outside sport. For example, chapter 2, on designing and managing learning experiences, and chapter 3, on questioning, emphasize the need to understand the athlete as a whole person and not just rely upon an objective analysis of progress. Throughout this book readers are encouraged to understand how athletes *experience* the task or activity and its challenges from both the objective, external position and through tapping into their subjective experience to provide more comprehensive understandings of learning. The importance of understanding athletes' subjective experiences of practice and competition is confirmed by recent work coming out of France such as that of Mouchet (2014) who suggests how an understanding of rugby players' subjective experience in competition can be used by coaches as a resource for improving at-action decision-making.

All the practical examples of Positive Pedagogy at work in Part III reflect the influence of humanistic coaching. The ways in which Positive Pedagogy places experience at the centre of learning and emphasizes it as a whole-person experience reflects Maslow's (1968) view that studies on learning should focus on experience. Many of the examples provided in Part III emphasize whole-person experience through 'feel'. This includes feeling the contact of fingers, hands and parts of the forearm to connect with the water during breaststroke (chapter 8), focusing on the feel of a clean hit in croquet (chapter 9) and karate (chapter 15), and developing awareness of (or feel for) the climber's centre of gravity as they traverse the rock face (chapter 13). Recognition of the learner as a complex and unique human being is also evident in how many chapters in Part III use reflection on action by integrating subjective experience for the learner and analysis from the external perspective (objective) of a partner through interaction.

Holistic coaching

The emphasis on the game as a complex phenomenon rather than on its discrete techniques or skills in GBA has gained significant acceptance and makes sense to many coaches of team sports (see Jones, 2015). Positive Pedagogy also takes an holistic approach to coaching sports in which this may seem to present a challenge, due to their focus on technique and skill, but the nine practical examples of coaches using Positive Pedagogy in Part III provide good examples of how an holistic approach can be used for coaching technique and skill. Team sports clearly offer great opportunities for using athlete-centred, inquiry-based coaching but coaching skill does not mean you have to revert to a mechanistic approach. For example, in chapter 12, the approach Chris North takes to helping kayakers learn how to perform a roll focuses on the whole experience of the roll as a single, smooth and powerful movement. In his progression of activities he emphasizes feeling the smoothness of movement and the kayakers' connection with the fluid environment of the water as he builds the complexity of the learning challenges.

In using the term 'holistic coaching' and considering the holistic nature of Positive Pedagogy it is important to note the philosophical assumptions that it sits upon. Positive Pedagogy sits on assumptions that coaches should be aware of as a base for making decisions about their coaching and adapting to the challenges that arise. It is informed by the constructivist epistemology (the nature of knowledge and how we acquire it) and of an holistic view of the world (that can be seen as ontology). It challenges dualistic conceptions of learning in and through sport that have shaped traditional approaches to coaching while encouraging rethinking about the relationship between mind and body as something that is emphasized in this book.

Although the philosophical division of mind and body can be traced to the Greeks, such as Aristotle, it is more commonly linked with the epistemology of sixteenth-century French philosopher René Descartes. His claim that 'I think therefore I am (*Je pense donc je suis*)' and his presentation of an argument that mind and body are distinctly different has had a profound influence upon Western thinking since then. Dualistic views of learning separate the mind from the body to see it as an exclusively intellectual process that movement such as sport intrudes upon (Dewey, 1916/1997). This reduces our understanding of human existence and of how we learn, what we learn and what learning is, as well as what the body's role in learning is. Dewey (1916/1997) goes as far as to describe dualism as an 'evil' influence on education, the negative effects of which cannot be underestimated. This has serious implications for coaching and teaching sport and other physical activity and helps explain some of the challenges that coaches so often face in adopting humanistic and holistic approaches to coaching. A growing literature on GBA consistently identifies and addresses specific challenges facing coaches and teachers such as using appropriate questioning, designing and managing practice games and analyzing learning (see Turner, 2014; Harvey and Light, 2015; Harvey and Robertson, 2015) but perhaps the problem lies much deeper.

Concern with the limits that Western dualism places on understanding the role that the body and its sensations play in learning over the past few decades has led to some interest in Eastern conceptions of learning (see Varela et al., 1991). This interest has extended to the appropriation of the Buddhist concept of mindfulness by Western psychologists (see Seligman and Csikszentmihalyi, 2000), interest in coaching informed by Zen practices (see for example Gallwey, 1974), the development of the concept of flow (Csikszentmihalyi, 1990) and recent suggestions for using the concept of *mushin* to explain learning in sport (Light, 2014c). These developments suggest frustration with Cartesian dualism and a search for concepts, ways of seeing the world and ways of thinking that can better help understand the role and significance of the body and movement in human learning.

My own long engagement in Japanese martial arts, the time I spent in Japan and the research I have been involved in on sport and learning in Japan has sensitized me to a more holistic view of the world that is finding voice in my more recent work on Game Sense and, now, Positive Pedagogy (see Light, 2014c). This became very apparent to me when writing chapter 15 on teaching karate. I had not originally planned to include anything on martial arts but when one of the readers of my book proposal for Routledge asked why I had not included a Japanese martial art, I had no answer. As I wrote this reflective practical chapter it brought the holistic theme that runs through this book to the fore for me and reminded me of the monist philosophical traditions underpinning the practice and meaning of Japanese and other Eastern martial arts.

There is an apparent paradox with teaching in traditional Japanese martial arts that certainly deserves some research attention in the future. Using karate as an example, training focuses on embedding correct technique through endless repetition with a focus on fine technical detail. This seems at odds with athlete-centred coaching yet it is underpinned by holistic ontology and the cultural concepts that are informed by it (see Light, 2014c). Care needs to be taken here in making judgements about practice in another culture without adequate understanding.

There has been significant interest in holistic approaches to understanding sport coaching over the past ten to fifteen years with a focus on the socially situated nature of coaching (see Cassidy et al., 2009) as part of growing consideration of the context within which coaching and learning takes place and interacts with. Writing and research on games-based approaches such as TGfU and Game Sense have also argued for the holistic nature of learning game play (see Harvey et al., 2010).

Positive Pedagogy and coach development

I finish with some suggestions about how coaches might use this book for developing and growing as a coach. Positive Pedagogy sits upon what Fosnot (1996) calls the 'big ideas' that I feel are the key to developing Positive Pedagogy for coaching individual sports. These are outlined and discussed in detail in chapters 2 and 3 and are evident throughout the book – including the nine practical examples of how Positive Pedagogy can be used across a range of individual sports. As I have already noted in this chapter, it is also important to understand and consider the humanistic and holistic nature of Positive Pedagogy and the assumptions about human learning that underpin it when putting it into practice. A reader could be tempted to skip Parts I and II and just go to the examples in Part III for ideas about how to use Positive Pedagogy in his or her sport. Although this might work for one specific situation it will do little to empower the coach to make important decisions about coaching that are required on an almost daily basis and which should be informed by the big ideas underpinning the approach.

Just as the examples in Part III emphasize helping the athlete understand core concepts to make sense of the technical detail, a coach interested in using a Positive Pedagogy approach needs an understanding of its underpinning ideas to further develop as a coach. No coach – no human – knows it all. Life involves learning as an ongoing process with Begg (2001) suggesting that living = learning. If there is one disposition required by a coach to be successful it is that s/he needs to always be open-minded and see him/herself as a learner. The idea that living = learning is a reference to lifelong learning as a *process* rather than to the notion of lifelong learning through informal and formal settings over the lifespan. With the increasingly rapid rate at which society is changing the idea of graduating students at secondary or tertiary level with a set body of knowledge that will serve them well over their professional lives has been replaced by the need to help them learn how to learn. The same goes for sport coaches, who need to be able to adapt to the changing social contexts within which they coach, the players they work with and the constantly changing demands of coaching.

Anyone who has read this book to this point is probably curious, possibly open-minded, interested in innovation in coaching, reflective and prepared to think about new ways of coaching. They are also likely to be well disposed towards the notion of developing as a coach being a lifelong process of learning within which they see themselves as active learners. As research conducted on coach development and writing on it suggests, implicit, non-conscious learning arising from experience as an athlete and coach over long periods of time forms the most powerful influence on how coaches coach (see Cushion et al., 2003; Nash et al., 2008; Hassanin and Light, 2014). However, as powerful as this implicit learning is, coaches who are open to learning and who are reflective practitioners (Schön, 1983, 1987) can identify and account for the ways in which it influences their thoughts and actions and their interpretation of innovation such as Positive Pedagogy.

The thinking and reflection involved in writing this book highlighted for me the complexity involved in adopting an athlete-centred and inquiry-based approach to coaching skill in individual sports. For me this makes it even more important to resist the temptation to try to reduce it to a model or a clearly defined number of steps for 'implementation'. The intent of the framework I provide by suggesting three Pedagogical features of Positive Pedagogy and how to make learning positive is aimed at providing guidance and the space or freedom for coaches to find what works for them but it is underpinned by a particular philosophical position and disposition toward coaching. This is why I emphasize the need for coaches to develop an understanding of the themes and concepts underpinning the approach and the need for them to think, reflect and be creative in their use of Positive Pedagogy. I want to empower them to take the ideas I put forward in this book and develop them to suit their dispositions, experiences and the nature of the context they coach in.

For some, this book may change their coaching dramatically, for others it may have a more subtle influence on how they think about coaching and go about their practice. Indeed, it may have little explicit influence upon some readers' coaching but it will hopefully encourage all readers to think deeply about what is possible in their coaching and what Positive Pedagogy can add to their coaching and their athletes' experiences of practice.

BIBLIOGRAPHY

Allen, J. (2003) 'Social motivation in youth sport', *Journal of Sport and Exercise Psychology*, 25(4): 551–567.

Almond, L. (1983) 'Games making', *Bulletin of Physical Education*, 19(1): 32–35.

Alvio, F. (2005) 'Bridging the gap between declarative and procedural knowledge in the training of translators: Meta-reflection under scrutiny', *Meta: Translators' Journal*, 50(4): 12–24.

Antonovsky, A. (1979) *Health, stress and coping*, San Francisco: Jossey-Bass.

Antonovsky, A. (1987) *Unraveling the mystery of health*, San Francisco: Jossey-Bass.

Antonovsky, A. (1996) 'The salutogenic model as a theory to guide health promotion', *Health Promotion International*, 11(1): 11–17.

Arnoldi, J. (2006) 'Autopoiesis', *Theory, Culture and Society*, 23: 116–117.

Barker, D., Quennerstedt, M. and Annerstedt, C. (2013) 'Inter-student interactions and student learning in health and physical education: A post-Vygotskian analysis', *Physical Education and Sport Pedagogy*, 20(4): 409–426.

Barrow, L. H. (2006) 'A brief history of inquiry: From Dewey to standards', *Journal of Science Teacher Education*, 17: 265–278.

Begg, A. (2001) 'Why more than constructivism is needed' in S. Gunn and A. Begg, eds, *Mind, Body and Society: Emerging Understanding of Knowing and Learning*, Melbourne: Department of Mathematics and Statistics, University of Melbourne, 13–20.

Begg, A. (2013) 'Interpreting enactivism for learning and teaching', *Education Sciences & Society*, 4(1): 81–96.

Beghetto, R. A. and Plucker, J. A. (2006) 'The relationship among schooling, learning, and creativity: "All roads lead to creativity" or "You can't get there from here?"', in J. C. Kaufman and J. Bear, eds, *Creativity and Reason in Cognitive Development*, Cambridge, NY: Cambridge University Press, 316–332.

Bohler, H. (2009) 'Sixth grade sudents' tactical understanding and decision-making in a TGM volleyball unit', in T. Hopper, J. Butler and B. Storey, eds, *TGfU...Simply Good Pedagogy: Understanding a Complex Challenge*, Toronto: PHE Canada, 87–100.

Borghi, A. M. and Cimatti, F. (2010) 'Embodied cognition and beyond: Acting and sensing the body', *Neuropsychologia*, 48: 763–773.

Boud, D., Cohen, R. and Sampson, J. (eds.) (2001) *Peer learning in higher education: Learning from and with each other*, London: Kogan Page.

Boud, D., Keogh, R. and Walker, D. (eds.) (1985) *Reflection: Turning experience into learning*, London: Kogan Page.

Bourdieu, P. (1986) *Distinction*, London: Routledge and Kegan Paul.

Bourdieu, P. (1990) *The logic of practice*, Stanford: Stanford University Press.

Bourdieu, P. and Wacquant, L. (1992) *An invitation to reflexive sociology*, Chicago: University of Chicago Press.

Brookfield, S. (1995) *Becoming a critically reflective teacher*, San Francisco: Jossey-Bass.

Bruner, J. S. (1961) 'The art of discovery', *Harvard Educational Review*, 31: 21–32.

Bruner, J. (1990) *Acts of Meaning*, Cambridge, MA: Harvard University Press.

Bruner, J. (1999) 'Folk pedagogies', in B. Leach and B. Moon, eds, *Learners and Pedagogy*, London: Open University Press, 4–20.

Bunker, D. and Thorpe, R. (1982) 'A model for teaching games in secondary school', *Bulletin of Physical Education*, 10: 9–16.

Burton, D. and Raedeke, T. D. (2008) *Sport psychology for coaches*, Champaign, IL: Human Kinetics.

Cassidy, T. and Kidman, L. (2010) 'Initiating a national coaching curriculum: A paradigmatic shift?', *Physical Education and Sport Pedagogy*, 15(3): 307–322.

Cassidy, T., Jones, R. and Potrac, P. (2009) *Understanding sports coaching: The social, cultural and pedagogical foundations of coaching* (2nd edn), London and New York: Routledge.

Chappell, G. and Light, R. L. (2015) 'Back to the future: Developing batting talent through Game Sense', Special issue of *Active + Healthy Magazine*, 23(2/3): 31–34.

Charlesworth, R. (2002) *Staying at the top*, Sydney: Pan MacMillan.

Chen, W. (2001) 'Description of an expert and novice teachers' constructivist-oriented teaching: Engaging students' critical thinking in learning creative dance', *Research Quarterly for Exercise and Sport*, 72(4): 366–375.

Chen, Q. and Light, R. (2006) '"I thought I'd hate cricket but I love it!": Year six students' responses to Game Sense pedagogy', *Change: Transformations in Education*, 9(2): 7–15.

Chen, W. and Rovegno, I. (2000) 'Examination of expert and novice teachers' constructivist-oriented teaching practices using a movement approach to elementary physical education', *Research Quarterly for Exercise and Sport*, 71(4): 357–372.

Clarke, J. C. (2016) 'Teaching older athletes new tricks: Coaching croquet through Game Sense', Paper presented at the 2015 Game Sense for Teaching and Coaching Conference, Christchurch, New Zealand.

Clarke, J. and Dembowski, S. (2006) 'The art of asking great questions', *The International Journal of Mentoring and Coaching*, 4(2): 1–6. Available from: http://www.solutionsurfers.com/pdf/TheArtOfAskingGreatQs.pdf. Accessed 21 January 2015.

Cobb, P. (1996) 'Where is the mind? A coordination of sociocultural and cognitive perspectives', in C.T. Fosnot, ed, *Constructivism: Theory, Perspectives and Practice*, New York, London: Teachers College, Columbia University, 34–52.

Cohen, E. (2010) 'From the Bodhi tree to the analyst's couch then into the MRI scanner: The psychologisation of Buddhism', *Annual Review of Critical Psychology*, 8: 97–119.

Colombetti, G. (2014) *The feeling body: Affective science meets the enactive mind*, Boston: MIT Press.

Cope, E. J. and Pearce, G. (2013) 'Why do children take part in, and remain involved in sport? A literature review and discussion of implications for sports coaches', *International Journal of Coaching Science*, 7(1): 55–74.

Cropley, A. (2006) 'In praise of convergent thinking', *Creativity Research Journal*, 18(3): 391–404.

Csikszentmihalyi, M. (1990) *Flow: The psychology of optimal experience*, New York: Harper & Row.

Cuddy-Keane, M. (2010) 'Narration, navigation, and non-conscious thought: Neuroscientific and literary approaches to the thinking body', *University of Toronto Quarterly*, 79(2): 680–701.

Cushion, C. J., Armour, K. M. and Jones, R. L. (2003) 'Coach education and continuing professional development: Experience and learning to coach', *Quest*, 55: 215–230.

Cushion, C. J., Nelson, L., Armour, K. M., Lyle, J., Jones, R., Sandford, R. and O'Callahan, C. (2010) *Coach learning & development: A review of literature*, Leeds: Sports Coach UK.

Daines, D. (1986) 'Are teachers asking higher level questions?', *Education*, 106: 368–374.

Dashper, K. (2012) 'Together, yet still not equal? Sex integration in equestrian sport', *Asia-Pacific Journal of Health, Sport and Physical Education*, 3(3): 213–226.

Davids, K. (2010) 'The constraints-based approach to motor learning: Implications for a nonlinear pedagogy in sport and physical education', in I. Renshaw, K. Davids and G. J. P. Savelsberg, eds, *Motor Learning in Practice: A Constraints-led Approach*, New York: Routledge, 3–17.

Davis, B. and Sumara, D. J. (1997) 'Cognition, complexity, and teacher education', *Harvard Educational Review*, 67(1): 105–125.

Davis, B. and Sumara, D. (2001) 'Learning communities: Understanding the workplace as a complex system', *New Directions for Adult and Continuing Education*, 92: 85–96.

Davis, B. and Sumara, D. (2003) 'Why aren't they getting this? Working through the regressive myths of constructivist pedagogy', *Teaching Education*, 14(2): 123–140.

Davis, B. and Sumara, D. (2008) 'Complexity as a theory of education', *Transnational Curriculum Inquiry*, 5(2): 33–44.

Davis, B., Sumara, D. and Luce-Kapler, R. (2000) *Engaging minds: Learning in a complex world*, Mahwah, NJ: Lawrence Erlbaum Associates, Inc.

De Jaegher, H. and Di Paolo, E. A. (2007) 'Participatory sense-making: An inactive approach to social cognition', *Phenomenology and the Cognitive Sciences*, 6(4): 485–507.

De Martelaer, K., De Bouw, J. and Struyven, K. (2012) 'Youth sport ethics: Teaching prosocial behaviour', in S. Harvey and R. Light, eds, *Ethics in Youth Sport: Policy and Pedagogical Applications*, London and New York: Routledge, 55–73.

Deci, E. L. and Ryan, R. M. (2000) 'The "what" and "why" of goal pursuits: Human needs and the self-determination of behavior', *Psychological Enquiry*, 11: 227–268.

den Duyn, N. (1997) *Game Sense: Developing thinking players*, Canberra: Australian Sports Commission.

DeVries, R. and Zan, B. (1996) 'A constructivist perspective on the role of the sociomoral atmosphere in promoting children's development', in C. T. Fosnot, ed, *Constructivism: Theory, Perspectives and Practice*, New York and London: Teachers College, Columbia University, 55–72.

Dewey, J. (1916/1997) *Democracy and education*, New York: Free Press.

Dewey, J. (1933) *How we think: A restatement of the relation of reflective thinking to the educative process*, Boston: D. C. Heath.

Dewey, J. (1934/1989) 'Art as experience', in J. Boydston, ed, *John Dewey: The Later Works, 1925–1953*, vol. 10, Carbondale: Southern Illinois University Press, 1–4.

Dewey, J. (1938a) *Experience and education*, Indianapolis, IN: Kappa Delta Di.

Dewey, J. (1938b/1972) *Experience and education* (15th edn), New York: Collier Books.

Dewey, J. (1939) 'Experience, knowledge and value: A rejoinder', in P. A. Schilpp, ed, *The Philosophy of John Dewey*, Evanston, IL: Northwestern University Press, 515–608.

Diener, E. (2000) 'Subjective well-being: The science of happiness and a proposal for a national index', *American Psychologist*, 55(1): 34–43.

Docherty, D. and Morton, A.R. (2008) 'A focus on skill development in teaching educational gymnastics', *Physical & Health Education Journal*, 74(2): 40–44.

Douge, B. and Hastie, P. (1993) 'Coach effectiveness', *Sport Science Review*, 2(2): 14–29.

Duffy, T. M. and Jonassen, D. H. (1992) *Constructivism and the technology of instruction: A conversation*, Hillsdale, NJ: Lawrence Erlbaum Associates, Inc.

Dyson, B. (2001) 'Cooperative learning in an elementary physical education program', *Journal of Teaching in Physical Education*, 20(3): 264–281.

Dyson, B. (2005) 'Integrating cooperative learning and tactical games models: Focusing on social interactions and decision-making', in L. L. Griffin and J. I. Butler, eds, *Teaching Games for Understanding: Theory, Research, and Practice*, Champaign, IL: Human Kinetics, 149–168.

Erriker, J. (2009) 'The importance of happiness to children's education and wellbeing', in M. de Souza, L. J. Francis, J. O'Higgins-Norman and D. Scott, eds, *International Handbook of Education for Spirituality, Care and Wellbeing*, New York: Springer, 739–752.

Esfeld, M. (1998) 'Holism and analytic philosophy', *Mind*, 107(426): 365–380.

Evans, J. R. (2012) 'Elite rugby union coaches' interpretation and use of Game Sense in New Zealand', *Asian Journal of Exercise & Sports Science*, 9(1): 85–97.

Evans, J. R. (2014) 'The nature and importance of coach-player relationships in the uptake of Game Sense by elite rugby coaches in New Zealand', in R. L. Light, J. Quay, S. Harvey and A. Mooney, eds, *Contemporary Developments in Games Teaching*, London & New York: Routledge, 133–145.

Evans, J. and Light, R. (2008) 'Coach development through Collaborative Action Research: A rugby coach's implementation of Game Sense pedagogy', *Asian Journal of Exercise & Sports Science*, 5(1), 31–37.

Evans, J., Davies, B. and Rich, E. (2009) 'The body made flesh: Embodied learning and the corporeal device', *British Journal of Sociology and Education*, 30(4): 391–406.

Fenwick, T. (2001) 'Work knowing on the fly: Post-corporate enterprise cultures and coemergent epistemology', *Studies in Continuing Education*, 23(1): 243–259.

Fernandez-Balboa, J. M. (1995) 'Reclaiming physical education in higher education through critical pedagogy', *Quest*, 47: 91–114.

Fitzsimons, R. and Light, R. L. (2016) 'Young people's experiences of being in a surfriders club', in R. L. Light, *Children, young people and sport: Studies on experience and meaning*, Newcastle, UK: Cambridge Scholars Press.

Ford, P. R., Yates, I. and Williams, M. A. (2010) 'An analysis of practice activities and instructional behaviours used by youth soccer coaches during practice: Exploring the link between science and application', *Journal of Sports Sciences*, 28: 483–495.

Forrest, G. (2014) 'Questions and answers: Understanding the connection between questioning and knowledge in game-centred approaches', in R. Light., J. Quay., S. Harvey and A. Mooney, eds, *Contemporary Developments in Games Teaching*, London: Routledge, 167–177.

Fosnot, C. T. (1996) 'Constructivism: A psychological theory of learning', in C. T. Fosnot, ed, *Constructivism: Theory, Perspectives and Practice*, New York and London: Teachers College, Columbia University, 103–119.

Foucault, M. (1977) *Discipline and punish: The birth of the prison*, New York: Vintage Books.

Foucault, M. (1979) *The history of sexuality volume I*, Harmondsworth: Penguin.

Fowler, J. H. and Christakis, N. A. (2008) 'Dynamic spread of happiness in a large social network: Longitudinal analysis over 20 years in the Framingham Heart Study', *British Medical Journal*, 337(a2338): 1–9.

Fraser-Thomas, J. L., Côté, J. and Deakin, J. (2005) 'Youth sport programs: An avenue to foster positive youth development', *Physical Education and Sport Pedagogy*, 10(1): 19–40.

Freire, P. (1970) *Pedagogy of the oppressed*, New York: Continuum.

Freire, P. (1998) *Pedagogy of freedom: Ethics, democracy, and civic courage*, Lanham, MD: Rowman and Littlefield.

Fry, J., Tan, C., McNeill, M. and Wright, S. (2010) 'Children's perspectives on conceptual games teaching: A value-adding experience', *Physical Education and Sport Pedagogy*, 15(20): 139–158.

Gallwey, W. T. (1974) *The inner game of tennis* (1st edn), New York: Random House.

Garn, A. C. and Cothran, D. J. (2006) 'The fun factor in physical education', *Journal of Teaching in Physical Education*, 25: 282–297.

Geertz, C. (1973) *The interpretation of cultures: Selected essays*, New York: Basic Books.

George, M. G. (2006) 'The power of positive pedagogy'. Available from: http://www.musiclearningcommunity.com/NewsletterArchive/2006October.The%20Power%20of%20Positive%20Pedagogy.htm. Accessed 17 November 2013.

Gorski, J. (2003) 'Chapter 5: Javelin', in J. Sylvester, ed, *Complete Book of Throws*, Champaign, IL: Human Kinetics, 101–130.

Gorski, J. (2014) 'Javelin' [online]. Available from: http://www.speerschule.ch/docs/doc-gorskijav.pdf. Accessed 26 December 2014.

Grant, A. M. (2011) 'The solution-focused inventory: A tripartite taxonomy for teaching, measuring and conceptualising solution focused approaches to coaching', *The Coach Pyschologist*, 7(2): 98–105.

Gréhaigne, J.-F., Richard, J.-F. and Griffin, L. L. (2005) *Teaching and learning team sports and games*, London and New York: Routledge.

Griffin, L. L. and Patton, K. (2005) 'Two decades of Teaching Games for Understanding: Looking at the past, present, and future', in L. Griffin and J. Butler, eds, *Teaching Games for Understanding: Theory, Research, and Practice*, Champaign, IL: Human Kinetics, 1–18.

Griffin, L. L., Chandler, T. J. and Sariscsany, M. J. (1993) 'What does "fun" mean in physical education?', *Journal of Physical Education, Recreation, and Dance*, 64(7): 63–66.

Griffin, L., Mitchell, S. and Oslin, J. (1997) *Teaching sport concepts and skills: A Tactical Games Approach*, Champaign, IL: Human Kinetics.

Harvey, S. (2009) 'A study of interscholastic soccer players' perceptions of learning with Game Sense', *Asian Journal of Exercise & Sports Science*, 6(1): 29–38.

Harvey, S. and Jarrett, K. (2014) 'Recent trends in research literature on game-based approaches to teaching and coaching games', in R. L. Light, J. Quay, S. Harvey, and A. Mooney, eds, *Contemporary Developments in Games Teaching*, London and New York: Routledge, 87–102.

Harvey, S. and Light, R. L. (2015) 'Questioning for learning in games-based approaches to teaching and coaching', *Asia-Pacific Journal of Health, Sport and Physical Education*, 6(2): 175–190.

Harvey, S. and Robertson, D. (2015) 'Enhancing practitioner's observation and analysis skills in a game centred approach', *Active + Healthy Magazine*, 22(2/3): 23–26.

Harvey, S., Cushion, C. and Massa-Gonzalez, A. (2010) 'Learning a new method: Teaching Games for Understanding in the coaches' eyes', *Physical Education and Sport Pedagogy*, 15(4): 361–382

Harvey, S., Kirk, D. and O'Donovan, T. M. (2014) 'Sport Education as a pedagogical application for ethical development in physical education and youth sport', *Sport, Education and Society*, 19(1): 41–62.

Harvey, S., Wegis, H. M., Beets, W. M., Bryan, R., Massa-Gonzalez, A.–N. and van der Mars, H. (2009) 'Changes in student perceptions of their involvement in a multi-week TGfU unit of soccer: A pilot study', in T. Hopper, J. Butler and B. Storey, eds, *TGfU… Simply Good Pedagogy: Understanding a Complex Challenge*, Toronto: PHE Canada, 101–114.

Haskett Smith, W. P. (1894) *Climbing in the British Isles*, Facsimile edition by The Ernest Press, 1986.

Hassanin, R. and Light, R. (2014) 'The influence of cultural context on rugby coaches' beliefs about coaching', *Sports Coaching Review*, 3(2): 132–144.

Hastie, P. (2010) *Student-designed games: Strategies for promoting creativity, co-operation and skill development*, Champaign, IL: Human Kinetics.

Hellison, D. R. (2003) *Teaching responsibility through physical activity* (2nd edn), Champaign, IL: Human Kinetics.

Henry, G. (2013) *Graham Henry: Final word*, London: Harper Collins.

Holt, N. L., Sehn, Z. L., Spence, J. C., Newton, A. S. and Ball, G. D. (2012) 'Physical education and sport programs at an inner city school: Exploring possibilities for positive youth development', *Physical Education and Sport Pedagogy*, 17(1): 97–113.

Holton, D. (2010) 'Constructivism + embodied cognition = enactivism: Theoretical and practical implications for conceptual change', paper presented at the 2010 AERA Conference. Denver, CO.

Hopkins, R. L. (1994) *Narrative schooling: Experiential learning and the transformation of American education*, New York: Teachers College Press.

Horn, J. and Wilburn, D. (2005) 'The embodiment of learning', *Educational Philosophy and Theory*, 37(5): 745–760.

Horst, E. (2016) *Training for climbing: The definitive guide to improving your performance*, Lanham, MD: Rowman & Littlefield.

Husserl, E. (1962) *Ideas: General introduction to pure phenomenology*, London: Collier Books.

Jackson, S. A. and Czikszentmihalyi, M. (1999) *Flow in sports*, Champaign, IL: Human Kinetics.

Jeffery, N. (2012) 'Hoogie blown away by Magnussen's times', *The Australian*, 9 February, 36.

Jonassen, D. H. (1992) 'Evaluating constructivistic learning', in T. M. Duffy and D. H. Jonassen, eds, *Constructivism and the Technology of Instruction: A Conversation*, Hillsdale: Lawrence Erlbaum Associates, Inc., 137–148.

Jones, E. (2015) 'Transferring skill from practice to the match in rugby through Game Sense', *Healthy + Active Magazine*, 22(2/3): 56–58.

Jones, R. L. (2006) *The sports coach as educator: Reconceptualising sports coaching*, London: Routledge.

Jones, R. L. (2009) 'Coaching as caring (the smiling gallery): Accessing hidden knowledge', *Physical Education and Sport Pedagogy*, 14(4): 377–390.

Jones, R. L. and Turner, P. (2006) 'Teaching coaches to coach holistically: Can problem-based learning (PBL) help?', *Physical Education and Sport Pedagogy*, 11(2): 181–202.

Jowett, S., Yang, X. and Lorimer, R. (2012) 'The role of personality, empathy, and satisfaction with instruction within the context of the coach-athlete relationship', *International Journal of Coaching Science*, 6(2): 3–20.

Kagan, S. (2005) 'Rethinking thinking. Does bloom's taxonomy align with brain science?', *Kagan Online Magazine* (Fall). Available from: www.KaganOnline.com. Accessed 22 February 2014.

Kidman, L. (ed.) (2005) *Athlete-centered coaching: Developing inspired and inspiring people*, Christchurch: Innovative Print Communications.

Kidman, L. and Lombardo, B. J., eds, (2010) *Athlete-centred coaching: Developing decision makers*, Worcester, UK: IPC Print Resources.

Kiraly, D. (2000) *A Social Constructivist approach to translator education: Empowerment from theory to practice*, Manchester: St. Jerome.

Kirk, D. (2005a) 'Future prospects for Teaching Games for Understanding', in L. Griffin and J. Butler, eds, *Teaching Games for Understanding: Theory, Research, and Practice*. Champaign, IL: Human Kinetics, 213–226.

Kirk, D. (2005b) 'Physical education, youth sport and lifelong participation: The importance of early learning experiences', *European Physical Education Review*, 11(3): 239–255.

Kirk, D. (2010) 'Towards a socio-pedagogy of sports coaching', in J. Lyle and C. Cushion, eds, *Sport Coaching: Professionalisation and Practice*, Edinburgh: Elsevier, 165–176.

Kirk, D. and MacPhail, A. (2002) 'Teaching games for understanding and situated learning: Re-thinking the Bunker-Thorpe model', *Journal of Teaching in Physical Education*, 21: 177–192.

Kirk, D. and MacPhail, A. (2003) 'Social positioning and the construction of a youth sports club', *International Review for the Sociology of Sport*, 38(1): 23–44.

Kitson, R. (2005, July 2) 'How All Blacks went back to their roots', *The Guardian*, 8–9. Available from: http://www.guardian.co.uk/sport/2005/jul/02/lions2005.rugbyunion2. Accessed 13 May 2009.

Kracl, C. L. (2012) 'Review or true? Using higher level thinking questions in social studies instruction', *The Social Studies*, 103: 57–60.

Kretchmar, S. (2005) 'Teaching Games for Understanding and the delights of human activity', in L. L. Griffin and J. Butler, eds, *Teaching Games for Understanding: Theory, Research, and Practice*, Champaign, IL: Human Kinetics, 199–212.

Lakoff, G. and Johnson, M. (1999) *Philosophy in the flesh: The embodied mind and its challenge to Western thought*, New York: Basic Books.

Lang, M. and Light, R. L. (2010) 'Interpreting the Long Term Athlete Development Model: English swimming coaches' views on the (swimming) LTAD in practice', *International Journal of Sports Science & Coaching*, 5(3): 389–403.

Launder, A. G. (2001) *Play practice: The games approach to teaching and coaching sports*, Champaign, IL: Human Kinetics.

Launder, A. and Piltz, W. (2013) *Play practice: Engaging and developing skilled players from beginner to elite*, Champaign, IL: Human Kinetics.

Lave, J. and Wenger, E. (1991) *Situated learning: Legitimate peripheral participation*, Cambridge: University of Cambridge Press.

Lémonie, Y., Light, R. L. and Sarremejane, P. (2015) 'The nature of teacher–student interactions and their influence on learning in swimming lessons', Published ahead of print, *Sport, Education and Society*, doi:10.1080/13573322.2015.1005068.

Light, R. (2002) 'The social nature of games: Pre-service primary teachers' first experiences of TGfU', *European Physical Education Review*, 8(3): 291–310.

Light, R. (2003) 'The joy of learning: Emotion, cognition and learning in games through TGfU', *New Zealand Journal of Physical Education*, 36(1): 94–108.

Light, R. (2004) 'Australian coaches' experiences of Game Sense: Opportunities and challenges', *Physical Education and Sport Pedagogy*, 9(2): 115–132.

Light, R. (2006) 'Situated learning in an Australian surf club', *Sport, Education and Society*, 11(2): 155–172.

Light, R. (2008a) *Sport in the lives of young Australians*, Sydney: Sydney University Press.

Light, R. (2008b) '"Complex" learning theory in physical education: An examination of its epistemology and assumptions about how we learn', *Journal of Teaching in Physical Education*, 27(1): 21–37.

Light, R. and Fawns, R. (2001a) 'The thinking body: Constructivist approaches to games teaching in Physical Education', *Melbourne Studies in Education*, 42(2): 69–87.

Light, R. and Fawns, R. (2001b) 'The embodied mind: Blending speech and action in games teaching through TGfU', *Quest*, 55: 161–176.

Light, R. and Fawns, R. (2003) 'Knowing the game: Integrating speech and action in games teaching through TGfU', *Quest*, 55: 161–176.

Light, R. and Tan, S. (2006) 'Culture, embodied understandings and primary school teachers' development of TGfU in Singapore and Australia', *European Physical Education Review*, 12(1): 100–117.

Light, R. and Wallian, N. (2008) 'A constructivist approach to teaching swimming', *Quest*, 60(3): 387–404.

Light, R. L. (2010) 'Children's social and personal development through sport: A case study of an Australian swimming club', *Journal of Sport and Social Issues*, 34(4): 266–282.

Light, R. L. (2013a) *Game Sense: Pedagogy for performance, participation and enjoyment*, London and New York: Routledge.

Light, R. L. (2013b) 'Game Sense pedagogy in youth sport: An applied ethics perspective', in S. Harvey and R. L. Light, eds, *Ethics in Youth Sport: Pedagogical and Policy Applications*, London and New York: Routledge, 229–234.

Light, R. L. (2014a) 'Learner-centred pedagogy for swim coaching: A complex learning theory informed approach', *Asia-Pacific Journal of Health, Sport and Physical Education*, 5(2): 167–180.

Light, R. L. (2014b) 'Positive Pedagogy for physical education and sport: Game Sense as an example', in R. L. Light, J. Quay, S. Harvey and A. Mooney, eds, *Contemporary Developments in Games Teaching*, London and New York: Routledge, 29–42.

Light, R. L. (2014c) 'Mushin and learning in and beyond Budo', *Ido Movement for Culture. Journal of Martial Arts Anthropology*, 14(3): 47–53, doi: 10.14589/ido.14.3.6.

Light, R. L. (2015) 'Managing practice activities and games in Game Sense coaching: Reflections upon teaching in Asia', *Proceedings for 2015 ACHPER International Conference*, 246–254. Available from: https://www.achper.org.au/professionallearning/past-international-con ference-proceedings/2015-international-conference-proceedings. Accessed 27 March 2016.

Light, R. L. (2016) *Children, young people and sport: Studies on experience and meaning*, Newcastle, UK: Cambridge Scholars Press.

Light, R. L. and Evans, J. R. (2010) 'The impact of Game Sense pedagogy on elite level Australian rugby coaches' practice: A question of pedagogy', *Physical Education and Sport Pedagogy*, 15(2): 103–115.

Light, R. L. and Evans, J. R. (2013) 'Dispositions of elite-level Australian rugby coaches towards Game Sense: Characteristics of their coaching habitus', *Sport, Education and Society*, 18(3): 407–423.

Light, R. L. and Harvey, S. (2015) 'Positive Pedagogy for sport coaching', *Sport, Education and Society*, 1–17, doi:10.1080/13573322.2015.1015977.

Light, R. L. and Kentel, J. A. (2015) 'Mushin: Learning in technique-intensive sport as uniting mind and body through complex learning theory', *Physical Education and Sport Pedagogy*, 20(4): 381–396.

Light, R. L. and Lémonie, Y. (2012) 'Constructivisme et pédagogie dans l'enseignement de la natation' [Constructivism and pedagogy for coaching in swimming], *eJRIEPS*, 26: 34–52.

Light, R. L. and Light, A. (2016) 'Fostering creativity: The games lesson as the laboratory of the possible', proceedings of the 2015 Game Sense for Teaching and Coaching Conference, University of Canterbury, Christchurch, New Zealand, 17–18 November, 74–86.

Light, R. L., Curry, C. and Mooney, A. (2014) 'Game Sense as a model for delivering quality teaching in physical education', *Asia-Pacific Journal of Health, Sport and Physical Education*, 5(1): 67–81.

Light, R. L., Harvey, S. and Memmert, D. (2013) 'Why children join and stay in sports clubs: Case studies in Australian, French and German swimming clubs', *Sport Education and Society*, 18(4): 550–566.

Light, R. L., Harvey, S. and Mouchet, A. (2014) 'Improving 'at-action' decision-making in team sports through a holistic coaching approach', *Sport, Education and Society*, 19(3): 258–275.

Light, R. L., Evans, J. R., Harvey, S. and Hassanin, R. (2015) *Advances in rugby coaching: An holistic approach*, London and New York: Routledge.

Light, R. L., Quay, J., Harvey, S. et al., (eds.) (2014) *Contemporary developments in games teaching*, London and New York: Routledge.

Lin, S. H. and Reifel, S. (1999) 'Context and meaning in Taiwanese kindergarten play', in S. Reifel, ed, *Play Contexts Revisited: Play and Culture Studies 2*, Greenwich, CT: Ablex, 151–176.

Lloyd, R. J. and Smith, S. S. (2010) 'Feeling flow motion in games and sports', in J. I. Butler and L. L. Griffin, eds, *More Teaching Games for Understanding: Moving Globally*, Champaign, IL: Human Kinetics, 89–104.

Lombardo, B. J. (1987) *Humanistic coaching: From theory to practice*, Springfield, IL: Charles C. Thomas.

Lyle, J. (2002) *Sports coaching concepts: A framework for coaches' behaviour*, London: Routledge.

MacPhail, A., Kirk, D. and Griffin, L. L. (2008) 'Throwing and catching as relational skills in game play: Situated learning in a modified game', *Journal of Teaching in Physical Education*, 27: 100–115.

Mahlo, F. (1974) *Act Tactique en Jeu* [Tactical action in play], Paris: Vigot.

Mandigo, J., Holt, N., Anderson, A. and Sheppard, J. (2008) 'Children's motivational experiences following autonomy-supportive games lessons', *European Physical Education Review*, 14(3): 407–425.

Martens, R. (2004) *Successful coaching* (3rd edn), Champaign, IL: Human Kinetics.

Maslow, A. H. (1968) *Toward a psychology of being*, New York: D. Van Nostrand Company.

Maslow, A. H. (1970) *Motivation and personality*, New York: Harper & Row.

Maturana, H. R. and Varela, F. J. (1987) *The Tree of Knowledge: The biological roots of human understanding*, Boston, MA: Shambhala.

Mauldon, E. and Layson, J. (1979) *Teaching gymnastics*, London: MacDonald & Evans.

McCuaig, L., Queenerstedt, M. and Macdonald, D. (2013) 'A salutogenic, strengths-based approach as a theory to guide HPE curriculum change', *Asia-Pacific Journal of Health, Sport and Physical Education*, 4(2): 109–125.

McCullough, J. and Mulliner, S. (1987) *The world of croquet*, Wiltshire, UK: Crowood.

McGeown, S. P., Johnston, R. S., Walker, J., Howatson, K., Stockburn, A. and Dufton, P. (2015) 'The relationship between young children's enjoyment of learning to read, reading attitudes, confidence and attainment', *Educational Research*, 57(4): 389–402.

McInerney, M. and McInerney, V. (1998) *Educational psychology: Constructing learning*, Sydney: Prentice Hill.

McNeill, M., Fry, J. M., Wright, S., Tan, S. and Rossi, A. (2008) 'Structuring time and questioning to achieve tactical awareness in games lessons', *Physical Education and Sport Pedagogy*, 13(3): 231–249.

Merleau-Ponty, M. (1962) *Phenomenology of perception*, London: Routledge.

Metzler, M. W. (2005) 'Implications of models-based instruction for research on teaching: A focus on Teaching Games for Understanding', in L. L. Griffin and J. Butler, eds, *Teaching Games for Understanding: Theory, Research, and Practice*, Champaign, IL: Human Kinetics, 193–198.

Mitchell, S. A., Oslin, J. L. and Griffin, L. L. (1995) 'The effects of two instructional approaches on game performance', *Pedagogy in Practice – Teaching and Coaching in Physical Education and Sports*, 1: 36–48.

Mosston, M. (1972) *From command to discovery*, Belmont, CA: Wadsworth.

Mosston, M. and Ashworth, S. (1986) *Teaching Physical Education* (3rd edn), Columbus, OH: Merrill.

Mouchet, A. (2005) 'Subjectivity in the articulation between strategy and tactics in team sports: An example in rugby', *Italian Journal of Sport Sciences*, 12(1): 24–33.

Mouchet, A. (2008) 'La subjectivité dans le décisionstactiques des joeurs experts en rugby' [Subjective tactical decision-making in elite rugby players], *eJRIEPS*, 14: 96–116.

Mouchet, A. (2014) 'Subjectivity as a resource for improving players' decision making in team sport', in R. L. Light, J. Quay, S. Harvey and A. Mooney, eds, *Contemporary Developments in Game Teaching*, London and New York: Routledge, 151–166.

Mouchet, A., Harvey, S. and Light, R. L. (2014) 'An holistic study on in-match rugby coach communications with players', *Physical Education and Sport Pedagogy*, 19(3): 320–336.

Nash, C. S., Sproule, J. and Horton, P. (2008) 'Sport coaches' perceived role frames and philosophies', *International Journal of Sports Science & Coaching*, 3(4): 535–550.

Nelson, L., Cushion, C. J., Potrac, P. and Groom, R. (2014) 'Carl Rogers, learning and educational practice: Critical considerations and applications in sports coaching', *Sport, Education and Society*, 19(5): 513–531.

Newmann, F. (1992) *Student engagement and achievement in American secondary schools*, New York: Teachers College Press.

Nilges, L. (2002) 'Pedagogical content knowledge: Teaching educational gymnastics effectively', *Teaching Elementary Physical Education*, 13(3): 7–9.

O'Reilly, E., Tompkins, J. and Gallant, M. (2001) '"They ought to enjoy physical activity, you know?" Struggling with fun in physical education', *Sport, Education, and Society*, 6(2): 211–221.

Ortner, S. B. (1999) 'Thick resistance: Death and the cultural construction of agency in Himalayan mountaineering', in S. B. Ortner, ed, *The Fate of Culture: Geertz and Beyond*, Berkley, Los Angeles and London: University of California Press, 136–164.

Oslin, J. and Mitchell, S. (2006) 'Game-centered approaches to teaching Physical Education', in D. Kirk., D. Macdonald and M. O'Sullivan, eds, *The Handbook of Physical Education*, London: Sage Publications, 627–651.

Ovens, A., Hopper, T. and Butler, J. (eds.) (2013) *Complexity thinking in physical education: Reframing curriculum, pedagogy and research*, London and New York: Routledge.

Papert, S. (1980) *Mindstorms: Children, computers, and powerful ideas*, New York: Basic Books.

Partington, M., Cushion, C. J. and Harvey, S. (2014) 'An investigation of the effect of athletes' age on the coaching behaviours of professional top-level youth soccer coaches', *Journal of Sport Sciences*, 35(2): 403–414.

Peterson, D. S. and Taylor, B. M. (2012) 'Using higher order questioning to accelerate students' growth in reading', *The Reading Teacher*, 65(5): 295–304.

Piaget, J. (1950) *The psychology of intelligence*, New York: Routledge.

Piaget, J. (1958) *The growth of logical thinking from childhood to adolescence*, New York: Basic Books.

Piaget, J. (1975/1985) *The equilibrium of cognitive structures* (T. Brown and K. J. Thampy, Trans), Chicago: University of Chicago Press.

Pill, S. (2011) 'Teacher engagement with games for understanding – game sense in physical education', *Journal of Physical Education and Sport*, 11(2): 115–123.

Placek, J. (1983) 'Conceptions of success in teaching: Busy, happy and good', in *Teaching in Physical Education*, Champaign, IL: Human Kinetics, 46–56.

Ploegh, K., Tillema, H. H. and Segers, M. S. R. (2009) 'In search of quality criteria in peer assessment practices', *Studies in Educational Evaluation*, 35(2–3): 102–109.

Poerksen, B. (2005) 'Learning how to learn', *Kybernetes*, 34(3/4): 471–484.

Potrac, P., Jones, R. and Armour, K. (2002) '"It's all about getting respect": The coaching behaviours of an expert English soccer coach', *Sport, Education and Society*, 7(2): 183–202.

Prince, M. J. and Felder, R. M. (2006) 'Inductive teaching and learning methods: Definitions, comparisons, and research bases', *Journal of Engineering Education*, 95: 123–138.

Pringle, R. (2010) 'Finding pleasure in physical education: A critical examination of the educational value of positive movement affects', *Quest*, 62(2): 119–134.

Proulx, J. (2004) 'The enactivist theory of cognition and behaviorism: An account of the processes of individual sense-making', proceedings of the 2004 Complexity Science and Educational Research Conference, 30 September–3 October, Chaffey's Locks, Ontario, 115–120.

Quay, J. and Stolz, S. (2014) 'Game as context in physical education: A Deweyan philosophical perspective', in R. Light, J. Quay, S. Harvey and A. Mooney, eds, *Contemporary Developments in Games Teaching*, London and New York: Routledge, 15–28.

Rach, S., Ufer, S. and Heinze, A. (2013) 'Learning from errors: Effects of teachers' training on students' attitudes towards and their individual use of errors', *PNA*, 8(1): 21–30.

Renshaw, I., Oldham, A. R. and Bawden, M. (2012) 'Non-linear pedagogy underpins intrinsic motivation in sports coaching', *The Open Sports Sciences Journal*, 5: 1–12.

Renshaw, I., Chow, I. Y., Davids, K. and Hammond, J. (2010) 'A constraints-led perspective to understanding skill acquisition and game play: A basis for integration of motor learning theory and physical education praxis?', *Physical Education and Sport Pedagogy*, 15(2): 117–137.

Richard, J.-F. and Wallian, N. (2005) 'Emphasizing student engagement in the construction of game performance', in L. L. Griffin and J. Butler, eds, *Teaching Games for Understanding: Theory, Research, and Practice*, Champaign, IL: Human Kinetics, 19–32.

Roberts, S. J. (2011) 'Teaching Games for Understanding: The difficulties and challenges experienced by participation cricket coaches', *Physical Education and Sport Pedagogy*, 16(1): 33–48.

Rogers, C. (1951) *Client-centered therapy: Its current practice, implications and theory*, London: Constable.

Rogoff, B. (1994) 'Developing understanding of communities of learners', *Mind, Culture and Activity*, 1(4): 209–229.

Rusnak, J. (2008) 'From age group to elite', *Swimming in Australia*, 24(3): 42–43.

Saleebey, D. (2005) *The strengths perspective in social work practice* (4th edn), Boston, MA: Allyn & Bacon.

Samurçay, R. and Rabardel, P. (2004) 'Modèles pour l'analyse de l'activité et des compétences, propositions' [Models for analysing activity and competency: proposals], in R. Samurçay and P. Pastré, eds, *Recherches en didactique professionnelle* [Research in professional didactics], Toulouse: Octares, 163–180.

Scanlan, T. K. and Simons, J. P. (1992) 'The construct of sport enjoyment', in G. C. Roberts, ed, *Motivation in Sport And Exercise*, Champaign, IL: Human Kinetics, 199–215.

Schmidt, H. G. (1998) 'Problem-based learning: Does it prepare medical students to become better doctors?', *The Medical Journal of Australia*, 168: 429–430.

Schön, D. A. (1983) *The reflective practitioner: How professionals think in action*, New York: Basic Books.

Schön, D. A. (1987) *Educating the reflective practitioner*, San Francisco, CA: Jossey-Bass.

Schön, D. A. (1992) 'The theory of inquiry: Dewey's legacy to education', *Curriculum Inquiry*, 22(2): 119–139.

Seligman, M. E. P. (2012) *Flourish: A visionary new understanding of happiness and wellbeing*, Sydney: Random House.

Seligman, M. E. P. and Csikszentmihalyi, M. (2000) 'Positive Psychology: An introduction', *American Psychologist*, 55(1): 5–14.

Sellappah, S., Hussey, T., Blackmore, A. M. and MacMurray, A. (1998) 'The use of questioning strategies by clinical teachers', *Journal of Advanced Nursing*, 28(1): 142–148.

Sheppard, J. and Mandigo, J. (2009) 'PlaySport: Teaching life skills for understanding through games', in T. Hopper, J. L. Butler and B. Storey, eds, *TGfU…Simply Good Pedagogy: Understanding a Complex Challenge*, Toronto: HPE Canada, 73–86.

Siedentop, D. (1994) *Sport education: Quality PE through positive sport experiences*, Champaign, IL: Human Kinetics.

Silvester, J. (2003) *Complete book of throws*, Champaign, IL: Human Kinetics.

Smith, W. (2005) 'Wayne Smith international rugby coach', in L. Kidman, ed, *Athlete Centered Coaching: Developing Inspired and Inspiring People*, Christchurch, New Zealand: Innovative Print Communications, 187–207.

Sport and Recreation New Zealand, *Effective Coaching*, http://www.sportnz.org.nz/assets/Uploads/attachments/managing-sport/coaching/Growing-Coaches-Programme-Guide.pdf. Accessed 6 January 2016.

Steffe, L. and Gale, J., eds, (1995) *Constructivism in education*, Hillsdale, NJ: Lawrence Erlbaum Associates, Inc.

Stolz, S. (2015) 'Embodied learning', *Educational Philosophy and Theory*, 47(5): 474–487.

Stolz, S. and Pill, S. (2015) 'A narrative approach to exploring TGfU – GS', *Sport, Education and Society*, 21(2): 239–261.

Stranger, M. (2011) *Surfing life: Surface, substructure and the commodification of the sublime*, Surrey, UK: Ashgate Publishing Ltd.

Strean, W. B. and Holt, N. L. (2000) 'Coaches', athletes', and parents' perceptions of fun in youth sports: Assumptions about learning and implications for practice', *Avante-Ontario*, 6(3): 84–98.

Sullivan, P. and Clarke, D. (1991) *Communication in the classroom: The importance of good questioning*, Geelong, Australia: Deakin University.

Suzuki, D. T. (1959) *Zen and Japanese culture*, Tokyo: Tuttle.

Tabeian, H., Zaravar, F., Shokrpour, N. and Baghooli, H. (2015) 'Impact of mental happiness on athletic success', *British Journal of Arts and Social Sciences*, 15(1): 75–84.

Tan, C. W. K., Chow, J. Y. and Davids, K. (2011) '"How does TGfU work?": Examining the relationship between learning design in TGfU and a nonlinear pedagogy', *Physical Education and Sport Pedagogy*, 17(4): 331–348.

Taylor, B. and Garrett, D. (2010) 'The professionalization of sport coaching: Relations of power, resistance and compliance', *Sport, Education and Society*, 15(1): 121–139.

Thomas, K. T. and Thomas, J. R. (1994) 'Developing expertise in sport: The relation of knowledge and performance', *International Journal of Sport Psychology*, 25: 295–312.

Thorpe, R. (1990) 'New dimensions in games teaching', in N. Armstrong, ed, *New Directions in Physical Education*, Champaign, IL: Human Kinetics, 79–100.

Thorpe, R. and Bunker, D. (2008) 'Teaching Games for Understanding – Do current developments reflect original intentions?' Paper presented at the fourth Teaching Games for Understanding conference, Vancouver, BC, Canada, May 14–17.

Train, P. (2012) 'Re-pleasuring physical education: A work in progress', in J. Butler, ed, *Reconceptualizing Physical Education through Teaching Games for Understanding*, Vancouver, Canada: Faculty of Education, University of British Columbia, 121–140.

Turner, A. (2014) 'Learning games concepts by design', in R. L. Light, J. Quay, S. Harvey and A. Mooney, eds, *Contemporary Developments in Games Teaching*, London and New York: Routledge, 193–206.

Turner, A. and Martineck, T. J. (1992) 'A comparative analysis of two models of teaching games: Technique approach and game-centred (tactical focus)', *International Journal of Physical Education*, 29(4): 15–31.

van Zee, E. H. and Minstrell, J. (1997) 'Using questioning to guide student thinking', *The Journal of the Learning Sciences*, 6(2): 227–269.

Varela, F. J., Thompson, E. and Rosch, E. (1991) *The embodied mind: Cognitive science and human experience*, Cambridge, MA: MIT Press.

Varvey, J. (2009) 'From hermeneutics to the translation classroom: Current perspective on effective learning', *Translation and Interpreting*, 1(1): 27–43.

Vickers, J. N., Livingston, L. F., Umeris-Bohnert, S. and Holden, D. (1999) Decision training: The effects of complex instruction, variable practice and reduced delayed feedback on the acquisition and transfer of a motor skill, *Journal of Sport Sciences*, 17(5): 357–367.

Vygotsky, L. S. (1962) *Thought and language*, Cambridge, MA: MIT Press.

Vygotsky, L. S. (1978) *Mind in society*, Cambridge, MA: Harvard University Press.

Wade, A. (1967) *The F.A. guide to training and coaching*, London: Heinemann.

Wallian, N. and Chang, C. W. (2007) 'Language, thinking and action: Towards a semi-constructivist approach in physical education', *Physical Education and Sport Pedagogy*, 12(3): 289–311.

Wang, C. L. and Ha, A. (2009) 'Pre-service teachers' perception of Teaching Games for Understanding: A Hong Kong perspective', *European Physical Education Review*, 15(3): 407–429.

Weimer, M. (2002) *Learner-centered teaching*, San Francisco, CA: Jossey-Bass.

Werner, P. H., Williams, L. H. and Hall, T. J. (2012) *Teaching children gymnastics* (3rd edn), Champaign, IL: Human Kinetics Publishers, Inc.

Williams, A. M. and Hodges, N. J. (2005) 'Practice, instruction and skill acquisition in soccer: Challenging tradition', *Journal of Sports Sciences*, 23: 637–650.

Wood, D., Bruner, J. and Ross, G. (1976) 'The role of tutoring in problem solving', *Journal of Child Psychology and Child Psychiatry*, 17: 89–100.

Wright, J. and Forrest, G. (2007) 'A social semiotic analysis of knowledge construction and games centred approaches to teaching', *Physical Education and Sport Pedagogy*, 12(3): 273–287.

Yakhlef, A. (2010) 'The corporeality of practice-based learning', *Organization Studies*, 31(4): 409–430.

Yang, Y. T. C., Newby, T. J. and Bill, R. L. (2005) 'Using Socratic questioning to promote critical thinking skills through asynchronous discussion forums in distance learning environments', *The American Journal of Distance Education*, 19(3): 163–181.

INDEX